WHY "WAIST" TIME IN THE KITCHEN?™

DENISE HAMILTON, L.P.N.
&
CHANTAL JAKEL, R.N.

FITNESS PROGRAM BY
CYNTHIA KERELUK, P.D.P.

Published in 1998 by Fit to Cook Inc.,
Box 51152 B.P.O., Calgary, Alberta, Canada T3K 3V9
Phone: (403) 274-3442   Fax: (403) 730-3492   e-mail: fittocook@shaw.wave.ca

Canadian Cataloguing in Publication Data

Hamilton, Denise, 1947—
Fit to cook—why "waist" time in the kitchen?

Includes index
ISBN 0-9682543-0-6

1. Cookery. 2. Low-fat diet— —Recipes. 3. Exercise
I. Jakel, Chantal, 1961— II. Kereluk, Cynthia, 1960 — III. Title.

RM237.7.H34 1998   641.5   C98—900119—9

Food Styling	*Fit to Cook Inc.*
Food Photography	*Junction Studio, Calgary*
Fitness Plan Photography	*Dwayne Brown Photography, Calgary*
Design, Illustration and Page Layout	*Sherry Ward Design, Calgary*
Film Output and Printing	*Sundog Printing Limited, Calgary*

Cover Photo
Red Sky in the Morning, *page 151*
Citrus Salad, *page 150*

Printed and bound in Canada

Acknowledgements

*We want to thank all of our friends and relatives who so often asked for our recipes, and who supported us in the writing of this book. We are grateful to Kim, Dorothy, Lorraine and Angie who trusted us with their family treasures and heirlooms as photo props. Special thanks to Folker, Ray, Darin, Joni, Ryan and Kim for their "editing". Bless Folker and Ken for their accounting knowledge, and Darin for teaching us **some** computer skills. We thank our lucky stars for leading us to Letty, our photographer, and most of all to Sherry, who is our creative genius.*

Chantal and Denise

Heartfelt thanks to my family, friends and fans for their ever-present love. You know who you are so please don't even consider hiding from this " hug of words".

Cynthia

MENU PLAN CONTENTS

Exercise Plan Contents

WHATEVER POSSESSED US?

All of our reviewers ask, "Why did you write this book?" Well, quite simply, we are nurses and nurses want to help everyone. We tried, oh, how we tried, but budget cuts limited the amount of time we could spend with each patient. A brief lecture on why to eat right left no time to say how to eat right, let alone talk about exercise. We said, "Just follow Canada's Food Guide and your health will improve!" The patient usually asked, "Really? How?" It seemed simple enough to us—we'd been helping our mothers cook since we were children. In fact, nutritional cooking became our lifelong hobby.

So, we quit our jobs, risked the "family farm", put our heads together and devised this plan for you. We thought our idea was so great and so easy to duplicate that we refused to tell anyone the details of our project. After all, we believed we could pop out a book every two months; in no time we would have a series!

We thank our lucky stars for our supportive husbands, because this book took not two months but two years to complete; a slight miscalculation!

Now we know why our patients said, "How?" when we told them to "just" follow Canada's Food Guide. They were all too busy and too stressed to actually **plan** healthy, low-fat, affordable meals that didn't start the whole family whining because they "don't like it".

We also know how important exercise is, yet how difficult it is to find even a brief time for a work-out. That's why we asked for Cynthia Kereluk's help. She is a most delightful lady who won't make you feel like a failure if you don't look like *Wonder Woman* or *Superman*.

This book is our contribution to preventive medicine. So, leave the planning to us. The work is done: just follow our simple recipes and you will **eat well, get moving and feel better!**

Denise Hamilton, L.P.N.   Chantal Jakel, R.N.

EAT WELL, GET MOVING, FEEL BETTER!

A Taste for Change

This is not just a cookbook — it's a plan to ease your cooking chores and simplify your search for balanced nutrition. We have given you some basic information in the beginning pages of this book. It won't take more than 15 minutes to read them, but it will save you hours in the kitchen and in the supermarket.

If you pick up a magazine or a newspaper, you will surely find an article lecturing you about how your poor eating habits are affecting your health. However, our experience as nurses taught us that lecturing people was purely a waste of time. Words, words and more words were futile. Patients returned to us knowing the theory but lacking the practical skills needed to change their eating habits. Even among our fellow health professionals, theory was frequently not being put into practice.

Health care professionals and the media theorize about the need to follow your country's Food Guide and about the need to reduce dietary fat. Still, most people have no idea how to fit the Food Guide recommendations into their daily lives. Most people do a better job of planning their vehicle maintenance than they do of planning their body maintenance. After all, the car comes with an instruction manual; we have yet to see a baby arrive the same way.

In the past, feeding the baby and the rest of the family just happened. The farm produce had to be used. There were no boxes of macaroni dinners or pizza hot-lines to call, so meals were created out of home-grown provisions. Food was eaten while fresh in season or preserved at home for winter use. Eating was more basic then.

Now, people must rediscover the real food in the chemistry lab that we call a supermarket. Variety in our grandparents' days meant seasonal fruits and vegetables. Today, variety means a pink cereal or a blue cereal: the decision is based on the toy in the box.

It is now apparent that we have eaten too much pink and blue cereal. Our folks were right after all — we should have kept the whole grains in our diet.

Just as we realize that our eating habits need to change, we realize that our teaching style needs to change. We have replaced our lecturing style with this new pampering style. The planning is done. We give you the step-by-step instructions, you do the cooking. Voilà! Now you're eating more of the basics without standing over the hot stove for hours.

In this book, you leave the planning to us so that you have time to start an exercise and recreation program that suits you. Just get moving, eat well and you'll feel better! We want you to eat all the good, basic food recommended by Canada's Food Guide and the Food Guide Pyramid of the U.S., enjoy cooking healthy food and have time for fun. By following our plan, you will enjoy a wide variety of food and ethnic flavours to satisfy your modern cosmopolitan tastes. After all, you have the privilege of access to a limitless variety of food — everything is in season somewhere in the world and all that variety is delivered to your doorstep fresh, frozen or canned every day.

Because of this huge food selection, you can eat healthy yet still entertain, eat out and have your snacks. Just check your pantry needs, take your grocery list to the store, then turn the pages one by one. If you can read, you can cook.

Welcome to your new lifestyle. Try it, it's easy— you'll like it! This healthy, fast, easy, cooking and fitness plan has worked well for us and our families for many years. We've been eating well and exercising, so we feel well, and we know this will work for you too!

The purpose of this book is to make sense of Canada's Food Guide and/or the Food Guide Pyramid of the U.S. These food guides are just broad definitions for common sense. To make life easier, we converted the food guides into a complete menu plan. All you have to do is get your scissors, turn to the shopping lists for Week 1 and follow these steps:

- Cut out either the list for a FAMILY OF 2 or the list for a FAMILY OF 4.

- On the WEEK 1 MENU page, find the recipes with an asterisk (*): these recipes **may** need to be adjusted for extra portions for those who need more calories (see page 4). Adjust the quantities on the shopping list **only** if you need **extra** portions. The **shopping lists** have accounted for two portions and four portions respectively, **even when a recipe says that it makes only one portion.**

- Check the Pantry Needs list and add items you don't have to the shopping list.

- Go shopping. If you don't like our fruit or vegetable choices, replace them with your own favourites, but, as Canada's Food Guide suggests, "Choose dark green and orange vegetables and orange fruit more often". Also, be sure to choose whole grain breads, cereals and pastas. You can substitute milk items with other low-fat milk products, eg. puddings, skim milk cheeses, yogurt, cottage cheese, etc. Meats can be substituted as long as they are lean cuts. There are many types of fish available — choose your favourites. Make any substitutions from the same food group (see pages 8 to 11).

- Before putting the groceries away, read Saturday's Game Plan.

- Turn the pages and follow the instructions. If you can read, you can cook, **as can anyone else in the household**. If they can't read, you can delegate tasks.

- Leave this book open on the counter so that anyone can start the next meal.

- When you see this symbol ➡ remind yourself to save some portions for meals on following days.

- Follow the exercise plan. You'll find it to be fun and easy.

Repeat all steps on WEEK 2, WEEK 3, WEEK 4, WEEK 1 ...

Watch for our next book.

HOT TIP TOMATO™

Throughout our menu plan you will notice our mascot, "Hot Tip Tomato", helping you through your day.

Cook Saver
Cooking tips to ease kitchen chores!

Heart Saver
Tips to trim the fat!

Time Saver
Step-saving tips save you time!

Waist Saver
Tips to remodel you from "Beefsteak" to "Roma"!

Game Plan
Helping you plan your day!

Nutrition Information

This book contains a 4 week menu plan.

Each week's plan has complete menus for—

7 BREAKFASTS:

5 quick to prepare, 1 longer and 1 brunch.

6 LUNCHES:

some hot , some cold and 1 of your own choosing.

7 DINNERS:

5 with start-to-sit-down times of 20 to 60 minutes, 1 casual (can be a T.V. dinner) and 1 elegant enough for guests.

7 SNACKS:

all easy to prepare.

IS A CALORIE A CALORIE?

No. All calories are units of energy, but some calories are "empty". That is, they are low in vitamins and minerals that are necessary for bodily functions. Empty calories are found in heavily refined foods. Those "foods" often contain excessive amounts of fat, sugar and salt, and are usually low in fibre. Leave a potato chip, candy or other heavily processed junk food on a shelf for a month and what happens? Nothing. Seldom will a self-respecting "bug" cause such junk food to mold or rot because those "foods" probably will not support life. If they won't support a bug's life, they won't support your life. Consider processed junk food to be a rare treat only.

What **does** support life is food made of "nutrient dense" calories. Such food contains high levels of nutrients, i.e. vitamins, minerals, complex (not refined) carbohydrates, lean protein, vegetable oil and fibre. Nutrient dense foods provide your body with its building blocks. So, just as the three little pigs build stronger houses with bricks than with straw, you need to build your body with nutrient dense calories rather than with empty calories.

The amount of calories needed varies with each individual. Energy needs are dependent on age, sex, body size and activity level. If you are unsure of your caloric requirements, consult a Registered Dietitian or a Physician. In this book, the menu plans provide the **minimum** calories needed to supply your body's essential nutrients as outlined by the Canadian and U.S. Food Guides.

DO "YO-YO" DIETS WORK?

No. When food consumption consistently drops below 1200 calories per day, your body goes into survival mode. That is, your body senses a famine, so the rate at which it burns calories slows. Below 1200 calories per day, your body will begin to burn lean muscle tissue for its blood sugar needs. It is easier for your body to draw energy from muscle tissue than from the fat that it has locked away in storage. **Therefore, when you stop dieting, you will gain weight very quickly for two reasons:**

1. Your rate of burning calories is now very slow.

2. You have less muscle tissue, and it is muscle that burns energy.

You gain weight, go on another diet, further slow your rate of burning calories, lose more muscle tissue and so on and so on, every time you go on a low calorie diet...

...and if you think that skipping breakfast is the solution to losing weight, think again. Breakfast means just what it sounds like: break the overnight fast and restock your depleted energy stores. How can you expect your body to shift into full gear when it's running on fumes? Even if you refuel with a "high-octane" fuel at lunchtime, you cannot make up the energy and nutrients you missed at breakfast time.

IS THERE A SOLUTION TO ACHIEVING A HEALTHY WEIGHT?

Yes. There are two steps in the solution:

1. Make every calorie count (eat nutrient dense foods).
2. Build muscle tissue (this can be done at any age).

HOW DO YOU MAKE THE CHANGES?

Easily — if you follow the menu and exercise plans in this book.

Cynthia Kereluk has outlined a plan to get you moving. The more you use your muscles, the more muscle tissue you will have (that's what helps you burn calories).

Chantal and Denise have devised menu plans that follow Canada's Food Guide and the Food Guide Pyramid of the U.S. The foods recommended in both Food Guides provide nutrient dense calories.

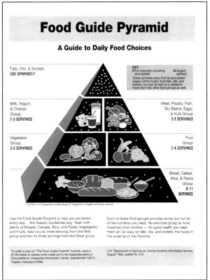

EAT WELL, GET MOVING, FEEL BETTER!

Each week's menu includes at least one each of the following dinners:

pasta,
poultry,
fish,
red meat,
vegetarian.

Each week's menu plan provides:

pantry needs reminder (items you should always have on hand) and grocery shopping lists for a family of 2 **or** *for a family of 4.*

Each daily menu includes one or more of the following tips:

time saver,
waist saver,
heart saver,
cook saver,
game plan.

Try all of our recipes. They're tasty and easy on the cook!

You'll find Cynthia Kereluk's exercise plan throughout the book!

Interpreting the Nutrition Information Tables

Our menu plan has succeeded in keeping the average daily fat content below 20% of total calories.

This will help minimize "donut syndrome": when you eat donuts and other fatty foods, your middle will look like a donut (round and plump).

 Individual recipes will not always provide less than 20% of calories from fat, but the daily total will usually be less than 20%. Therefore, follow the menu "as is" to maintain a balanced diet. Add extra calories by eating more vegetables, fruits, whole grains or fat-free dairy products, rather than extra meat or dessert portions.

To help you monitor the number of calories you are consuming and keep track of your fat intake, we have placed a NUTRITION INFORMATION table with each day's menu. The foods listed below are the generic choices we have used in the tables: they are used for ease of calculation. If you make substitutions, your calories will vary slightly.

Generic Food Choice	Caloric Standard Used in this Book
Fruit	1 medium apple
Bread	1 slice whole wheat bread
Cereal	1 oz (30 g) or 1 cup (250 mL) bran flakes
Milk	8 oz (250 mL) skim milk
Fruit Juice	6 oz (175 mL) unsweetened orange juice
Vegetable Sticks	1/2 cup (125 mL) each carrots and broccoli
Tossed Salad	2 cups (500 mL) mixed vegetables with 1 tbsp (15 mL) fat-free salad dressing
Vegetable Juice	6 oz (175 mL) tomato juice
Jam	1 tbsp (15 mL) fruit-only jam

- We want you to be creative. If you don't like a particular recipe, don't throw the baby out with the bath water. It's okay to substitute with one of your favourite low-fat recipes; just remember to adjust your SHOPPING LIST and the calories for that day (if you are counting them).

- If you don't like our fruit or vegetable suggestions, choose something else but remember the advice of Canada's Food Guide, "Choose dark green and orange vegetables and orange fruit more often".

- When buying bread, cereal, rice and pasta, be sure to choose whole grain products more often.

- Canada's Food Guide recommends the use of lower-fat dairy products, but there now are many new delicious no-fat products available. **Try them!**

- Because orange juice is so popular, we have used orange juice calories. Expand your horizons by trying other juices, but read the labels. Products saying "beverage", "cocktail" or "drink" may be mostly sugar and water.

- Vegetable juice choices may be limited in your area, so use your juicer if you have one.

- Some people make their own jams: the few extra calories from sugar need not be a concern.

- Meat choices are not generic but when buying meat, choose lean cuts. Remove all visible fat: that means bare-naked chicken (skinless). When a recipe calls for a chicken breast, we mean the right or the left, not both! A meat portion equals 4 oz (120g) raw or 3 oz (90g) cooked: that's about the size of a deck of cards.

Navigating the Supermarket

Where is the real food? Supermarket shopping is like being on a scavenger hunt in which you have been given coded clues. Most people search the aisles for real food, but where is it? The oatmeal is most likely up so high that a stepladder should be provided with the shopping cart, or down so low that kneepads should be mandatory shopping equipment. Where are the "pink" and "blue" cereals? Why, at eye level of course, or better yet, at kid level.

The basic foods are concentrated around the perimeter of the store. Think about the location of the produce, meat, dairy and bakery departments. Most likely they are on the outer edges. So if a food is within easy reach in an aisle, beware.

THE BASIC RULE: READ THE LABEL!

If the food item that you choose lists fat, sugar, salt or any refined starch as one of the first three ingredients, use it with caution. It is very likely a source of empty calories. As you read the nutrition information on a label, the energy is listed first. That means the number of calories.

Sometimes the calories are listed by weight or volume. Be aware that you must know the calories per serving. For example, if a serving of salad dressing is 30 calories, does that mean per teaspoon or per tablespoon? Sometimes the calorie count is deceiving. If the nutrition information is given in dry weight, the calories of butter, cheese, milk, etc. needed to reconstitute the package are not included. That is one reason why the most confusing part of label reading is interpreting the fat content of a food.

DOES LOW-FAT EQUAL LIGHT OR LITE? NO WAY!

Light means many things: light colour, light taste, low in salt, less alcohol, less sugar and sometimes even low in fat!

Confused yet? Well, to make matters even worse, cholesterol-free means no **animal** fat and/or little **saturated** fat but it can still be **100%** fat (e.g. vegetable oil).

So how light is light? To calculate the percentage of fat in a food, we have devised a simple formula called the "Less than 3 Fat Rule". If you're like us and don't carry a calculator to the grocery store, use our formula; it uses small numbers.

THE "LESS THAN 3 FAT RULE"

- Divide the total number of calories in a serving by 100.
- Multiply the answer by 3. That will give the maximum number of grams of fat allowed per serving for a food to contain **less than 30%** fat.
- If the fat grams per serving on the label equal less than your answer, you have selected a low-fat item.

EXAMPLE OF THE "LESS THAN 3 FAT RULE":

(Calories $\div$ 100) x 3 = the maximum grams of fat allowed for a food to be **less than 30%** fat.

Or: (Calories $\div$ 100) x 2 = the maximum grams of fat allowed for a food to be **less than 20%** fat, which is an even **better** choice.

Standard Label:	Total Calories:	500 cal
	CARB	70 g
	PROTEIN	32 g
	FAT	10 g

Therefore: (500 cal $\div$ 100) x 3 = 15 g. The above food choice contains only 10 grams of fat, making it a very good selection.

Don't be deceived by labels that claim to be low-fat. Low-fat does not necessarily equal nutritious or that the food should be eaten in unlimited quantities.

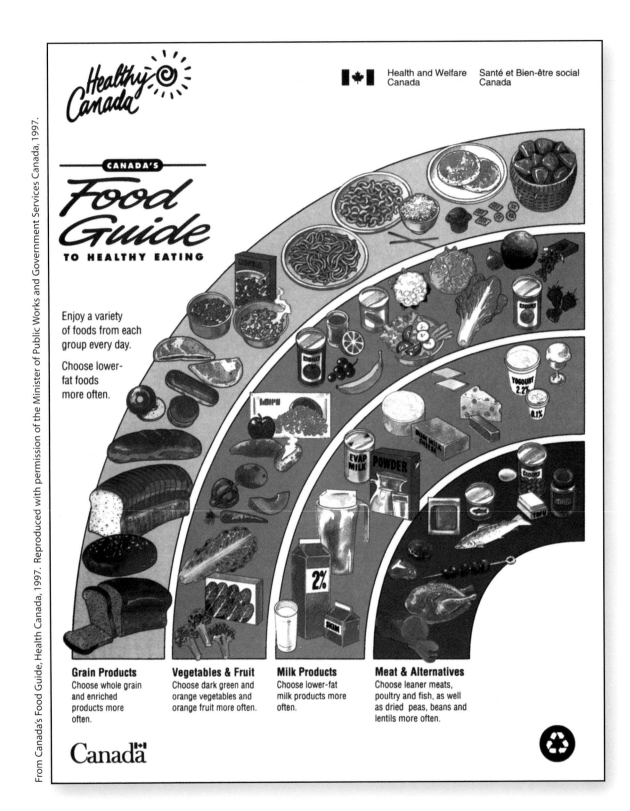

From Canada's Food Guide, Health Canada, 1997. Reproduced with permission of the Minister of Public Works and Government Services Canada, 1997.

Health and Welfare Canada   Santé et Bien-être social Canada

CANADA'S
Food Guide
TO HEALTHY EATING

Enjoy a variety of foods from each group every day.

Choose lower-fat foods more often.

Grain Products
Choose whole grain and enriched products more often.

Vegetables & Fruit
Choose dark green and orange vegetables and orange fruit more often.

Milk Products
Choose lower-fat milk products more often.

Meat & Alternatives
Choose leaner meats, poultry and fish, as well as dried peas, beans and lentils more often.

Canada

Different People Need Different Amounts of Food

The amount of food you need every day from the 4 food groups and other foods depends on your age, body size, activity level, whether you are male or female and if you are pregnant or breast-feeding. That's why the Food Guide gives a lower and higher number of servings for each food group. For example, young children can choose the lower number of servings, while male teenagers can go to the higher number. Most other people can choose servings somewhere in between.

Grain Products
5-12 SERVINGS PER DAY

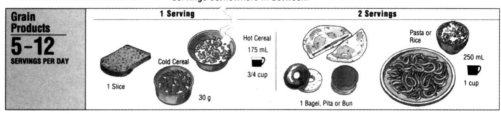

1 Serving — 1 Slice — Cold Cereal 30 g — Hot Cereal 175 mL 3/4 cup

2 Servings — 1 Bagel, Pita or Bun — Pasta or Rice 250 mL 1 cup

Vegetables & Fruit
5-10 SERVINGS PER DAY

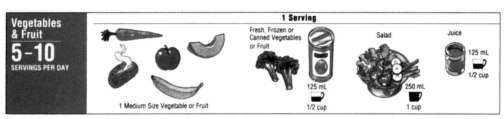

1 Serving — 1 Medium Size Vegetable or Fruit — Fresh, Frozen or Canned Vegetables or Fruit 125 mL 1/2 cup — Salad 250 mL 1 cup — Juice 125 mL 1/2 cup

Milk Products
SERVINGS PER DAY
Children 4–9 years: 2–3
Youth 10–16 years: 3–4
Adults: 2–4
Pregnant & Breast-feeding Women: 3–4

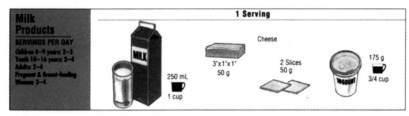

1 Serving — 250 mL 1 cup — Cheese 3"x1"x1" 50 g — 2 Slices 50 g — 175 g 3/4 cup

Other Foods

Taste and enjoyment can also come from other foods and beverages that are not part of the 4 food groups. Some of these foods are higher in fat or Calories, so use these foods in moderation.

Meat & Alternatives
2-3 SERVINGS PER DAY

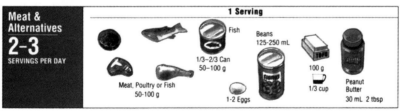

1 Serving — Meat, Poultry or Fish 50-100 g — 1-2 Eggs — Fish 1/3–2/3 Can 50–100 g — Beans 125-250 mL — Tofu 100 g 1/3 cup — Peanut Butter 30 mL 2 tbsp

Enjoy eating well, being active and feeling good about yourself. That's VITALIT⋵

From Canada's Food Guide, Health Canada, 1997. Reproduced with permission of the Minister of Public Works and Government Services Canada, 1997.

Food Guide Pyramid

A Guide to Daily Food Choices

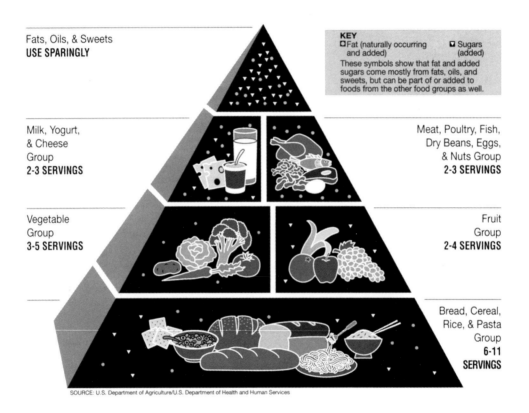

Fats, Oils, & Sweets
USE SPARINGLY

KEY
☐ Fat (naturally occurring and added)   ▼ Sugars (added)
These symbols show that fat and added sugars come mostly from fats, oils, and sweets, but can be part of or added to foods from the other food groups as well.

Milk, Yogurt,
& Cheese
Group
2-3 SERVINGS

Meat, Poultry, Fish,
Dry Beans, Eggs,
& Nuts Group
2-3 SERVINGS

Vegetable
Group
3-5 SERVINGS

Fruit
Group
2-4 SERVINGS

Bread, Cereal,
Rice, & Pasta
Group
6-11
SERVINGS

SOURCE: U.S. Department of Agriculture/U.S. Department of Health and Human Services

Use the Food Guide Pyramid to help you eat better every day. . .the Dietary Guidelines way. Start with plenty of Breads, Cereals, Rice, and Pasta; Vegetables; and Fruits. Add two to three servings from the Milk group and two to three servings from the Meat group.

Each of these food groups provides some, but not all, of the nutrients you need. No one food group is more important than another — for good health you need them all. Go easy on fats, oils, and sweets, the foods in the small tip of the Pyramid.

To order a copy of "The Food Guide Pyramid" booklet, send a $1.00 check or money order made out to the Superintendent of Documents to: Consumer Information Center, Department 159-Y, Pueblo, Colorado 81009.

U.S. Department of Agriculture, Human Nutrition Information Service, August 1992, Leaflet No. 572

How to Use The Daily Food Guide

What counts as one serving?

Breads, Cereals, Rice, and Pasta
1 slice of bread
1/2 cup of cooked rice or pasta
1/2 cup of cooked cereal
1 ounce of ready-to-eat cereal

Vegetables
1/2 cup of chopped raw or
  cooked vegetables
1 cup of leafy raw vegetables

Fruits
1 piece of fruit or melon wedge
3/4 cup of juice
1/2 cup of canned fruit
1/4 cup of dried fruit

Milk, Yogurt, and Cheese
1 cup of milk or yogurt
1-1/2 to 2 ounces of cheese

Meat, Poultry, Fish, Dry Beans, Eggs, and Nuts
2-1/2 to 3 ounces of cooked lean
  meat, poultry, or fish
Count 1/2 cup of cooked beans,
  or 1 egg, or 2 tablespoons of
  peanut butter as 1 ounce of lean
  meat (about 1/3 serving)

Fats, Oils, and Sweets
LIMIT CALORIES FROM THESE
especially if you need to lose weight

> The amount you eat may be more than one serving. For example, a dinner portion of spaghetti would count as two or three servings of pasta.

How many servings do you need each day?

	Women & some older adults	Children, teen girls, active women, most men	Teen boys & active men
Calorie level*	about 1,600	about 2,200	about 2,800
Bread group	6	9	11
Vegetable group	3	4	5
Fruit group	2	3	4
Milk group	**2-3	**2-3	**2-3
Meat group	2, for a total of 5 ounces	2, for a total of 6 ounces	3 for a total of 7 ounces

*These are the calorie levels if you choose lowfat, lean foods from the 5 major food groups and use foods from the fats, oils, and sweets group sparingly.

**Women who are pregnant or breastfeeding, teen-agers, and young adults to age 24 need 3 servings.

A Closer Look at Fat and Added Sugars

The small tip of the Pyramid shows fats, oils, and sweets. These are foods such as salad dressings, cream, butter, margarine, sugars, soft drinks, candies, and sweet desserts. Alcoholic beverages are also part of this group. These foods provide calories but few vitamins and minerals. Most people should go easy on foods from this group.

 Some fat or sugar symbols are shown in the other food groups. That's to remind you that some foods in these groups can also be high in fat and added sugars, such as cheese or ice cream from the milk group, or french fries from the vegetable group. When choosing foods for a healthful diet, consider the fat and added sugars in your choices from all the food groups, not just fats, oils, and sweets from the Pyramid tip.

☆ GPO : 1992 O – 330–958

Avoiding the Gym

Eating well is not the only element of well-being. Do you feel the best you can feel? There is a definite correlation between quality of food intake, activity level and the body's performance. You may already believe that you eat well, but your energy level is not what it should be. Why? You no longer live like the pre-automobile generations, walking "five miles to school through three feet of snow in bare feet". The point is, they were more active, forcing the circulatory system to work more efficiently. Circulation is just like spreading a rumor...the more people know it, the faster it spreads. The same is true of the blood...the more blood vessels that are open, the more nutrients are spread.

The body has two pumps involved in the circulation of nutrients. The first pump, the heart, sends 4 to 6 litres of nutrient and oxygen rich blood out through 100,000 km of blood vessels, mostly capillaries (tiny blood vessels). These capillaries distribute nutrients and oxygen to the body's tissues. The second pump is the muscles, especially the large muscle groups of the arms and legs. When muscles are at rest, only a few capillaries are open. When the muscles are working, such as when walking briskly, 50 times more capillaries are open and nourishing the body's cells.

Brisk walking and other forms of exercise activate the muscles. Vigorously working the muscles squeezes the blood back to the heart where it replenishes its nutrients and continues its circulatory journey. Therefore, eating nutrient dense food and distributing those nutrients properly is the key to increasing your energy level.

How much exercise is enough to keep both pumps working effectively? The Canadian Heart and Stroke Foundation recommends beginning an exercise program slowly and working up to a more vigorous level. The **minimum** activity recommended is 20 minutes on 3 non-consecutive days each week.

How long it will take you to feel the benefits of healthy eating and exercising depends on your level of fitness, how nourished your body is, and how dedicated you are to your new lifestyle plan. **You don't need to belong to a gym, you just need to get moving!** Please be sensible. Don't try to run a marathon tomorrow and don't lose more than 1 or 2 pounds per week.

We believe so much in the combination of healthy eating and exercise that we invited Cynthia Kereluk, an internationally-known fitness celebrity and star of "*Everyday Workout*", to design an exercise program for you.

Cynthia's effective exercise program will benefit you in three ways:
- You will improve your flexibility by learning the proper way to stretch.
- You will improve your heart and lung fitness by following her walking program.
- You will firm and strengthen your muscles by doing the toning exercises.

So join in the program and—

EAT WELL, GET MOVING, FEEL BETTER!

CYNTHIA KERELUK, P.D.P.

One million nine hundred twelve thousand five hundred seventy five (1,912,575) leg lifts later (beads of sweat unknown), Cynthia Kereluk *(Kur-luck)*, **writer and host of T.V.'s internationally syndicated "Everyday Workout" comes to help us with "Fit to Cook-Why 'Waist' Time in the Kitchen?"**

Since 1985 Cynthia has written and hosted 845 episodes of the *"Everyday Workout"* which airs across Canada, the U.S., Hong Kong, Thailand and Saudi Arabia. Exercise physiologists for "Self", "Longevity" and "Good Housekeeping" magazines rank Cynthia as T.V.'s #1 female exercise host. Cynthia also has seven videos to her credit. This former Miss Canada (1984) says, "Exercise should complement your daily routine not dictate it". Her soft-mannered, humorous yet kinetically-correct approach has *"moved"* millions, literally.

Of course, it's not always easy to move those millions because of the law of inertia: an object that isn't moving continues to be motionless unless a force puts it into motion. So please read on– you'll find yourself moving too in spite of all your creative excuses (rain, cold, heat, creaky joints, etc.). Follow **Cynthia's Exercise Program** and you'll find that moving makes you smile, relax and hear yourself thinking, "This is fun. I feel strong. This gets easier every day." Go ahead, say it out loud, "I feel great!"

WATCH FOR CYNTHIA'S ICONS

Exercise Program

Exercise Techniques

Fitness Tips

TO EXERCISE OR NOT?

When did you exercise last? If there is some humming and hawing it is in your best interests to see your family doctor and explain your good intentions. He or she may have some specific guidelines for you to follow that will make exercising a more welcoming experience for your body. This is especially true if you have never exercised, are on medication or have any type of health ailment or potential health ailment. Once you get your doctor's vote of approval, please read page 14 and get moving.

MEASUREMENT CHART

Trying to lose weight? Lose the scale. Take these measurements:

Neck _____ in/cm

Chest _____ in/cm

Bicep _____ in/cm

Waist _____ in/cm

Hips _____ in/cm

Thigh _____ in/cm

Calf _____ in/cm

Use inches rather than centimeters (25 inches sounds better than 63.5 centimeters). Measure your progress by inches/centimeters lost instead of pounds/kilograms because muscle tissue is denser than fat tissue, therefore 1 cup (250 mL) of muscle weighs more than 1 cup (250 mL) of fat. Their functions in the body are also different: muscle is an energy-burning tissue and fat is an energy-storing tissue. If you are caught up in the numbers game, 1 inch (2.5 cm) equals approximately 1 pound (454 g).

Exercise program by

Cynthia Xerelux ™

AEROBIC PACING

Before you high-tail it out the door for a brisk walk or tune into "Everyday Workout" for aerobics, let's discuss pacing.

As integral as using the right ingredients in a recipe, so too, pacing is as essential when you are exercising. Whether you are walking, cycling, swimming or cross-country skiing, it is important that you exercise at a comfortable-to-you pace:

■ a pace that allows you to continue the activity for 20 to 30 minutes if you so choose;

■ a pace that causes you to breathe deeply, but not pant or gasp for air;

■ a pace that makes you feel winded yet allows you to carry on a conversation.

That is probably **your** pace and within **your** heart rate target zone. I like the pace concept since it is based on you individually. If you find it hard to use the pace concept, please refer to the *Heart Rate Target Zone Chart* below. Please remember that this chart is designed for the average person. I don't happen to feel that you're average! Another quirk I have about the chart is the assumption that you have to drop your pace as you age. Balderdash! Read *Ageless Body, Timeless Mind – The Quantum Alternative to Growing Old* by Deepak Chopra, M.D.

HEART RATE TARGET ZONE CHART

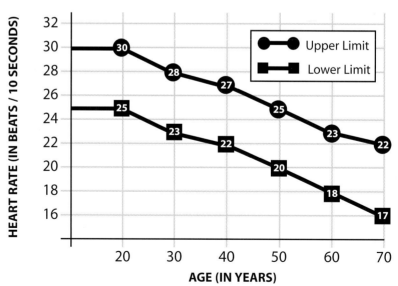

Published by the authority of the Minister of State Fitness and Amateur Sport. FAS 7347 5/1988

See page 29 to begin your exercise program.

WEEK 1 MENU

Recipes are provided in this chapter for menu items in **BOLD** on the day they are first prepared.

DAY	BREAKFAST	LUNCH	DINNER	SNACK
S SAT *pg. 21*	Half Grapefruit, ***Basted Egg on Whole Grain Toast**, Milk	**Cheese and Spinach Calzone**, Fruit of Choice, Milk	***Sweet and Sour Pork on a Bed of Rice Noodles**, Fortune Cookie (*optional*)	**Good Old Tapioca Pudding**
S SUN *pg. 27*	BRUNCH **Multi-Grain Soda Bread** ➡ ***Vanilla Fruit Salad** ➡ Low-fat Cheddar Cheese, **Orange-Cinnamon Coffee**		***Cream of Broccoli Soup** ➡ **"Ignore Me" Roast Beef** ➡ **Gravy,** ***Slight Smashed Spuds, *Glazed Carrot and Turnip Chunks**	**No-Guilt Chocolate Cake** ➡ Milk
M MON *pg. 33*	Whole Grain Cereal of Choice, Fruit Juice of Choice, Milk	Cream of Broccoli Soup, Multi-Grain Soda Bread ➡ No-Guilt Chocolate Cake ➡	***Noodles with Sherried Mushroom Sauce,** Multi-Grain Soda Bread	Vanilla Fruit Salad
T TUE *pg. 41*	Whole Grain Bagel, Fat-Free Cream Cheese, Fruit-Only Jam, Fruit Juice of Choice, Milk	***"Fit to Cook" Egg Salad Sandwich**, Green Pepper & Carrot Sticks, Fruit of Choice	***Creamy Dijon Chicken, *Baked Potato, Sour Cream & Chives, *Oven Roasted Carrots,** ***Mixed Fruit Cup**	Fig Bars, Milk
W WED *pg. 45*	***Vanilla-Raisin Oatmeal**, Milk	***Roast Beef Gyro**, Fruit of Choice, Vegetable Juice of Choice	***Fish Fillet in Mushroom Sauce,** ***Long Grain Brown Rice,** ***Lemon-Parmesan Asparagus**	**Oatmeal Blueberry Muffin** ➡ Milk
T THU *pg. 51*	Whole Grain Toast, Reduced-Fat Peanut Butter, Fruit-Only Jam, Half Banana, Milk	Oatmeal Blueberry Muffin, Fat-Free Vanilla Yogurt, Fruit of Choice	**Mexican Meatball Stew,** Whole Grain Bun, ***Black Forest Pudding**	Half Banana
F FRI *pg. 55*	Whole Grain Cereal of Choice, Fruit of Choice, Milk	T.G.I.F. (Use up leftovers or buy a lunch.)	***Veggie Pizza**, Fruit of Choice, Milk	Have a beer (that's **root** beer for the kids)!

* These recipes provide **EXACT MINIMUM PORTIONS** and may need to be adjusted for extra portions.

➡ This symbol will remind you to save portions of this recipe for use later this week.

PANTRY NEEDS

These items might be in your pantry now.

If not, add them to your shopping list on the following pages, as well as any personal preferences such as shampoo, toothpaste, cleaning supplies and so on.

Please note: ground spices and dried herbs are used in recipes unless otherwise specified.

- ☐ **ALLSPICE**
- ☐ **BASIL**
- ☐ **CHILI POWDER**
- ☐ **CINNAMON**
- ☐ **CORIANDER**
- ☐ **CUMIN**
- ☐ **CURRY POWDER** (optional)
- ☐ **LEMON-PEPPER SEASONING**
- ☐ **NUTMEG**
- ☐ **OREGANO**
- ☐ **PAPRIKA**
- ☐ **PARSLEY** (optional)
- ☐ **PEPPER**, black
- ☐ **PEPPER**, white
- ☐ **RED PEPPER FLAKES**
- ☐ **SALT**
- ☐ **ALMOND EXTRACT**
- ☐ **KIRSCH FLAVOURING**
- ☐ **VANILLA EXTRACT**
- ☐ **BOUILLON CONCENTRATE**, beef
- ☐ **BAKING POWDER**
- ☐ **BAKING SODA**
- ☐ **CORNSTARCH**
- ☐ **FLOUR**, all-purpose
- ☐ **FLOUR**, whole wheat
- ☐ **QUICK-COOKING TAPIOCA**
- ☐ **RAISINS**
- ☐ **SKIM MILK POWDER**
- ☐ **SUGAR**, brown
- ☐ **SUGAR**, icing
- ☐ **SUGAR**, white

- ☐ **CEREALS**, whole grain, breakfast
- ☐ **NATURAL WHEAT BRAN**
- ☐ **OAT BRAN**
- ☐ **QUICK OATS**
- ☐ **FIG BARS**
- ☐ **JAMS**, fruit-only
- ☐ **PEANUT BUTTER**, reduced-fat
- ☐ **COCOA POWDER**
- ☐ **COFFEE**
- ☐ **JUICES**, fruit, assorted
- ☐ **JUICES**, vegetable, assorted
- ☐ **LEMON JUICE**, bottled or fresh
- ☐ **RED WINE OR SHERRY**, dry
- ☐ **TEAS**, assorted
- ☐ **COOKING SPRAY**, butter-flavoured
- ☐ **COOKING SPRAY**, plain
- ☐ **OIL**, olive and/or canola
- ☐ **MUSTARD**, dijon and/or prepared
- ☐ **VINEGAR**, white
- ☐ **WORCESTERSHIRE SAUCE**
- ☐ **RICE**, brown, long grain
- ☐ **SOY SAUCE**, salt-reduced
- ☐ **JALAPEÑO PEPPERS**, sliced
- ☐ **MARASCHINO CHERRIES** (optional)
- ☐ **PARMESAN CHEESE**, low-fat, grated
- ☐ **SUN-DRIED TOMATOES**, dry packed
- ☐ **TOOTHPICKS**, non flavoured

*S*HOPPING LIST

Review all recipes for portion requirements (see page 22). Add any missing pantry items to your grocery list.

PRODUCE

☐ **APPLES** 1

☐ **BANANAS** 3

☐ **FRUIT**, assorted 12 portions

☐ **GRAPEFRUIT** 1

☐ **LEMON** 1 (*optional*)

☐ **ORANGE** 1

☐ **ASPARAGUS**, fresh or frozen 1 lb (450 g)

☐ **BROCCOLI** 4 stalks

☐ **CARROTS** 1-5 lb (2.3 kg) bag

☐ **CELERY** 1 bunch

☐ **CUCUMBER** 1 small

☐ **GARLIC** 2 heads

☐ **MUSHROOMS** ¾ lb (340 g)

☐ **GREEN ONIONS** 2 bunches

☐ **ONIONS** 2 medium

☐ **ONIONS** 2 small

☐ **RED ONION** 1 medium

☐ **PARSLEY OR MINT** 1 sprig (*optional*)

☐ **PEPPERS**, green 2 medium

☐ **PEPPERS**, red 3 medium

☐ **POTATOES** 10 medium

☐ **ROMA TOMATOES** 2

☐ **TURNIP** 1 small

☐ **VEGETABLES FOR SNACKS**, assorted (*see side panel page 67*)

GROCERIES

☐ **CORN SYRUP** 1 bottle

☐ **EVAPORATED SKIM MILK** 1-14 oz (385 mL) can

☐ **APPLE SAUCE**, unsweetened 1-14 oz (398 mL) can

☐ **CHERRY PIE FILLING** 1-19 oz (540 mL) can

☐ **FRUIT OF CHOICE**, in juice 2-14 oz (398 mL) cans

☐ **PINEAPPLE TIDBITS**, in juice 1-14 oz (398 mL) can

☐ **MUSHROOMS**, sliced 2-10 oz (284 mL) cans

☐ **TOMATOES,** diced 1-19 oz (540 mL) can

☐ **TOMATO PASTE** 1-5.5 oz (156 mL) can

☐ **TOMATO SAUCE** 1-7.5 oz (213 mL) can

☐ **TOMATO SAUCE** 1-19 oz (540 mL) can

☐ **TOMATO SAUCE**, Italian 1-14 oz (398 mL) can

☐ **NOODLES**, extra broad, yolk-free 1-12 oz (340 g) pkg

☐ **CHICKEN BROTH** 2-10 oz (284 mL) cans

☐ **KIDNEY BEANS** 1-14 oz (398 mL) can

☐ **MUSHROOM SOUP**, fat-reduced 1-10 oz (284 mL) can

☐ **BAMBOO SHOOTS** 1-8 oz (227 mL) can

☐ **FORTUNE COOKIES** (*optional*)

☐ **RICE VERMICELLI** 1-12 oz (340 g) pkg

(*continued on reverse*)

MEAT

- [ ] **CHICKEN BREASTS**, boneless, skinless 8
- [ ] **EYE OF ROUND ROAST OF BEEF**
  1-5 lb (2.3 kg)
- [ ] **LEAN GROUND BEEF** 1 lb (450 g)
- [ ] **PORK TENDERLOIN** 1 lb (450 g)
- [ ] **WHITE FISH FILLETS**, frozen
  (*not individually wrapped*) 1-14 oz (400 g) pkg

BAKERY

- [ ] **BAGELS**, whole grain 2
- [ ] **BREAD**, whole grain 1 loaf
- [ ] **BUNS**, whole grain 2
- [ ] **PITA BREAD**, whole wheat 2

FROZEN

- [ ] **BREAD DOUGH**, whole wheat
  2-1 lb (450 g) loaves
- [ ] **BLUEBERRIES** 2 cups (500 mL)
- [ ] **GREEN BEANS**, cut 2 cups (500 mL)
- [ ] **KERNEL CORN** 2 cups (500 mL)
- [ ] **SPINACH**, chopped 1-10 oz (300 g) pkg
- [ ] **ORANGE JUICE CONCENTRATE**
  1-12 oz (355 mL) can

DAIRY

- [ ] **BUTTERMILK**, 1% milk fat 1 quart (1 L)
- [ ] **MILK** 7 quarts (7 L)
- [ ] **YOGURT**, plain, fat-free ¾ cup (175 mL)
- [ ] **YOGURT**, vanilla, low-fat 2½ cups (625 mL)
- [ ] **SOUR CREAM**, fat-free 1¼ cups (300 mL)
- [ ] **RICOTTA CHEESE**, low-fat 1 cup (250 mL)
- [ ] **CREAM CHEESE**, fat-free 1 cup (250 mL)
- [ ] **CHEDDAR CHEESE**, low-fat 6 oz (180 g)
- [ ] **EGGS** 16

PANTRY & OTHER

- [ ] _____
- [ ] _____
- [ ] _____
- [ ] _____
- [ ] _____
- [ ] _____
- [ ] _____
- [ ] _____
- [ ] _____
- [ ] _____
- [ ] _____
- [ ] _____

SHOPPING LIST

Review all recipes for portion requirements (see page 22). Add any missing pantry items to your grocery list.

PRODUCE

☐ **APPLES** 1

☐ **BANANAS** 3

☐ **FRUIT**, assorted 12 portions

☐ **GRAPEFRUIT** 1

☐ **LEMON** 1 *(optional)*

☐ **ORANGE** 1

☐ **ASPARAGUS**, fresh or frozen 1 lb (450 g)

☐ **BROCCOLI** 4 stalks

☐ **CARROTS** 1-5 lb (2.3 kg) bag

☐ **CELERY** 1 bunch

☐ **CUCUMBER** 1 small

☐ **GARLIC** 2 heads

☐ **MUSHROOMS** ¾ lb (340 g)

☐ **GREEN ONIONS** 2 bunches

☐ **ONIONS** 2 medium

☐ **ONIONS** 2 small

☐ **RED ONION** 1 medium

☐ **PARSLEY OR MINT** 1 sprig *(optional)*

☐ **PEPPERS**, green 2 medium

☐ **PEPPERS**, red 3 medium

☐ **POTATOES** 10 medium

☐ **ROMA TOMATOES** 2

☐ **TURNIP** 1 small

☐ **VEGETABLES FOR SNACKS**, assorted
(*see side panel page 67*)

GROCERIES

☐ **CORN SYRUP** 1 bottle

☐ **EVAPORATED SKIM MILK**
1-14 oz (385 mL) can

☐ **APPLE SAUCE**, unsweetened
1-14 oz (398 mL) can

☐ **CHERRY PIE FILLING** 1-19 oz (540 mL) can

☐ **FRUIT OF CHOICE**, in juice
2-14 oz (398 mL) cans

☐ **PINEAPPLE TIDBITS**, in juice
1-14 oz (398 mL) can

☐ **MUSHROOMS**, sliced 2-10 oz (284 mL) cans

☐ **TOMATOES,** diced 1-19 oz (540 mL) can

☐ **TOMATO PASTE** 1-5.5 oz (156 mL) can

☐ **TOMATO SAUCE** 1-7.5 oz (213 mL) can

☐ **TOMATO SAUCE** 1-19 oz (540 mL) can

☐ **TOMATO SAUCE**, Italian 1-14 oz (398 mL) can

☐ **NOODLES**, extra broad, yolk-free
1-12 oz (340 g) pkg

☐ **CHICKEN BROTH** 2-10 oz (284 mL) cans

☐ **KIDNEY BEANS** 1-14 oz (398 mL) can

☐ **MUSHROOM SOUP**, fat-reduced
1-10 oz (284 mL) can

☐ **BAMBOO SHOOTS** 1-8 oz (227 mL) can

☐ **FORTUNE COOKIES** *(optional)*

☐ **RICE VERMICELLI** 1-12 oz (340 g) pkg

(continued on reverse)

MEAT

- [ ] **CHICKEN BREASTS**, boneless, skinless 8
- [ ] **EYE OF ROUND ROAST OF BEEF**
  1-5 lb (2.3 kg)
- [ ] **LEAN GROUND BEEF** 1 lb (450 g)
- [ ] **PORK TENDERLOIN** 1 lb (450 g)
- [ ] **WHITE FISH FILLETS**, frozen
  (*not individually wrapped*) 1-14 oz (400 g) pkg

BAKERY

- [ ] **BAGELS**, whole grain 2
- [ ] **BREAD**, whole grain 1 loaf
- [ ] **BUNS**, whole grain 2
- [ ] **PITA BREAD**, whole wheat 2

FROZEN

- [ ] **BREAD DOUGH**, whole wheat
  2-1 lb (450 g) loaves
- [ ] **BLUEBERRIES** 2 cups (500 mL)
- [ ] **GREEN BEANS**, cut 2 cups (500 mL)
- [ ] **KERNEL CORN** 2 cups (500 mL)
- [ ] **SPINACH**, chopped 1-10 oz (300 g) pkg
- [ ] **ORANGE JUICE CONCENTRATE**
  1-12 oz (355 mL) can

DAIRY

- [ ] **BUTTERMILK**, 1% milk fat 1 quart (1 L)
- [ ] **MILK** 7 quarts (7 L)
- [ ] **YOGURT**, plain, fat-free ¾ cup (175 mL)
- [ ] **YOGURT**, vanilla, low-fat 2½ cups (625 mL)
- [ ] **SOUR CREAM**, fat-free 1¼ cups (300 mL)
- [ ] **RICOTTA CHEESE**, low-fat 1 cup (250 mL)
- [ ] **CREAM CHEESE**, fat-free 1 cup (250 mL)
- [ ] **CHEDDAR CHEESE**, low-fat 6 oz (180 g)
- [ ] **EGGS** 16

PANTRY & OTHER

- [ ] _____
- [ ] _____
- [ ] _____
- [ ] _____
- [ ] _____
- [ ] _____
- [ ] _____
- [ ] _____
- [ ] _____
- [ ] _____
- [ ] _____
- [ ] _____

SHOPPING LIST

Review all recipes for portion requirements (see page 22). Add any missing pantry items to your grocery list.

PRODUCE

- ☐ **APPLES** 2
- ☐ **BANANAS** 6
- ☐ **FRUIT**, assorted 24 portions
- ☐ **GRAPEFRUIT** 2
- ☐ **LEMON** 1 (*optional*)
- ☐ **ORANGES** 2
- ☐ **ASPARAGUS**, fresh or frozen 1 lb (450 g)
- ☐ **BROCCOLI** 6 stalks
- ☐ **CARROTS** 1-5 lb (2.3 kg) bag
- ☐ **CELERY** 1 bunch
- ☐ **CUCUMBER** 1 small
- ☐ **GARLIC** 2 heads
- ☐ **MUSHROOMS** ¾ lb (340 g)
- ☐ **GREEN ONIONS** 2 bunches
- ☐ **ONIONS** 4 medium
- ☐ **ONIONS** 2 small
- ☐ **RED ONION** 1 medium
- ☐ **PARSLEY OR MINT** 1 sprig (*optional*)
- ☐ **PEPPERS**, green 3 medium
- ☐ **PEPPERS**, red 3 medium
- ☐ **POTATOES** 10 medium
- ☐ **ROMA TOMATOES** 4
- ☐ **TURNIP** 1 small
- ☐ **VEGETABLES FOR SNACKS**, assorted
  (*see side panel page 67*)

GROCERIES

- ☐ **CORN SYRUP** 1 bottle
- ☐ **EVAPORATED SKIM MILK**
  1-14 oz (385 mL) can
- ☐ **APPLE SAUCE**, unsweetened
  1-14 oz (398 mL) can
- ☐ **CHERRY PIE FILLING** 1-19 oz (540 mL) can
- ☐ **FRUIT OF CHOICE**, in juice
  2-14 oz (398 mL) cans
- ☐ **PINEAPPLE TIDBITS**, in juice
  1-14 oz (398 mL) can
- ☐ **MUSHROOMS**, sliced 2-10 oz (284 mL) cans
- ☐ **TOMATOES**, diced 1-19 oz (540 mL) can
- ☐ **TOMATO PASTE** 1-5.5 oz (156 mL) can
- ☐ **TOMATO SAUCE** 1-7.5 oz (213 mL) can
- ☐ **TOMATO SAUCE** 1-19 oz (540 mL) can
- ☐ **TOMATO SAUCE**, Italian 1-14 oz (398 mL) can
- ☐ **NOODLES**, extra broad, yolk-free
  1-12 oz (340 g) pkg
- ☐ **CHICKEN BROTH** 3-10 oz (284 mL) cans
- ☐ **KIDNEY BEANS** 1-14 oz (398 mL) can
- ☐ **MUSHROOM SOUP**, fat-reduced
  1-10 oz (284 mL) can
- ☐ **BAMBOO SHOOTS** 1-8 oz (227 mL) can
- ☐ **FORTUNE COOKIES** (*optional*)
- ☐ **RICE VERMICELLI** 1-12 oz (340 g) pkg

...continued on reverse

MEAT

☐ **CHICKEN BREASTS**, boneless, skinless 8

☐ **EYE OF ROUND ROAST OF BEEF**
1-5 lb (2.3 kg)

☐ **LEAN GROUND BEEF** 1 lb (450 g)

☐ **PORK TENDERLOIN** 1 lb (450 g)

☐ **WHITE FISH FILLETS**, frozen
(*not individually wrapped*) 1-14 oz (400 g) pkg

BAKERY

☐ **BAGELS**, whole grain 4

☐ **BREAD**, whole grain 2 loaves

☐ **BUNS**, whole grain 4

☐ **PITA BREAD**, whole wheat 4

FROZEN

☐ **BREAD DOUGH**, whole wheat
2-1 lb (450 g) loaves

☐ **BLUEBERRIES** 2 cups (500 mL)

☐ **GREEN BEANS**, cut 2 cups (500 mL)

☐ **KERNEL CORN** 2 cups (500 mL)

☐ **SPINACH**, chopped 1-10 oz (300 g) pkg

☐ **ORANGE JUICE CONCENTRATE**
1-12 oz (355 mL) can

DAIRY

☐ **BUTTERMILK,** 1% milk fat 1 quart (1 L)

☐ **MILK** 13 quarts (13 L)

☐ **YOGURT,** plain, fat-free 1 cup (250 mL)

☐ **YOGURT,** vanilla, low-fat 5 cups (1.25 L)

☐ **SOUR CREAM**, fat-free 1½ cups (375 mL)

☐ **RICOTTA CHEESE**, low-fat 1 cup (250 mL)

☐ **CREAM CHEESE**, fat-free 1 cup (250 mL)

☐ **CHEDDAR CHEESE**, low-fat 8 oz (240 g)

☐ **EGGS** 25

PANTRY & OTHER

☐ _____

☐ _____

☐ _____

☐ _____

☐ _____

☐ _____

☐ _____

☐ _____

☐ _____

☐ _____

☐ _____

☐ _____

BREAKFAST
Half Grapefruit, **Basted Egg on Whole Grain Toast**, Milk

LUNCH
Cheese and Spinach Calzone,
Fruit of Choice, Milk

DINNER
Sweet and Sour Pork on a Bed of Rice Noodles, Fortune Cookie *(optional)*

SNACK
Good Old Tapioca Pudding

NUTRITION INFORMATION
See page 6 for standards used.

MENU ITEMS (single portion)	calories	carbs (grams)	protein (grams)	fat (grams)
Grapefruit — 1/2	38.5	9.65	0.75	0.1
Basted Egg — 1	75	0.6	6.4	5.1
Whole Grain Toast — 1	63	12.4	2.7	0.8
Milk	86	11.9	8.3	0.4
Cheese & Spinach Calzone — 1	194.9	32.8	10.6	3.7
Fruit of Choice	81	21	0.2	0.5
Milk	86	11.9	8.3	0.4
Sweet & Sour Pork	290.8	27.1	27.2	8
Rice Noodles	286.6	71.5	0.8	0
Good Old Tapioca Pudding	82.6	13.5	4.9	1
Total for day	1298	215.7	70.8	27.3
			percentage fat ➤	**19%**

REMEMBER, these are the MINIMUM REQUIREMENTS of the Canada and U.S. Food Guides. Some people will need more calories.

GAME PLAN

Make sure that you have eggs, bread, milk and grapefruit on hand for breakfast.

We assume that you will go grocery shopping before lunch on Saturday, because the organization of your week starts then.

When you unpack your groceries, put the roast beef and pork tenderloin in the fridge. Freeze all remaining meat. Freeze the buns. Freeze all bread sliced. Freeze pitas in packages of 4 or the number needed for Wednesday. Freeze bagels pre-sliced so they are toaster-ready.

... continued on page 24

Fill a plastic container with washed, raw vegetable pieces. Chantal's husband calls them "**mouse food**" (see page 67)— they are free calories for nibbling and they keep him out of the chocolate chip jar.

If you want to lose weight, the worst thing you can do is to skip meals, especially breakfast. Your metabolism will slow down to compensate, meaning that you will burn less energy.

If you want to keep a fire burning, you must keep it fueled: your body's calorie-burning process works the same way.

Skipping meals also deprives your body of the nutrients it needs for cell repair. Therefore, eat regularly.

Check with a physician or a dietitian if you are unsure of your daily caloric requirements.

BEFORE YOU BEGIN...

Check **ALL** recipes on the weekly menu page for this symbol: ✳ (you may need to adjust for extra portions). Some recipes make 1 portion only, however the shopping lists for **"Family of Two"** or for **"Family of Four"** provide the ingredients for 2 and 4 portions respectively. Some family members may need more than 1 portion each: this is where you need to do a little work to adjust the shopping lists and recipes to accommodate your individual needs (*check with your physician or your dietitian for individual caloric needs — see page 4*). Make the adjustments on the shopping lists and on the recipes so that you make the changes once only.

Make sure you read the **GAME PLAN** daily — the recipes are given in order of preparation. Hot Tip Tomato is your cooking guide. We have planned your grocery lists so that you have all of the ingredients for the whole week <u>and</u> Saturday morning breakfast. However, you can shop on Friday night instead of Saturday morning as we have suggested. **ENJOY!**

BASTED EGG ON WHOLE GRAIN TOAST

This is the <u>one</u> recipe Denise learned from her husband — we could have called this the "Bachelor Special".

1	egg	1
1 tbsp	water	15 mL
1	slice whole grain bread, toasted	1

1. Coat a nonstick skillet with cooking spray.

2. Heat skillet to medium-high (a few drops of water sprinkled into pan will sizzle — it takes about 2 minutes).

3. Crack egg into pan.

4. Add 1 tbsp (15 mL) water. Cover. Egg cooks quickly (as soon as egg white covering yolk is opaque, it is done — about 30 seconds).

5. Serve on toast.

Makes 1 portion.

CAPELLI MEDLEY WITH ROASTED TOMATOES
page 88

CHEESE & SPINACH CALZONES

To thaw the bread dough, place the dough on a microwaveable dish and cover with a damp cloth. Place in the microwave on defrost for 3 minutes. Cut the dough into 8 pieces. Cover and defrost an additional 3 minutes. Let rest under the damp cloth while preparing the filling.

1	**1 lb (454 g) loaf frozen whole wheat bread dough, thawed, cut into 8 pieces** **OR** **1 recipe "Homemade Pizza Dough "** *(page 175)*	1
½ **cup**	**red onion, diced**	125 mL
1	**clove garlic, minced**	1
1	**red pepper, diced**	1
1	**10 oz (300 g) pkg frozen, <u>chopped</u> spinach, thawed, drained & patted dry**	1
½ **cup**	**low-fat ricotta cheese**	125 mL
½ **cup**	**fat-free cream cheese**	125 mL
¼ **tsp**	**black pepper**	1 mL
¼ **tsp**	**paprika**	1 mL
½ **tsp**	**oregano**	2 mL
1	**egg**	1
1 1¾ **cups**	**14 oz (398 mL) can Italian tomato sauce** **OR** **"Homemade Italian Tomato Sauce "** *(page 175)*	1 425 mL

1. Cook onion, garlic and red pepper for 3 minutes over medium heat in a non-stick skillet coated with cooking spray. Stir constantly. Remove from heat.

2. Add spinach, cheeses, spices and egg. Mix well. Set aside.

3. Roll each piece of dough into a 6 " (15 cm) circle on a lightly floured board.

4. Spoon ⅓ cup (75 mL) spinach mixture onto each circle. Moisten edge of circle with water. Fold dough over filling to form a half moon. Seal edge by pressing with a fork.

5. Bake at 375°F (190°C) for 20 to 25 minutes, or until lightly browned, on a cookie sheet coated with cooking spray.

6. Meanwhile, heat Italian tomato sauce in a small covered saucepan over medium-low heat for 2 to 3 minutes. Serve as topping.

Makes 8 portions. *One portion = 1 calzone topped with 3 tbsp (45 mL) Italian tomato sauce. Freezes well.*

Calzones and Italian tomato sauce freeze well and both reheat easily in the microwave for a fast lunch.

For future lunches, wrap calzones individually and package sauce separately in individual portions, then freeze.

Read the Game Plan tip on the next page <u>now</u>.

... continued from page 21

At lunch time, the calzones take 20 minutes to bake, so use that time to prepare the **No-Guilt Chocolate Cake** for tomorrow's snack.

Decrease the oven temperature to 350°F (180°C) before placing the cake in the oven. Enjoy your lunch while the cake bakes; this will maximize the use of an already hot oven.

For your convenience, the cake recipe is placed here, but nutrient calculations are given with tomorrow's menu.

Please read the **Good Old Tapioca Pudding** recipe now.

There is only one recipe needed to make dinner, so just follow the simple steps.

Total preparation and cooking time: **30 min.**

NO-GUILT CHOCOLATE CAKE

Denise's husband says, "This is the best chocolate cake you've ever made!" This is a real compliment coming from a butter lover (he still doesn't know it's fat-free).

1 cup	all-purpose flour	250 mL
⅓ cup	cornstarch	75 mL
⅓ cup	cocoa powder	75 mL
½ cup	sugar	125 mL
1 tsp	baking powder	5 mL
½ tsp	baking soda	2 mL
½ tsp	salt	2 mL
2	egg whites	2
½ cup	canned evaporated skim milk	125 mL
¾ cup	unsweetened apple sauce *(Use the leftovers as a fruit of choice selection.)*	175 mL
½ cup	corn syrup	125 mL
2 tsp	vanilla extract	10 mL
1 tbsp	icing sugar	15 mL

1. Mix dry ingredients (except for icing sugar) in a medium bowl. Set aside.

2. Whisk together wet ingredients in a large bowl.

3. Add dry ingredients all at once to wet ingredients. Stir until well moistened.

4. Pour into an 8" (20 cm) square baking pan coated with cooking spray. Bake at 350°F (180°C) for 30 to 40 minutes or until toothpick inserted into centre comes out clean.

5. Cool in pan. Sprinkle with icing sugar.

Makes 12 portions. *Doubles easily. Freezes well.*

 Save one portion per person for lunch on Monday and again for **Black Forest Pudding** on Thursday.

SWEET AND SOUR PORK ON A BED OF RICE NOODLES

If you don't have a wok, don't feel you can't cook Chinese food. Use a deep pan and decrease the heat to medium-high. Less heat is needed because the pan makes direct contact with the heat but the wok does not.

12 oz	rice vermicelli	340 g
1 tbsp	olive or canola oil	15 mL
1 lb	pork tenderloin, cut into 1" (2.5 cm) cubes	450 g
1	medium onion, cut into eight pieces	1
1	clove garlic, minced	1
1	green pepper, cut into 1" (2.5 cm) pieces	1
1	red pepper, cut into 1" (2.5 cm) pieces	1
2	medium carrots, sliced thinly on the diagonal	2
1	8 oz (227 mL) can bamboo shoots, drained	1
1	14 oz (398 mL) can pineapple tidbits, juice reserved	1
SAUCE:		
¾ cup	reserved pineapple juice	175 mL
¼ cup	salt-reduced soy sauce	50 mL
¾ cup	orange juice	175 mL
¼ cup	tomato paste	50 mL
2 tbsp	cornstarch	30 mL
1 tbsp	white vinegar	15 mL

1. Boil water in a Dutch oven. Meanwhile, prepare meat and vegetables. Set aside. Add vermicelli to boiling water. Stir. Cook according to package instructions. Drain vermicelli well. Set aside.

2. Add oil to a hot wok, then add pork, onion and garlic. Stir-fry until lightly browned.

3. Add peppers, carrots, bamboo shoots and pineapple to wok. Stir-fry 3 to 5 minutes. Reduce heat to medium. Add 1 tbsp (15 mL) water. Cover and steam 3 to 5 minutes.

4. Mix all sauce ingredients together. Add to pork mixture and cook 2 to 3 minutes, stirring constantly, until sauce thickens. Serve over vermicelli.

Makes 4 portions. *One portion = ¼ of the pork mixture over 1 cup (250 mL) vermicelli. Doubles easily. Freezes well.*

If freezing leftovers, cover the noodles with sauce to prevent drying.

Freeze the leftover tomato paste from **Sweet and Sour Pork** for use on Saturday, Week 2. **Do not freeze tomato paste in the can.**

For **Good Old Tapioca Pudding** or any other milk puddings or gravy, invest in an "underpot wire" to prevent scorching. You still must stir, but burning is less likely.

GOOD OLD TAPIOCA PUDDING

Some like it hot, some like it cold. It only takes 10 minutes to prepare, so if you like it hot, prepare just before eating. If you prefer it cold, prepare early in the day; you never know when the growlies will attack!

1. Prepare 1 recipe quick-cooking minute tapioca pudding according to package instructions, using <u>skim</u> milk.

2. To dress it up and add calories, top with fresh, frozen, canned or dried fruit (raspberries, strawberries, raisins or peaches).

Makes 6 — ½ cup (125 mL) portions.
(*Leftovers can be used as an extra milk portion.*)

TIPS ON BUYING SNEAKERS

You may feel rooted to your couch but it is possible at any age to get started on a few moves! Slip into some loose, comfortable clothes and put your new sneakers on.

Wait! Do you have the right sneakers?

It is paramount to wear well-made, not necessarily expensive, footwear while exercising. The right footwear lowers your risk of injury, providing you don't get zealous, jump up into the air and land in full splits; at least not the first time. Most athletic shops have trained staff to help you choose the best shoe for your activity and believe me, there is a special shoe for your activity. For example, you do not want to wear a court shoe (tennis, racquetball, squash) for walking or running. Court shoes are designed for repeated lateral movements (different grip and sole padding, etc). Please confer with a sales person who may suggest a specially designed walking shoe or a versatile cross-training shoe.

When should you buy your sneakers?

Time of day is important when shopping for the right fit. You need your feet to be the size they are during exercise, so shop for shoes in the afternoon. Your feet expand throughout the day, especially when you are on them — as in walking.

BRUNCH

Multi-Grain Soda Bread, **Vanilla Fruit Salad**,
Low-Fat Cheddar Cheese,
Orange-Cinnamon Coffee

DINNER

Cream of Broccoli Soup,
"Ignore Me" Roast Beef, **Beef Gravy**,
Slight Smashed Spuds, **Glazed Carrot & Turnip Chunks**

SNACK

No-Guilt Chocolate Cake *(see page 24)*, Milk

GAME PLAN

Begin your day by moving the chicken for tomorrow's spaghetti from the freezer to the fridge. Thawing in the fridge will reduce the risk of food poisoning.

... continued on page 28

Be sure to read page 6, *Interpreting the Nutrition Information Tables*

NUTRITION INFORMATION
See page 6 for standards used.

MENU ITEMS (single portion)	calories	carbs (grams)	protein (grams)	fat (grams)
Multi-Grain Soda Bread	146.4	28.1	5	1.3
Vanilla Fruit Salad	153	37	2.8	0.8
Low-Fat Cheddar Cheese — 1 oz (30 g)	71	6	5	4.1
Orange-Cinnamon Coffee — 6 oz (175 mL)	2	0	0	0
Cream of Broccoli Soup	89.2	8	9	2.5
"Ignore Me" Roast Beef	314	0.5	49.5	11
Beef Gravy	32.4	6.3	1.5	0.2
Slight Smashed Spuds	114	22.6	5.9	0.2
Glazed Carrot & Turnip Chunks	71.8	18.2	1.9	0.3
No-Guilt Chocolate Cake	157.8	33.2	3.9	1.2
Milk	86	11.9	8.3	0.4
Total for day	1236	171.8	92.8	17.9
			percentage fat ▶	13%

REMEMBER, these are the MINIMUM REQUIREMENTS of the Canada and U.S. Food Guides. Some people will need more calories.

... continued from page 27
While the **Multi-Grain Soda Bread** bakes for brunch, prepare the **"Ignore Me" Roast Beef** and the **Vanilla Fruit Salad**. As soon as the soda bread has baked, increase the oven temperature to 500°F (260°C). Place the roast in the pre-heated oven. After 15 minutes, decrease the temperature to 175°F (80°C) and forget it for the day!

About 45 to 60 minutes prior to dinner time, prepare the rest of the meal in this order and everything will be ready at once:

• potatoes,

• carrots/turnips,

• soup,

• gravy.

Total preparation and cooking time: **60 min.**

MULTI-GRAIN SODA BREAD

This bread is also great thinly sliced and toasted.

1²/₃ cups	all-purpose flour	400 mL
2 cups	whole wheat flour	500 mL
²/₃ cup	quick oats	150 mL
¼ cup	natural wheat bran	50 mL
¼ cup	sugar	50 mL
2 tsp	baking soda	10 mL
½ tsp	salt	2 mL
2 cups	1% buttermilk	500 mL
1 tbsp	1% buttermilk	15 mL
2 tbsp	quick oats	30 mL

1. Mix dry ingredients together in a large bowl (except 2 tbsp [30 mL] oats).

2. Add 2 cups (500 mL) buttermilk. Stir lightly with a fork just until moistened. Gather into a ball. Place onto a floured board. Using a spatula, **gently** rotate so that all sides are coated with flour and are no longer sticky.

3. Transfer to a cookie sheet coated with cooking spray. Pat into a 10" (25 cm) circle. Score into 16 wedges with a knife. Brush top with remaining buttermilk. Sprinkle with remaining oats.

4. Bake for 45 to 50 minutes at 350°F (180°C) or until golden brown.

5. Remove from oven. Place on a cooling rack. Cover bread with lightly dampened cloth and cool for 10 to 15 minutes before eating.

Makes 16 portions.

 Save 1 portion per person for tomorrow's lunch and 1 portion per person for tomorrow's dinner. Freeze remaining portions.

VANILLA FRUIT SALAD

Our version of a Waldorf salad.

1 cup	celery, diced	250 mL
1	medium banana, thinly sliced	1
1	medium apple, diced	1
1	medium orange, cut into bite-size pieces	1
½ cup	raisins	125 mL
½ cup	low-fat vanilla yogurt	125 mL
1	sprig fresh parsley or mint *(optional)*	1

1. Mix all fruits together in a large serving bowl.

2. Add yogurt. Toss lightly.

3. Garnish with parsley or mint if desired.

Makes 4 —1 cup (250 mL) portions.

 For family of four, make an extra portion per person for tomorrow's snack.

ORANGE-CINNAMON COFFEE

Save your pennies — flavour your own coffee!

4 to 6 tbsp	coffee, ground	60 to 90 mL
2 tbsp	orange rind, grated	30 mL
1 tsp	ground cinnamon	5 mL
4 cups	cold water	1L

1. Add orange rind and cinnamon to the coffee grounds in your coffee maker.

2. Add water as usual. Turn machine on.

Makes 6 —6 oz (170 mL) coffee cups.

Exercise program by

FIRST TIME STRETCHING:

Always warm up before you stretch (see page 35). Since you'll be starting your walking program next week, learn to stretch the muscles in your lower body first (see pages 36 to 40). Do each stretch slowly and deliberately to loosen your muscles. Avoid bouncing, which causes your muscles to contract rather than to expand and stretch. Your goal is relaxation, so remember to breathe deeply (see page 35).

Use stretching as a reward for your hard day's work—no equipment is required and it's free.

...continued on page 47

To kill bacteria carried by raw meat, use the following solution:

1 tbsp (15 mL) chlorine bleach per gallon (4 L) of warm, soapy water. Thoroughly wash all surfaces and utensils that have been in contact with the raw meat.

"IGNORE ME" ROAST BEEF

This really does need to be ignored, even though the aroma will drive you crazy!

1	**5 lb (2.3 kg) eye of round roast of beef**	1
8	**cloves garlic, halved**	8
2 tbsp	**beef bouillon concentrate**	30 mL
2 tbsp	**prepared mustard of choice**	30 mL
¼ tsp	**black pepper**	1 mL

1. Trim excess fat from meat. Make 16 slits 1" (2.5 cm) deep all around roast and insert 1 garlic piece into each slit.

2. In a small bowl, combine bouillon, mustard and pepper. Coat roast with mixture. Place on a rack in a covered roasting pan.

3. Place in pre-heated 500°F (260°C) oven for 15 minutes. Decrease heat to 175°F (80°C) and **IGNORE** for 6 to 8 hours.

Makes 16 - 3 oz (85 g) each, cooked portions. *Freezes well.*

 Reserve one portion per person for **Gyros** on Wednesday.

BEEF GRAVY

	pan drippings, fat removed	
1 cup	**water**	250 mL
½ cup	**all-purpose flour**	125 mL
½ tsp	**salt**	2 mL
optional	**beef bouillon concentrate**	optional

1. Remove roast from pan onto a serving platter. Cover with foil. Remove rack from roasting pan. The amount of drippings you have in your pan will vary.

2. Remove fat from drippings, using a spoon or a gravy separator. Pour drippings into a 4 cup (1 L) measuring cup. Fill to the 3 cup (750 mL) line with water. Return to roasting pan. Bring to a boil over medium-high heat.

3. Meanwhile, in a small jar with a tight-fitting lid, shake flour, salt and 1 cup (250 mL) of **cold** water vigorously until there are no lumps.

4. While stirring constantly, slowly add flour mixture to the boiling pan drippings. Continue stirring over medium heat until thickened. Add bouillon concentrate to taste, if desired.

Makes 8 —½ cup (125 mL) servings. *Freezes well.*

Freeze leftover roast beef by covering with leftover **Beef Gravy** to prevent drying.

SLIGHT SMASHED SPUDS

When you use the water from the potatoes, you retain the water-soluble vitamins and minerals.

4	medium potatoes, peeled & quartered	4
1 cup	water	250 mL
⅓ cup	skim milk powder	75 mL
¼ tsp	salt	1 mL
pinch	black pepper	pinch
1 tbsp	fat-free sour cream	15 mL
Optional:		
2 tbsp	fresh chives or green onion, finely chopped **OR**	30 mL
1 tsp	parsley	5 mL

1. Place potatoes and water in a medium saucepan.

2. Bring to a boil over medium-high heat. Reduce heat to medium-low, cover and simmer for 20 minutes or until fork-tender.

3. Remove from heat. **DO NOT DRAIN WATER**. Add all remaining ingredients. Smash well with potato masher. Add fresh skim milk if too dry.

Makes 4 -1 cup (250 mL) portions. *Halves or doubles easily. Freezes well.*

GLAZED CARROT AND TURNIP CHUNKS

Brown sugar complements the sweetness of carrots and turnips.

4	medium carrots, cut in 1 " (2.5 cm) pieces	4
4 cups	turnip, cut in 1 " (2.5 cm) cubes	1 L
1 tbsp	brown sugar	15 mL
pinch	black pepper	pinch

1. Place vegetables in the steamer insert of a medium saucepan. Add water to bottom of saucepan. Bring to a boil over medium-high heat.

2. Reduce heat to medium-low. Cover. Steam for 20 minutes or until fork-tender. Drain.

3. Place in a serving dish. Toss with brown sugar and pepper.

Makes 4 portions. *Halves or doubles easily. Freezes well.*

The recipes on this page can be halved easily

OR

if the recipes make too much for your family, freeze the extra portions as future time-savers.

Leftover canned skim milk is good in coffee or tea.

If your workplace does not have a microwave to reheat your soup, a good old thermos works well. If you **do** use a thermos, wait until the morning to pack the soup.

Package tomorrow's lunch this evening if you don't have the time (or the wits) in the morning.

CREAM OF BROCCOLI SOUP

If you think that homemade soup is difficult to create, try this. You'll dazzle your family and yourself.

1	10 oz (284 mL) can chicken broth, fat removed	1
1¼ cups	water	300 mL
	OR	
2½ cups	Homemade Chicken Broth *(page 176)*	625 mL
2 cups	broccoli, chopped *(florets and peeled stalks)*	500 mL
1	small onion, diced	1
½ cup	canned evaporated skim milk	125 mL
pinch	black pepper	pinch
¼ cup	low-fat Parmesan cheese, grated	50 mL

1. Combine canned broth, water, broccoli and onion in a large saucepan. Bring to a boil over medium-high heat. Reduce heat to medium-low and simmer for 15 minutes. Remove from heat. Allow to cool slightly.

2. Purée soup in a blender or food processor. Return to saucepan over medium heat.

3. Slowly add milk while stirring. Add pepper and Parmesan cheese. Remove from heat. Set aside.

4. Just before serving, reheat on medium-low for 5 minutes. Do not boil.

Makes 4 — 1 cup (250 mL) portions. *Doubles easily. Freezes well.*

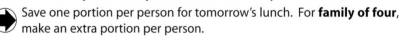 Save one portion per person for tomorrow's lunch. For **family of four**, make an extra portion per person.

BREAKFAST
Whole Grain Cereal of Choice, Fruit Juice of Choice, Milk

LUNCH
Cream of Broccoli Soup, Multi-Grain Soda Bread,
No-Guilt Chocolate Cake

DINNER
Noodles with Sherried Mushroom Sauce,
Multi-Grain Soda Bread

SNACK
Vanilla Fruit Salad

GAME PLAN

Before you leave for work, thaw the chicken for tomorrow's dinner in the fridge.

Don't forget to take your lunch with you!

... continued on page 34

NUTRITION INFORMATION
See page 6 for standards used.

MENU ITEMS (single portion)	calories	carbs (grams)	protein (grams)	fat (grams)
Whole Grain Cereal of Choice	126	20.3	2.6	4.4
Fruit Juice of Choice	80	20	1	0
Milk	86	11.9	8.3	0.4
Cream of Broccoli Soup	89.2	8	9	2.5
Multi-Grain Soda Bread	146.4	28.1	5	1.3
No-Guilt Chocolate Cake	157.8	33.2	3.9	1.2
Sherried Mushroom Sauce	213.2	15.1	29	4.1
Yolk-Free Noodles	298	60	13.6	1
Multi-Grain Soda Bread	146.4	28.1	5	1.3
Vanilla Fruit Salad	153	37	2.8	0.8
Total for day	1496	261.7	80.2	17
percentage fat ▶				10%

REMEMBER, these are the MINIMUM REQUIREMENTS of the Canada and U.S. Food Guides. Some people will need more calories.

... continued from page 33

Prior to cooking dinner, cook the eggs for tomorrow's lunch (see page 42), then follow the easy recipe for **Noodles with Sherried Mushroom Sauce**. See, cooking is "no sweat"!

Total preparation and cooking time: **30 min.**

You can make your sandwiches this evening or tomorrow morning.

Noodles with Sherried Mushroom Sauce doubles or triples easily, so make a bigger batch! Cover noodles with sauce and freeze in containers that hold 1 or 2 portions — convenient for days when you're in a rush!

NOODLES WITH SHERRIED MUSHROOM SAUCE

Submitted by Darin Hamilton, Calgary, Alberta. This recipe was invented by Denise's bachelor son — he loves to create unusual pasta recipes!

4	chicken breasts, boneless, skinless, cut into narrow strips	4
1	medium onion, diced	1
1	clove garlic, minced	1
2 cups	fresh mushrooms, sliced	500 mL
½ cup	dry sherry or dry red wine	125 mL
1	19 oz (540 mL) can tomato sauce	1
¼ tsp each:	black pepper white pepper red pepper flakes coriander allspice	1 mL each
1 tbsp	basil	15 mL
1	12 oz (340g) pkg extra broad, yolk-free noodles	1

1. Boil water in a Dutch oven.

2. Meanwhile, brown chicken over medium-high heat in a nonstick skillet coated with cooking spray. Set aside.

3. Cook onion, garlic and mushrooms for 3 to 5 minutes over medium-high heat in a Dutch oven coated with cooking spray. Add sherry or wine. Stir over medium heat for 3 more minutes. Add chicken, tomato sauce and spices to mushroom mixture. Simmer over medium-low heat while noodles are cooking.

4. Add noodles to boiling water. Cook according to package instructions.

5. Drain noodles well. Serve with sauce.

Makes 4 portions. *One portion = 1 cup (250 mL) of sauce over 1½ cups (375 mL) cooked noodles. Doubles easily. Freezes well.*

Warm-Up

ALWAYS warm up before you exercise. It is important that you warm your muscles by doing some light and fluid motions before you go for a run, a walk or before you stretch. When you're cold, you want to curl up by a warm fire to keep warm. The same thing applies to your muscles; so warm them up and they won't want to curl up. Warm, relaxed muscles are less likely to become injured than cold, stiff muscles. Marching is a good way to warm up. If you don't fancy marching, try walking up and down stairs for 3 to 5 minutes. Jumping rope, a light polka and moderate cycling are some activities that increase blood flow to your heart, then to your ligaments, tendons and muscles. My preference is marching.

BREATHING TECHNIQUE

Are you breathing correctly? Usually, shallow breathers complain of chronic neck and shoulder stiffness. Most of us shallow breathe: our shoulders rise and fall and the air we breathe enters the chest region only. The better and correct way to breathe is to inhale through your nose, forcing air down to the bottom of your lungs, therefore causing your tummy to expand. Then exhale, forcing your tummy in and air up and out. Inhale two, three and exhale two, three. Breathing correctly oxygenates your blood, energizing you to move more. In turn, this helps you to burn more calories, enabling you to lose weight more easily (I thought that you would like that last tip especially).

MARCHING TECHNIQUE

Marching is designed to increase blood flow and increase circulation. As you march, pump your arms; you can pump higher if you don't have any neck problems. Pumping your arms also increases your blood flow and circulation, which is very important before you stretch.

1. Please be light in your sneakers, think soft with your knee joints, maintain good posture and breathe deeply. Knees are always bent—they are your shock absorbers. Shoulders are back and down.

2. Make initial contact with the ball of your foot, then roll your foot through and touch your heel to the floor. This is the reverse foot motion of walking. If you suffer from neck problems, here's a trick: push your hands down by your sides, making sure that your head is back and that your ears are in line with your shoulders. Try not to lead with your head.

3. March for at least 3 to 5 minutes. Now you are ready to begin stretching.

LOWER BODY STRETCHES

STANDING QUADRICEP STRETCH

This is sometimes referred to as the runner's stretch. I once saw a photograph of President Clinton attempting this stretch on the cover of a U.S. national newspaper. Heaven have mercy! He was holding his toes instead of his ankle. Whoops. Just a tad of potential stress on that precious knee joint! Also, he did not keep his knees close together or his leg perpendicular to the floor. So, a short time later he was on the same front page on crutches. Is there a connection? This is the correct and safe way to stretch the quadricep:

1. Stand straight and tall as pictured, using a chair or a wall for support. Slightly bend your left knee. Always think soft with the knee joint.

2. With your hips and eyes forward, draw your right heel toward your buttock and try to keep your knees fairly close together. Keep your leg perpendicular to the floor. Grab your ankle with your right hand (or use a towel wrapped around your ankle if you can't reach). You should feel the stretch in the front of your thigh. Hold the stretch for 20 to 30 seconds.

3. Do this stretch twice on the right leg, then repeat on the other leg.

LOWER BODY STRETCHES

CALF STRETCH

All you wanna-be farmers, hear ye, hear ye: you have two "calves" to care for. The calves that walk around with you must be stretched so your knees don't stiffen up!

1. Stand as pictured, both feet facing forward, right leg back. Use a chair or wall for support. Place the ball of your right foot on the floor, holding your leg at a 45 degree angle from your body. Keep the knee of your front leg in line with its ankle.

2. Begin up on the ball of your right foot then slowly press your right heel down. At this point, please look forward for proper spine posture. You should feel the stretch in the back of your right lower leg. If not, place your right heel further back. Keep the heel of your back leg (stretching leg) down and hold the stretch for a slow count of 20 to 30.

3. Do this stretch twice on the right leg, then repeat on the other leg.

LOWER BODY STRETCHES

ADDUCTOR STRETCH

This inner-thigh stretch is a must for people just embarking on an exercise program and for veterans (did I omit anybody?).

1. Sit as pictured, best posture possible, with your back against a wall for support.

2. Place the soles of your feet together, grab your ankles to help stabilize your knees, and pull your feet as close to your body as is comfortable. Never grab your laces or your shoes because that mobilizes your knee joints.

3. Press the soles of your feet together while you slowly press your knees down, using only your adductors. If you feel a pull in your knee joints, you are over-stretching, so move your feet a little bit away from your body. You should feel the stretch in your adductors (inner thighs) only. Please remember to hold each stretch for a slow count of 20 to 30.

4. Try this stretch 2 to 3 times.

5. **More advanced people:** if you would like to apply resistance, do so at mid-thigh, never at the knee joint.

Lower Body Stretches

SEATED HAMSTRING STRETCH

This old standard stretch is good. However, it does employ some of the muscles in the lower back region, so try to focus on the hamstring (back of thigh) muscles.

1. Sit as tall as you comfortably can, back straight as pictured, knees bent, legs out in front and feet flexed.

2. Slowly lower your legs to touch the floor. If, on the way to touch the floor, you begin to feel a stretch in your hamstrings, please stop there. Hold the position, feeling the stretch while you repeat your full name slowly 15 times. Each time you do this exercise, your knees will be slightly closer to the floor.

3. Bring your knees up out of the position and try again.

4. Try this stretch 2 to 3 times.

Note: If you make full contact with your legs and do not feel a stretch, a slow bend forward from the waist, still with a straight back, should prove interesting. Please remember to breathe deeply and slowly while you are stretching, while the kids are running around the house playing tag, while the dog just walked in with muddy paws, while the cat has shed everywhere and your significant other is wondering where his gourmet dinner is!

Lower Body Stretches

ABDUCTOR STRETCH

This stretch is for the abductor region, a.k.a. the dreaded "saddle bags".

1. Lie on your back on a floor mat or towel. Bend your knees, placing your feet flat on the floor, shoulder width apart. Push your spine flat, making sure there is no arch in your lower back.

2. Cross your left leg over your right knee, placing your left ankle on the right knee.

3. Straighten your right leg as high as is comfortable for you by lifting your right foot toward the ceiling. Keep your right knee soft.

4. Clasp your hands behind your right knee, drawing your right leg toward your body until you feel the stretch in your outer thigh. Keep the left knee out by pushing it away from your head, using the abductor muscles only. Please remember to hold each stretch for a slow count of 20 to 30.

5. Do this stretch twice on the left leg, then repeat on the other leg.

COOL DOWN

I'm sure that you've all experienced stiff muscles after exercising. To prevent stiffness and to avoid injury, you must return your muscles to their pre-exercise condition. Always repeat the warm up exercise.

Your muscles will thank you!

BREAKFAST
Whole Grain Bagel, Fat-Free Cream Cheese, Fruit-Only Jam,
Fruit Juice of Choice, Milk

LUNCH
"Fit to Cook" Egg Salad Sandwich, Green Pepper and Carrot Sticks, Fruit of Choice

DINNER
Creamy Dijon Chicken, **Baked Potato with Sour Cream and Chives**,
Oven Roasted Carrots, **Mixed Fruit Cup**

SNACK
Fig Bars, Milk

NUTRITION INFORMATION
See page 6 for standards used.

MENU ITEMS (single portion)	calories	carbs (grams)	protein (grams)	fat (grams)
Whole Grain Bagel — 1	152	31.5	5.5	0.6
Fat-Free Cream Cheese — 1 tbsp (15 mL)	11.9	2	0.9	0
Fruit-Only Jam	43	11	0.1	0
Fruit Juice of Choice	80	20	1	0
Milk	86	11.9	8.3	0.4
"Fit to Cook" Egg Salad Sandwich	212	27.4	12.9	6.7
Green Pepper — 1/4	5	1.2	0.2	0
Carrot Sticks — 1 medium carrot	31	7.3	0.7	0.1
Fruit of Choice	81	21	0.2	0.5
Creamy Dijon Chicken	179	3.3	29.5	4.4
Baked Potato	76	17.1	2.1	0.1
Fat-Free Sour Cream & Chives	19	3.1	2.1	0
Oven Roasted Carrots	62	14.6	1.4	0.2
Mixed Fruit Cup	91	23.2	1	0
Fig Bars — 2	120	22	2	2
Milk	86	11.9	8.3	0.4
Total for day	1335	228.5	76.2	15.4
percentage fat ➧				10%

REMEMBER, these are the MINIMUM REQUIREMENTS of the Canada and U.S. Food Guides. Some people will need more calories.

GAME PLAN
Good Morning! If you didn't prepare your lunch, do so now. You should have hard-cooked eggs (prepared last night) in the fridge.

Enjoy your day!

...continued on page 43

Fig bars : these commercial cookies are low in fat and make an excellent snack when you get the "munchies" or crave chocolate. A recommended single portion is 2 fig bars.

Don't forget that your container full of snacking "veggies" (a.k.a."mouse food") is in the fridge.

"FIT TO COOK" EGG SALAD SANDWICHES

Our method for hard-cooking eggs prevents blackening of the yolks:

- pierce the wide end of each egg with a pin;

- place the eggs in a pan of cold water and bring just to the boiling point — cover;

- turn the heat off but leave the pan on the heat source for 15 minutes;

- drain and fill the pan with cold water — crack the shells;

- let the eggs sit in cold water until **thoroughly chilled** and drain — store in the fridge until ready to use.

If you need more than one sandwich per person, and want to be good to your heart, add one egg for each extra sandwich needed, but discard the yolk before mashing. This will decrease the fat by 5.6 g and the cholesterol by 272 mg for each yolk discarded.

2	**eggs, hard-cooked & peeled**	2
2 tbsp	**fat-free sour cream**	30 mL
2 tbsp	**celery, diced**	30 mL
1 tbsp	**green onion, chopped**	15 mL
pinch	**salt**	pinch
pinch	**black pepper**	pinch
4	**slices whole grain bread**	4
Serve with:		
1/2	**medium green pepper, cut in sticks**	1/2
2	**medium carrots, cut in sticks**	2

1. Mash eggs in a medium bowl. Add all remaining ingredients. Stir well.

2. For each sandwich, spread 1/2 of the mixture on a slice of whole grain bread. Top with the remaining bread slice. Repeat for second sandwich.

3. Serve with green pepper and carrot sticks.

Makes 2 sandwiches. *One portion = 1 sandwich served with 1/2 of the vegetable sticks. Halves or doubles easily.*

BAKED POTATOES WITH SOUR CREAM AND CHIVES

For a change of taste and a boost of vitamin A, replace the potatoes with yams or sweet potatoes.

4	medium potatoes, washed, skin pierced *(to prevent bursting)*	4
½ cup	fat-free sour cream	125 mL
¼ cup	fresh chives or green onion, chopped	50 mL

1. Preheat oven to 350°F (180°C).

2. Bake potatoes on oven rack for 60 minutes.

3. Serve with sour cream and chives.

Makes 4 portions. *One portion = 1 potato topped with 2 tbsp (30 mL) fat-free sour cream and 1 tbsp (15 mL) chives. Doubles easily. Freezes well.*

OVEN ROASTED CARROTS

Roasting rather than boiling carrots preserves nutrients and enhances the carrot flavour. This technique works well for many vegetables, for example, turnips, beets, asparagus, parsnips ...

8	medium carrots, peeled or scrubbed	8
	butter flavoured cooking spray	

1. Place carrots in an 8" (20 cm) square baking dish.

2. Coat carrots well with cooking spray.

3. Bake uncovered at 350°F (180°C) for 45 to 60 minutes, or until fork tender.

Makes 4 portions. *Doubles easily.*

...continued from page 41

Hi! You're back so soon. We missed you. Why don't you start dinner by putting the potatoes and the carrots in the oven and then put your feet up for 30 minutes!

Now that you're rested, preparing the **Creamy Dijon Chicken** and the **Mixed Fruit Cups** will be a snap!

Total preparation and cooking time: **60 min.**

To save cleaning the kitchen twice, immediately after dinner prepare the **Roast Beef Gyro** (see page 47) for tomorrow's lunch. Remember that you saved one portion of beef per person from dinner on Sunday for this recipe.

If you know that you'll be pressed for time tomorrow evening, cut the dinner preparation time in half by doing the following: cook the **Long Grain Brown Rice** tonight and thaw the fish in the fridge.

Note to Sports Parents— individual canned fruit cups travel well and when combined with cheese or yogurt, provide a healthy, energy snack.

CREAMY DIJON CHICKEN

Change the mustard, change the taste! If you're not a fan of Dijon mustard (like Denise), use prepared mustard. Either way, it's yummy!

4	**skinless, boneless, chicken breasts, all visible fat removed**	4
4 tsp	**Dijon mustard**	**20 mL**
½ cup	**chicken broth, undiluted** *(Use the leftover chicken broth in the rice on Wednesday.)*	**125 mL**
2	**cloves garlic, minced**	**2**
pinch	**black pepper**	**pinch**
½ cup	**fat-free plain yogurt**	**125 mL**

1. Coat each chicken breast with 1 tsp (5 mL) mustard.

2. Brown lightly over medium heat in a nonstick skillet coated with cooking spray (approximately 3 to 4 minutes per side).

3. Add broth, garlic and pepper. Cover. Simmer over medium-low heat for 10 minutes.

4. Whisk in yogurt while stirring constantly. Remove from heat.

Makes 4 portions. *Halves or doubles easily. Freezes well.*

MIXED FRUIT CUPS

The only one working here is the can opener! To look like you worked up a sweat, sprinkle water on your forehead.

2	**14 oz (398 mL) cans fruit, in juice (e.g. pears and pineapple)**	2

1. Mix together and place in individual fruit bowls.

Makes 4 portions. *Halves or doubles easily... chuckle, chuckle!*

BREAKFAST

Vanilla-Raisin Oatmeal, Milk

LUNCH

Roast Beef Gyro, Fruit of Choice, Vegetable Juice of Choice

DINNER

Fish Fillet in Mushroom Sauce, Long Grain Brown Rice,
Lemon-Parmesan Asparagus

SNACK

Oatmeal Blueberry Muffin, Milk

GAME PLAN

In the morning, place the ground beef in the fridge to thaw for tomorrow's dinner.

Do not fear, you won't miss the bus — you made your lunch last night so no worries there. Your oatmeal will be ready in only **4 minutes** and there won't be a sticky pot to wash!

... continued on page 48

NUTRITION INFORMATION
See page 6 for standards used.

MENU ITEMS (single portion)	calories	carbs (grams)	protein (grams)	fat (grams)
Vanilla-Raisin Oatmeal	202.4	40.7	7.7	1.8
Milk	86	11.9	8.3	0.4
Roast Beef Gyro	348.6	36.7	34	6.8
Fruit of Choice	81	21	0.2	0.5
Vegetable Juice of Choice	43	8.7	1.3	0.4
Fish Fillet in Mushroom Sauce	122.6	5	19.3	2.9
Long Grain Brown Rice	329.9	66.4	8.6	2.1
Lemon-Parmesan Asparagus	37.7	4.6	4.6	0.9
Oatmeal Blueberry Muffin	222	43	8.2	2.9
Milk	86	11.9	8.3	0.4
Total for day	1553.2	249.9	100.5	19.1
percentage fat ▶				11%

REMEMBER, these are the MINIMUM REQUIREMENTS of the Canada and U.S. Food Guides. Some people will need more calories.

Call Mom tonight and tell her you ate your oatmeal!

Microwave ovens vary in wattage. The first time you make **Vanilla-Raisin Oatmeal**, watch it carefully to prevent spillage.

Make note of your microwave cooking time here for future reference:

VANILLA-RAISIN OATMEAL

Oatmeal used to be messy to prepare, but cooked in a serving bowl in the microwave, even a child can prepare this favourite old-fashioned breakfast.

⅓ cup	quick oats	75 mL
pinch	salt	pinch
1 tbsp	raisins	15 mL
⅔ cup	water	150 mL
⅓ cup	skim milk	75 mL
½ tsp	vanilla extract	2 mL
1 tsp	brown sugar	5 mL

1. Place all ingredients in a microwaveable cereal bowl.

2. Microwave on high for 2 minutes. Stir. Microwave on medium for 2 minutes, stirring after 1 minute.

3. Serve with extra brown sugar and milk if desired (these will be additional calories).

Makes 1 portion. *This recipe will be used again with a variation on page 81.*

Did you know that, at rest, your stomach is usually no bigger than the size of your fist? When you are eating it is good to remember that it takes 20 minutes for your brain to realize that your stomach is full.

If you are an over-eater, remembering these two tips can lead to a comfortable feeling after a meal. However, if you forget and feel stuffed because you did stuff yourself, fennel or ginger tea aids digestion.

ROAST BEEF GYRO

Close your eyes and picture yourself cruising the Greek Isles!

3 oz	cooked roast beef, cut into thin, bite-size pieces	90 g
2 tbsp	fat-free plain yogurt	30 mL
1 tsp	prepared mustard	5 mL
1	Roma tomato, diced	1
¼ cup	cucumber, diced	50 mL
1 tbsp	red onion, diced	15 mL
pinch	salt	pinch
¼ tsp	black pepper	1 mL
1	whole wheat pita, halved	1
optional	¼ tsp (1 mL) curry powder	optional

1. Mix beef, yogurt, mustard, tomato, cucumber, onion, salt and pepper.

2. Place in a small, tightly sealed container if brown-bagging.

3. Insert one pita half into the other half. Wrap if brown-bagging.

4. When ready to eat, add beef mixture to pita.

Makes 1 portion.

Exercise program by

SECOND TIME STRETCHING:

Don't forget your warm-up (see page 35), then do the upper body stretches starting on page 92. Do each stretch slowly and breathe deeply. Stretching exercises are part of your overall fitness program, but they can also be used as stress releasers any time the boss is on your case, or your customers want an order yesterday, or the kids forgot to tell you they have to take cookies to school today.

... continued on page 53

... continued from page 45

To organize your evening meal, start the rice first, then prepare the **Fish Fillets in Mushroom Sauce** and place the fish in the oven.

About 20 minutes before the end of the rice cooking time, prepare and cook the **Lemon-Parmesan Asparagus**.

While dinner cooks, mix the **Oatmeal Blueberry Muffins**.

As soon as the fish is done, place the muffins in the oven and bake them while you eat dinner.

Total preparation and cooking time: **60 min.**

Don't forget to pack tomorrow's lunch.

LONG GRAIN BROWN RICE

Brown rice takes at least 45 minutes to cook, but the extra flavour makes the wait worthwhile.

1½ **cups**	**long grain brown rice**	**375 mL**
2¼ **cups**	**cold water**	**550 mL**
¾ **cup**	**chicken broth, undiluted** (*leftover from Tuesday*)	**175 mL**
¼ **cup**	**green onion, chopped**	**50 mL**
½ **tsp**	**paprika**	**2 mL**

1. Place rice and water in a large saucepan. Bring to a boil over medium-high heat.

2. Immediately reduce heat to low and simmer, tightly covered, for 45 minutes or until rice is tender and liquid is absorbed.

Makes 4 portions. *One portion = 1 cup (250 mL) rice topped with 1 tbsp (15 mL) green onion and a sprinkle of paprika. Doubles easily.*

FISH FILLETS IN MUSHROOM SAUCE

This is almost too easy to write down, but it tastes like you spent all day in the kitchen!

1	**14 oz (400 g) pkg frozen white fish fillets** *(eg., Sole, Boston Bluefish, Cod)*	1
1	**10 oz (284 mL) can fat-reduced mushroom soup, undiluted**	1

1. Place frozen fish in a baking dish coated with cooking spray. Cover fish with mushroom soup. Cover dish with lid or foil.

2. Bake at 350°F (180°C) for 40 to 45 minutes or until fish flakes easily.

Makes 4 portions. *Doubles easily. Freezes well.*

LEMON-PARMESAN ASPARAGUS

Asparagus adds colour and class to this super easy meal but it can be replaced by broccoli.

1 lb	**fresh or frozen asparagus**	450 g
2 tsp	**lemon juice** *(fresh is best)*	10 mL
2 tbsp	**low-fat Parmesan cheese**	30 mL
¼ tsp	**lemon-pepper seasoning**	1 mL
optional	**lemon rind curls** *(garnish)*	optional

1. Snap off tough ends of asparagus, if using fresh.

2. Place in a microwaveable dish. Drizzle with lemon juice. Sprinkle with Parmesan and lemon-pepper seasoning. Cover with plastic wrap, leaving one corner vented.

3. Microwave on high for 10 to 15 minutes, rotating every 5 minutes, until fork-tender.

4. Garnish with lemon rind curls.

Makes 4 portions. *Doubles easily. Freezes well.*

For quick and easy freezer-to-microwave lunches, freeze leftover rice, fish and asparagus in single size portions. Cover rice with fish and sauce to prevent drying.

If using frozen asparagus, follow package instructions for cooking time.

OATMEAL BLUEBERRY MUFFINS

These are large muffins so use 2¾" (7 cm) diameter muffin tins.

2 cups	quick oats	500 mL
2 cups	1% buttermilk	500 mL
2 cups	whole wheat flour	500 mL
2 tsp	baking powder	10 mL
1 tsp	baking soda	5 mL
½ tsp	salt	2 mL
1½ tsp	cinnamon	7 mL
½ tsp	nutmeg	2 mL
2	eggs	2
½ cup	fat-free sour cream	125 mL
¾ cup	brown sugar, packed	175 mL
1 tsp	vanilla extract	5 mL
2 cups	blueberries, still frozen, or fresh	500 mL

1. Mix oats and buttermilk in a medium bowl. Set aside.

2. Combine flour, baking powder, baking soda, salt, cinnamon and nutmeg in a medium bowl. Set aside.

3. Combine eggs, sour cream, brown sugar and vanilla in a large bowl. Beat well. Add oat mixture. Stir.

4. Add dry ingredients all at once to wet ingredients. Stir only until moistened.

5. Add blueberries. Stir gently.

6. Spoon batter into 12 muffin cups coated with cooking spray. Bake 15 to 20 minutes at 350°F (180°C), or until toothpick inserted into centre of a muffin comes out clean.

Makes 12 portions. *Freezes well.*

➡ Save one portion per person for tomorrow's lunch.

BREAKFAST
Whole Grain Toast, Reduced-Fat Peanut Butter, Fruit-Only Jam,
Half Banana, Milk

LUNCH
Oatmeal Blueberry Muffin, Fat-Free Vanilla Yogurt, Fruit of Choice

DINNER
Mexican Meatball Stew, Whole Grain Bun, **Black Forest Pudding**

SNACK
Half Banana

GAME PLAN

If using commercial frozen bread dough for tomorrow's pizza, put it in the fridge in the morning. It will thaw and rise well if placed in a bowl coated with cooking spray. Cover tightly.

...continued on page 52

NUTRITION INFORMATION
See page 6 for standards used.

MENU ITEMS (single portion)	calories	carbs (grams)	protein (grams)	fat (grams)
Whole Grain Toast — 2	126	24.8	5.4	1.6
Reduced-Fat Peanut Butter	82	5.2	2.7	5.6
Fruit-Only Jam	43	11	0.1	0
Banana — 1/2	55	13.8	0.6	0.3
Milk	86	11.9	8.3	0.4
Oatmeal Blueberry Muffin	222	43	8.2	2.9
Fat-Free Vanilla Yogurt — 1 cup (250 mL)	180	34	11	0
Fruit of Choice	81	21	0.2	0.5
Mexican Meatball Stew	286.5	26.1	16.7	12.6
Whole Grain Bun — 1	93	18.8	3.6	1
Black Forest Pudding	325	65.2	10	2.9
Banana — 1/2	55	13.8	0.6	0.3
Total for day	1635	288.6	67.4	28.1
percentage fat ▶ 16%				

REMEMBER, these are the MINIMUM REQUIREMENTS of the Canada and U.S. Food Guides. Some people will need more calories.

... continued from page 51

Because simmering time is 30 minutes, begin preparing the **Mexican Meatball Stew** one hour before you plan to eat dinner. While the stew simmers, prepare the **Black Forest Pudding** so that it has time to cool.

Total preparation and cooking time: **60 min.**

Friday lunch is a good time to use up leftovers or to eat out.

The **Mexican Meatball Stew** recipe makes a large quantity but don't worry, you'll be happy to have some in the freezer for those nights when you really have no time to cook. Freeze in single-size portions for quick lunches or for when you're dining alone.

Mexican Meatball Stew

If eating this makes you jump up and shout "OLÉ", it's too hot! Decrease the amount of jalapeño. If you like shouting "OLÉ", add more!

1 lb	lean ground beef	450 g
¼ cup	oat bran	50 mL
1	egg white	1
½ tsp	cumin	2 mL
2 tbsp	jalapeño pepper, finely chopped	30 mL
¼ tsp	black pepper	1 mL
2	medium potatoes, washed & diced	2
2 cups	frozen kernel corn	500 mL
2 cups	frozen green beans, chopped	500 mL
1	19 oz (540 mL) can tomatoes, diced	1
1	14 oz (398 mL) can kidney beans, undrained	1
1 tsp	beef bouillon concentrate	5 mL
1 tbsp	chili powder	15 mL
1 tsp	oregano	5 mL
2 cups	cold water, divided	500 mL
¼ cup	all-purpose flour	50 mL

1. Combine ground beef, oat bran, egg white, cumin, jalapeño and black pepper. Shape into meatballs using 2 tsp (10 mL) of mixture per meatball.

2. Arrange meatballs on a rack in a broiler pan. Cover bottom of pan with hot water to prevent splattering. Broil 6" (15 cm) from heat for 5 to 10 minutes. Turn meatballs and broil an additional 5 minutes. Remove from oven.

3. Meanwhile, combine potatoes, corn, green beans, tomatoes, kidney beans, bouillon concentrate, chili powder, oregano and 1 cup (250 mL) of water in a Dutch oven. Bring to a boil over medium-high heat, stirring frequently. Add meatballs. Reduce heat to medium-low. Cover and simmer for 30 minutes.

4. Using a small jar with a tight-fitting lid, shake flour and 1 cup (250 mL) of **cold** water vigorously until there are no lumps.

5. Increase heat to medium. When mixture has returned to boiling point, slowly add flour mixture, stirring constantly. Simmer an additional 5 minutes, stirring frequently. Serve with whole grain buns.

Makes 8—1½ cup (375 mL) portions. *Doubles easily. Freezes well.*

Black Forest Pudding

Adding pudding is a good way to revitalize dry cake. Our mothers never threw away anything, especially leftover cake. With this recipe, you'll be glad to have leftovers.

1	**egg**	1
1 tsp	**vanilla extract**	5 mL
¼ tsp	**almond extract**	1 mL
½ tsp	**kirsch flavouring**	2 mL
¼ cup	**sugar**	50 mL
3 tbsp	**cornstarch**	45 mL
pinch	**salt**	pinch
2 cups	**skim milk**	500 mL
4 portions	**leftover No-Guilt Chocolate Cake**	4 portions
½ cup	**cherry pie filling** *(Freeze the remaining pie filling for dessert on Saturday, Week 3.)*	125 mL
1 tsp	**cocoa powder**	5 mL
optional	**maraschino cherries**	optional

1. Combine egg, vanilla extract, almond extract and kirsch flavouring in a medium bowl. Beat lightly. Set aside.

2. Combine sugar, cornstarch and salt in a medium saucepan (use an under-pot wire to prevent scorching). Add milk slowly and bring to a boil over medium heat. Stir constantly. Reduce heat to medium-low and cook for about 1 minute, continuing to stir. Remove from heat.

3. Stir approximately ½ cup (125 mL) of cornstarch mixture, slowly, into egg mixture. Whisk egg mixture back into the saucepan and continue cooking for 2 minutes over medium heat, stirring constantly. Remove pudding from heat.

4. Layer 1 portion cake, 2 tbsp (30 mL) cherry pie filling and ½ cup (125 mL) pudding into individual dessert dishes. Sprinkle with cocoa powder and top with a maraschino cherry if desired.

5. Refrigerate.

Makes 4 portions. *Doubles easily.*

Exercise program by

THIRD TIME STRETCHING:

After your warm-up, do a whole body stretch (that means lower and upper body, pages 36 and 92). Don't worry, you can't stretch too often—just look at the cat who stretches every day. You are familiar with stretching technique, so this time enjoy the stretch by constant, slooow deeep breathing—inhale one, two, three (tummy goes out), exhale one, two, three (tummy goes in) while you elongate each muscle. You will have a good sleep tonight!

If you end up in a pretzel position, you're probably stretching wrong.

... continued on page 71

RESTAURANT EATING TIPS

Demand forces change, so ask for low-fat when you eat out.

Some restaurants have already responded to the demand for low-fat food by marking healthy choices on the menu.

Don't fall for the fried stuff which is usually disguised in lots of batter. In fact, it's difficult to find the real food under that greasy batter. Face it, you don't want to have your body wrapped the same way.

You are what you eat, so let us see the real you!

We recognize that you won't always eat at home, but you can make healthy choices no matter where you eat. Your health is an every day concern, so here are some tips for ordering in a restaurant. Our suggestions for healthy choices are:

✔ **red sauce on pasta** over its white cousin that contains more butter and cream;

✔ **broth-based soup** (in a cream soup, need we say it —the key word is cream!);

✔ **broiled or grilled meat** over deep-fried or pan-fried;

✔ **oil and vinegar dressings** over creamy ones (ask for them on the side so you can control the amount);

✔ **butter, sour cream or cheese ordered on the side** to control the amount;

✔ **unbuttered whole grain toast or bagels with low-fat toppings** instead of high-fat commercial muffins;

✔ **fruit or fruit-based dessert** over rich and creamy desserts (okay, make an exception once in a while —*the moon is blue occasionally*!);

✔ **raw vegetables and low-fat dressings** at the salad bar (avoid mixed dishes such as pasta salad, potato salad and oil-marinated vegetables because of their high-fat dressings (another source of high fat is cheese);

✔ **mineral water instead of alcohol-based beverages** — it's not only O.K., it's trendy;

✔ **doggie bags instead of overeating** — restaurant portions are usually too large for the average person;

✔ **treats justified this way:** low-fat appetizer instead of a main course and then enjoy your favorite dessert — you don't even have to share it!

Don't let your eyes make the decision — they are always bigger than your stomach and so is the dessert display!

So, making choices in a restaurant is easy! Eat your favourite dish occasionally; just balance the extra calories by eating low-fat the next day. Eat breakfast and lunch on the day you are dining out; it is easier to control your appetite and to make wiser choices if your blood sugar is not too low.

(clockwise from top)

Black Forest Pudding
page 53

Good Old Tapioca Pudding
page 26

Heavy Artillery Cookies
page 168

Blueberry Bubbly
page 106

BREAKFAST

Whole Grain Cereal of Choice, Fruit of Choice, Milk

LUNCH

T.G.I.F. (Use up leftovers or buy a lunch.)

DINNER

Veggie Pizza, Fruit of Choice, Milk

SNACK

Have a beer (that's **root** beer for the kids)!

GAME PLAN

You are now ready to venture into "restaurant land" on your own, or you can plan your own lunch.

ENJOY YOUR OWN SMART CHOICES!

If you choose to eat out, you may want to review the restaurant tips on the opposite page but if you plan to brown-bag it, there are plenty of leftovers in your freezer. All you have to cook today is the **Veggie Pizza** for a casual dinner.

Total preparation and cooking time: **30 min.**

As you can see, the snack is not planned. An occasional treat is recommended, *and you deserve it!*

NUTRITION INFORMATION
See page 6 for standards used.

MENU ITEMS (single portion)	calories	carbs (grams)	protein (grams)	fat (grams)
Whole Grain Cereal of Choice	126	20.3	2.6	4.4
Fruit of Choice	81	21	0.2	0.5
Milk	86	11.9	8.3	0.4
Veggie Pizza	497.9	74.1	30.5	13.7
Fruit of Choice	81	21	0.2	0.5
Milk	86	11.9	8.3	0.4
Total for day	957.9	160.2	50.1	19.9
percentage fat ▶				19%

REMEMBER, these are the MINIMUM REQUIREMENTS of the Canada and U.S. Food Guides. Some people will need more calories.

It's just as easy to make two pizzas as one, so make two and freeze one unbaked!

Congratulations on your first week of healthy eating... *and* you even started exercising!

Remember that Rome wasn't built in a day; you won't notice dramatic changes in your waist size instantly.

We did not design a yo-yo diet for you. What we did design is a feel-good plan that incorporates healthy eating and exercise habits into your daily routine.

Be persistent. This is a lifestyle change.

Success is a journey — not a destination.

VEGGIE PIZZA

It's a must to try our crust, but when in a hurry don't worry...commercial bread dough works well!

1	**1 lb (454 g) loaf frozen whole wheat bread dough, thawed** **OR** **1 recipe "Homemade Pizza Dough "** *(page 175)*	1
1	**7.5 oz (213 mL) can tomato sauce**	1
1 tsp	**oregano**	5 mL
½ tsp	**basil**	2 mL
1	**clove garlic, minced**	1
¼ tsp	**black pepper**	1 mL
1 tsp	**red pepper flakes** *(optional)*	5 mL
1 tbsp	**canola or olive oil**	15 mL
1	**medium onion, sliced**	1
1	**10 oz (284 mL) can mushrooms, sliced**	1
1/2	**green pepper, cut in strips**	1/2
1/2	**red pepper, cut in strips**	1/2
2 cups	**broccoli florets**	500 mL
½ cup	**low-fat ricotta cheese**	125 mL
½ cup	**low-fat cheddar cheese, grated**	125 mL
½ cup	**sun-dried tomatoes, cut in small pieces**	125 mL
½ cup	**low-fat Parmesan cheese, grated**	125 mL

1. Lightly dust dough with 2 tbsp (30 mL) all-purpose flour. Stretch and spread dough on a pizza pan coated with cooking spray. Let rest.
2. Meanwhile, combine tomato sauce, oregano, basil, garlic, black pepper and red pepper flakes in a small bowl. Set aside.
3. Heat canola oil in a large nonstick skillet over medium heat. Add onion, mushrooms and peppers. Stir-fry 2 to 3 minutes. Add broccoli and 1 tbsp (15 mL) water. Cover. Reduce heat to medium-low and cook an additional 3 to 4 minutes. **Drain well**. Stir in ricotta cheese. Set aside.
4. Spread tomato sauce evenly over dough. Distribute vegetable mixture over pizza. Top with cheddar cheese and sun-dried tomatoes. Sprinkle with Parmesan cheese.
5. Bake at 400°F (200°C) for 15 to 20 minutes. Remove from oven. Allow to rest for 5 minutes before slicing.

Makes 4 portions. *Doubles easily. Freezes well.*

WEEK 2 MENU

Recipes are provided in this chapter for menu items in **BOLD** on the day they are first prepared.

DAY	BREAKFAST	LUNCH	DINNER	SNACK
1 SAT pg. 63	*Garden Scramble, Whole Grain Toast, Fruit Juice of Choice	*"Fit to Eat" Grilled Cheese Sandwich, Dill Pickle, Fruit of Choice, Milk	Spaghetti with "Salsa di Carné", *Garden Salad	*Cinnamon Graham Fruit
2 SUN pg. 67	**BRUNCH** *Cinnamon Bagel French Toast, *Maple Cream Topping, Half Grapefruit, Milk		*Veggies & Dip ➡ *Toss & Bake Chicken, *Spinach-Stuffed Potato, *Garlic-Parmesan Tomato	*Saucy Apple Pudding ➡ Milk
3 MON pg. 73	Whole Grain Cereal of Choice, Banana, Fruit Juice of Choice, Milk	*Vegetarian Pita Pocket, Fruit of Choice, Vegetable Juice of Choice	*Fillet of Sole Veronique, *Le Riz Vert, *Broccoli "Noël", Veggies & Dip, Milk	*Saucy Apple Pudding ➡
4 TUE pg. 77	Toasted Whole Grain Bagel, Fat-Free Cream Cheese, Fruit-Only Jam, Fruit Juice of Choice	*Golden Cream of Carrot Soup, *Turkey Bunwich, Fruit of Choice	*Southwestern Black Bean Chicken Salad, *Garlic Toast, Milk	Fruit of Choice
5 WED pg. 81	*Apple-Cinnamon Oatmeal, Fruit Juice of Choice, Milk	*Tuna Sandwich, *Orange-Almond Salad, Fruit of Choice	*Black Forest Potatoes, *Garlic Green Beans	Banana-Pineapple Muffin ➡ Milk
6 THU pg. 85	Whole Grain Toast, Reduced-Fat Peanut Butter, Fruit-Only Jam, Fruit of Choice, Milk	*Fruity Cottage Cheese Salad, Banana-Pineapple Muffin	*Wild Oriental Chicken, Fruit of Choice, Milk	Saucy Apple Pudding, or Fig Bar & Apple
7 FRI pg. 87	Whole Grain Cereal of Choice topped with Canned Peach Slices, Fruit Juice of Choice, Milk	T.G.I.F. (Use up leftovers or buy a lunch.)	*Capelli Medley with Roasted Tomatoes, *Fruit & Crème Brulé, Milk	Your favourite treat (popcorn & a video)!

✱ These recipes provide **EXACT MINIMUM PORTIONS** and may need to be adjusted for extra portions.

➡ This symbol will remind you to save portions of this recipe for use later this week.

These items might be in your pantry now.

If not, add them to your shopping list on the following pages, as well as any personal preferences such as shampoo, toothpaste, cleaning supplies and so on.

Please note: ground spices and dried herbs are used in recipes unless otherwise specified.

- ☐ ALLSPICE
- ☐ BASIL
- ☐ BAY LEAVES
- ☐ CAYENNE PEPPER
- ☐ CINNAMON
- ☐ CUMIN
- ☐ GARLIC POWDER
- ☐ GINGER
- ☐ MUSTARD, dry
- ☐ ONION POWDER
- ☐ ORANGE PEEL, dried
- ☐ OREGANO
- ☐ PAPRIKA
- ☐ PARSLEY
- ☐ PEPPER, black
- ☐ PEPPER, white
- ☐ RED PEPPER FLAKES
- ☐ SALT
- ☐ SEASONING SALT
- ☐ THYME
- ☐ MAPLE EXTRACT
- ☐ VANILLA EXTRACT
- ☐ MAPLE-FLAVOURED SYRUP, light
- ☐ BOUILLON CONCENTRATE, chicken
- ☐ BAKING POWDER
- ☐ BAKING SODA
- ☐ FLOUR, all-purpose
- ☐ MOLASSES
- ☐ SKIM MILK POWDER
- ☐ SUGAR, brown
- ☐ SUGAR, icing
- ☐ SUGAR, white
- ☐ CEREALS, whole grain, breakfast

- ☐ NATURAL WHEAT BRAN
- ☐ OAT BRAN
- ☐ QUICK OATS
- ☐ CINNAMON GRAHAM WAFERS, low-fat
- ☐ FIG BARS
- ☐ JAMS, fruit-only
- ☐ PEANUT BUTTER, reduced-fat
- ☐ COFFEE
- ☐ JUICES, fruit, assorted
- ☐ JUICES, vegetable , assorted
- ☐ LEMON JUICE, bottled or fresh
- ☐ LIME JUICE, bottled or fresh
- ☐ TEAS, assorted
- ☐ WHITE WINE or apple juice
- ☐ COOKING SPRAY, butter-flavoured
- ☐ COOKING SPRAY, plain
- ☐ DILL PICKLES
- ☐ OIL, olive and/or canola
- ☐ MUSTARD, prepared
- ☐ SALAD DRESSINGS, assorted, fat-free
- ☐ SALAD DRESSING, Italian, fat-free
- ☐ SALAD DRESSING, Ranch, fat-free
- ☐ TABASCO SAUCE
- ☐ VINEGAR, white wine
- ☐ VINEGAR, red wine
- ☐ RICE, brown, long grain
- ☐ SOY SAUCE, salt-reduced
- ☐ DRIED BREAD CRUMBS, fine
- ☐ PARMESAN CHEESE, low-fat, grated
- ☐ SPAGHETTI, high-fibre

SHOPPING LIST

Review all recipes for portion requirements (see page 22). Add any missing pantry items to your grocery list.

PRODUCE

☐ **APPLES**, macintosh or spartan 7

☐ **BANANAS** 4

☐ **FRUIT**, assorted 14 portions

☐ **GRAPEFRUIT** 1

☐ **GREEN GRAPES**, seedless (*optional*)

☐ **KIWI FRUIT** 4

☐ **BROCCOLI** 6 stalks

☐ **CARROTS** 1-5 lb (2.3 kg) bag

☐ **CAULIFLOWER** 1 small head

☐ **CELERY** 1 bunch

☐ **CUCUMBER** 1 small

☐ **GARLIC** 2 heads

☐ **JICAMA** 1

☐ **LETTUCE**, red or green leaf 1 head

☐ **LETTUCE**, romaine 1 head

☐ **GREEN ONIONS** 3 bunches

☐ **ONION** 1 medium

☐ **ONION** 1 large

☐ **RED ONION** 1 medium

☐ **PEPPERS**, green 3

☐ **PEPPERS**, red 3 (*or substitute 2 red peppers with 2 small zucchini*)

☐ **POTATOES** 6 medium

☐ **POTATOES**, red 4 medium

☐ **SPROUTS**, alfalfa or mixed 1 pkg

☐ **TOMATOES** 5 medium

☐ **ROMA TOMATOES** 12

☐ **ZUCCHINI** 1 small

☐ **VEGETABLES FOR SNACKS**, assorted (*see side panel page 67*)

GROCERIES

☐ **ALMONDS**, slivered ¼ cup (50 mL)

☐ **EVAPORATED SKIM MILK**
1-14 oz (385 mL) can

☐ **TACO SEASONING** 1-1.5 oz (35 g) pkg

☐ **FRUIT OF CHOICE**, in juice
2-14 oz (398 mL) cans

☐ **MANDARIN ORANGE SEGMENTS**, in juice
1-10 oz (284 mL) can

☐ **PEACHES,** sliced, in juice
1-14 oz (398 mL) can

☐ **PINEAPPLE**, crushed, in juice
1-14 oz (398 mL) can

☐ **PINEAPPLE TIDBITS**, in juice
1-14 oz (398 mL) can

☐ **MUSHROOMS**, sliced 2-10 oz (284 mL) cans

☐ **TOMATOES**, diced 1-28 oz (798 mL) can

☐ **TOMATO PASTE** 1-14 oz (398 mL) can

☐ **TOMATO SAUCE** 1-26 oz (725 mL) can

☐ **CAPELLI OR ANGEL HAIR PASTA**
1-12 oz (375 g) pkg

☐ **CHICKEN BROTH** 2-10 oz (284 mL) cans

☐ **BLACK BEANS** 1-19 oz (540 mL) can

☐ **TUNA**, in water 1-7.5 oz (213 g) can

☐ **CHILI SAUCE** 1-10 oz (285 mL) bottle

☐ **ZESTY ONION RELISH** 1-14 oz (375 mL) jar

☐ **WILD RICE** ½ cup (125 mL)

(*continued on reverse*)

FAMILY OF 2

MEAT

- [ ] **CHICKEN BREASTS**, boneless, skinless 2
- [ ] **CHICKEN LEGS**, whole (*thigh & drumstick*) 2
- [ ] **CHICKEN THIGHS**, skinless, bone in 8
- [ ] **LEAN GROUND BEEF** 2 lbs (900 g)
- [ ] **SOLE FILLETS**, fresh or frozen
  1-14 oz (400 g) pkg
- [ ] **BLACK FOREST HAM**, sliced ½" (1 cm) thick
  8 oz (225 g)
- [ ] **ROASTED DELI TURKEY BREAST**,
  thinly sliced 4 oz (120 g)

BAKERY

- [ ] **BAGELS**, whole grain 4
- [ ] **BREAD**, whole grain 1 loaf
- [ ] **BUNS**, whole grain 2
- [ ] **FRENCH BREAD** , sliced 1 loaf
- [ ] **PITA BREAD**, whole wheat 2

FROZEN

- [ ] **BLUEBERRIES** 1 cup (250 mL)
- [ ] **GREEN BEANS**, cut 4 cups (1 L)
- [ ] **KERNEL CORN** 2 cups (500 mL)
- [ ] **SPINACH**, chopped 1-10 oz (300 g) pkg
- [ ] **ORANGE JUICE CONCENTRATE**
  1-12 oz (355 mL) can

DAIRY

- [ ] **MILK** 7 quarts (7 L)
- [ ] **YOGURT**, vanilla, fat-free ½ cup (125 mL)
- [ ] **SOUR CREAM**, fat-free 2¼ cups (550 mL)
- [ ] **COTTAGE CHEESE**, 1% milk fat
  1 cup (250 mL)
- [ ] **CREAM CHEESE**, low-fat ½ cup (125 mL)
- [ ] **CHEDDAR CHEESE**, low-fat, grated
  1 cup (250 mL)
- [ ] **FETA CHEESE**, low-fat 4 oz (120 g)
- [ ] **CHEESE SLICES**, 1% milk fat   8
- [ ] **MARGARINE**, non hydrogenated
- [ ] **EGGS** 7

PANTRY & OTHER

- [ ] _____
- [ ] _____
- [ ] _____
- [ ] _____
- [ ] _____
- [ ] _____
- [ ] _____
- [ ] _____
- [ ] _____
- [ ] _____
- [ ] _____

SHOPPING LIST

Review all recipes for portion requirements (see page 22). Add any missing pantry items to your grocery list.

PRODUCE

- ☐ **APPLES**, macintosh or spartan 7
- ☐ **BANANAS** 4
- ☐ **FRUIT**, assorted 14 portions
- ☐ **GRAPEFRUIT** 1
- ☐ **GREEN GRAPES**, seedless (*optional*)
- ☐ **KIWI FRUIT** 4
- ☐ **BROCCOLI** 6 stalks
- ☐ **CARROTS** 1-5 lb (2.3 kg) bag
- ☐ **CAULIFLOWER** 1 small head
- ☐ **CELERY** 1 bunch
- ☐ **CUCUMBER** 1 small
- ☐ **GARLIC** 2 heads
- ☐ **JICAMA** 1
- ☐ **LETTUCE**, red or green leaf 1 head
- ☐ **LETTUCE**, romaine 1 head
- ☐ **GREEN ONIONS** 3 bunches
- ☐ **ONION** 1 medium
- ☐ **ONION** 1 large
- ☐ **RED ONION** 1 medium
- ☐ **PEPPERS**, green 3
- ☐ **PEPPERS**, red 3 (*or substitute 2 red peppers with 2 small zucchini*)
- ☐ **POTATOES** 6 medium
- ☐ **POTATOES**, red 4 medium
- ☐ **SPROUTS**, alfalfa or mixed 1 pkg
- ☐ **TOMATOES** 5 medium
- ☐ **ROMA TOMATOES** 12
- ☐ **ZUCCHINI** 1 small
- ☐ **VEGETABLES FOR SNACKS**, assorted (*see side panel page 67*)

GROCERIES

- ☐ **ALMONDS**, slivered ¼ cup (50 mL)
- ☐ **EVAPORATED SKIM MILK** 1-14 oz (385 mL) can
- ☐ **TACO SEASONING** 1-1.5 oz (35 g) pkg
- ☐ **FRUIT OF CHOICE**, in juice 2-14 oz (398 mL) cans
- ☐ **MANDARIN ORANGE SEGMENTS**, in juice 1-10 oz (284 mL) can
- ☐ **PEACHES,** sliced, in juice 1-14 oz (398 mL) can
- ☐ **PINEAPPLE**, crushed, in juice 1-14 oz (398 mL) can
- ☐ **PINEAPPLE TIDBITS**, in juice 1-14 oz (398 mL) can
- ☐ **MUSHROOMS**, sliced 2-10 oz (284 mL) cans
- ☐ **TOMATOES**, diced 1-28 oz (798 mL) can
- ☐ **TOMATO PASTE** 1-14 oz (398 mL) can
- ☐ **TOMATO SAUCE** 1-26 oz (725 mL) can
- ☐ **CAPELLI OR ANGEL HAIR PASTA** 1-12 oz (375 g) pkg
- ☐ **CHICKEN BROTH** 2-10 oz (284 mL) cans
- ☐ **BLACK BEANS** 1-19 oz (540 mL) can
- ☐ **TUNA**, in water 1-7.5 oz (213 g) can
- ☐ **CHILI SAUCE** 1-10 oz (285 mL) bottle
- ☐ **ZESTY ONION RELISH** 1-14 oz (375 mL) jar
- ☐ **WILD RICE** ½ cup (125 mL)

(*continued on reverse*)

MEAT

- [ ] **CHICKEN BREASTS**, boneless, skinless 2
- [ ] **CHICKEN LEGS**, whole (*thigh & drumstick*) 2
- [ ] **CHICKEN THIGHS**, skinless, bone in 8
- [ ] **LEAN GROUND BEEF** 2 lbs (900 g)
- [ ] **SOLE FILLETS**, fresh or frozen
  1-14 oz (400 g) pkg
- [ ] **BLACK FOREST HAM**, sliced ½" (1 cm) thick
  8 oz (225 g)
- [ ] **ROASTED DELI TURKEY BREAST**,
  thinly sliced 4 oz (120 g)

BAKERY

- [ ] **BAGELS**, whole grain 4
- [ ] **BREAD**, whole grain 1 loaf
- [ ] **BUNS**, whole grain 2
- [ ] **FRENCH BREAD** , sliced 1 loaf
- [ ] **PITA BREAD**, whole wheat 2

FROZEN

- [ ] **BLUEBERRIES** 1 cup (250 mL)
- [ ] **GREEN BEANS**, cut 4 cups (1 L)
- [ ] **KERNEL CORN** 2 cups (500 mL)
- [ ] **SPINACH**, chopped 1-10 oz (300 g) pkg
- [ ] **ORANGE JUICE CONCENTRATE**
  1-12 oz (355 mL) can

DAIRY

- [ ] **MILK** 7 quarts (7 L)
- [ ] **YOGURT**, vanilla, fat-free ½ cup (125 mL)
- [ ] **SOUR CREAM**, fat-free 2¼ cups (550 mL)
- [ ] **COTTAGE CHEESE**, 1% milk fat
  1 cup (250 mL)
- [ ] **CREAM CHEESE**, low-fat ½ cup (125 mL)
- [ ] **CHEDDAR CHEESE**, low-fat, grated
  1 cup (250 mL)
- [ ] **FETA CHEESE**, low-fat 4 oz (120 g)
- [ ] **CHEESE SLICES**, 1% milk fat 8
- [ ] **MARGARINE**, non hydrogenated
- [ ] **EGGS** 7

PANTRY & OTHER

- [ ] _____
- [ ] _____
- [ ] _____
- [ ] _____
- [ ] _____
- [ ] _____
- [ ] _____
- [ ] _____
- [ ] _____
- [ ] _____
- [ ] _____

SHOPPING LIST

Review all recipes for portion requirements (see page 22). Add any missing pantry items to your grocery list.

PRODUCE

- [ ] **APPLES**, macintosh or spartan 9
- [ ] **BANANAS** 6
- [ ] **FRUIT**, assorted 28 portions
- [ ] **GRAPEFRUIT** 2
- [ ] **GREEN GRAPES**, seedless *(optional)*
- [ ] **KIWI FRUIT** 4
- [ ] **BROCCOLI** 6 stalks
- [ ] **CARROTS** 1-5 lb (2.3 kg) bag
- [ ] **CAULIFLOWER** 1 head
- [ ] **CELERY** 1 bunch
- [ ] **CUCUMBER** 1 large
- [ ] **GARLIC** 2 heads
- [ ] **JICAMA** 1
- [ ] **LETTUCE**, red or green leaf 1 head
- [ ] **LETTUCE**, romaine 2 heads
- [ ] **GREEN ONIONS** 4 bunches
- [ ] **ONION** 1 medium
- [ ] **ONION** 1 large
- [ ] **RED ONION** 1 medium
- [ ] **PEPPERS**, green 4
- [ ] **PEPPERS**, red 4 *(or substitute 2 red peppers with 2 small zucchini)*
- [ ] **POTATOES** 8 medium
- [ ] **POTATOES,** red 8 medium
- [ ] **SPROUTS**, alfalfa or mixed 2 pkgs
- [ ] **TOMATOES** 10 medium
- [ ] **ROMA TOMATOES** 14
- [ ] **ZUCCHINI** 1 small
- [ ] **VEGETABLES FOR SNACKS**, assorted *(see side panel page 67)*

GROCERIES

- [ ] **ALMONDS**, slivered ½ cup (125 mL)
- [ ] **EVAPORATED SKIM MILK** 1-14 oz (385 mL) can
- [ ] **TACO SEASONING** 1-1.5 oz (35 g) pkg
- [ ] **FRUIT OF CHOICE**, in juice 4-14 oz (398 mL) cans
- [ ] **MANDARIN ORANGE SEGMENTS**, in juice 1-10 oz (284 mL) can
- [ ] **PEACHES**, sliced, in juice 2-14 oz (398 mL) cans
- [ ] **PINEAPPLE**, crushed, in juice 1-14 oz (398 mL) can
- [ ] **PINEAPPLE TIDBITS**, in juice 1-14 oz (398 mL) can
- [ ] **MUSHROOMS**, sliced 2-10 oz (284 mL) cans
- [ ] **TOMATOES**, diced 1-28 oz (798 mL) can
- [ ] **TOMATO PASTE** 1-14 oz (398 mL) can
- [ ] **TOMATO SAUCE** 1-26 oz (725 mL) can
- [ ] **CAPELLI OR ANGEL HAIR PASTA** 1-12 oz (375 g) pkg
- [ ] **CHICKEN BROTH** 2-10 oz (284 mL) cans
- [ ] **BLACK BEANS** 1-19 oz (540 mL) can
- [ ] **TUNA**, in water 2-7.5 oz (213g) cans
- [ ] **CHILI SAUCE** 1-10 oz (285 mL) bottle
- [ ] **ZESTY ONION RELISH** 1-14 oz (375 mL) jar
- [ ] **WILD RICE** ½ cup (125 mL)

(continued on reverse)

MEAT

- ☐ **CHICKEN BREASTS**, boneless, skinless 4
- ☐ **CHICKEN LEGS**, whole (*thigh & drumstick*) 4
- ☐ **CHICKEN THIGHS**, skinless, bone in 8
- ☐ **LEAN GROUND BEEF** 2 lbs (900 g)
- ☐ **SOLE FILLETS**, fresh or frozen
  1-14 oz (400 g) pkg
- ☐ **BLACK FOREST HAM**, sliced ½" (1 cm) thick
  1 lb (450 g)
- ☐ **ROASTED DELI TURKEY BREAST**,
  thinly sliced 8 oz (240 g)

BAKERY

- ☐ **BAGELS**, whole grain 8
- ☐ **BREAD**, whole grain 2 loaves
- ☐ **BUNS**, whole grain 4
- ☐ **FRENCH BREAD** , sliced 1 loaf
- ☐ **PITA BREAD**, whole wheat 4

FROZEN

- ☐ **BLUEBERRIES** 1 cup (250 mL)
- ☐ **GREEN BEANS**, cut 6 cups (1.5 L)
- ☐ **KERNEL CORN** 2 cups (500 mL)
- ☐ **SPINACH**, chopped 1-10 oz (300 g) pkg
- ☐ **ORANGE JUICE CONCENTRATE**
  1-12 oz (355 mL) can

DAIRY

- ☐ **MILK** 13 quarts (13 L)
- ☐ **YOGURT**, vanilla, fat-free ½ cup (125 mL)
- ☐ **SOUR CREAM**, fat-free 2½ cups (625 mL)
- ☐ **COTTAGE CHEESE**, 1% milk fat
  2 cups (500 mL)
- ☐ **CREAM CHEESE**, low-fat ¾ cup (175 mL)
- ☐ **CHEDDAR CHEESE**, low-fat, grated
  1½ cups (375 mL)
- ☐ **FETA CHEESE**, low-fat 4 oz (120 g)
- ☐ **CHEESE SLICES** 1% milk fat 16
- ☐ **MARGARINE**, non hydrogenated
- ☐ **EGGS** 10

PANTRY & OTHER

- ☐ _____
- ☐ _____
- ☐ _____
- ☐ _____
- ☐ _____
- ☐ _____
- ☐ _____
- ☐ _____
- ☐ _____
- ☐ _____
- ☐ _____
- ☐ _____

SHOPPING LIST

Review all recipes for portion requirements (see page 22). Add any missing pantry items to your grocery list.

PRODUCE

- [ ] **APPLES**, macintosh or spartan 9
- [ ] **BANANAS** 6
- [ ] **FRUIT**, assorted 28 portions
- [ ] **GRAPEFRUIT** 2
- [ ] **GREEN GRAPES**, seedless (*optional*)
- [ ] **KIWI FRUIT** 4
- [ ] **BROCCOLI** 6 stalks
- [ ] **CARROTS** 1-5 lb (2.3 kg) bag
- [ ] **CAULIFLOWER** 1 head
- [ ] **CELERY** 1 bunch
- [ ] **CUCUMBER** 1 large
- [ ] **GARLIC** 2 heads
- [ ] **JICAMA** 1
- [ ] **LETTUCE**, red or green leaf 1 head
- [ ] **LETTUCE**, romaine 2 heads
- [ ] **GREEN ONIONS** 4 bunches
- [ ] **ONION** 1 medium
- [ ] **ONION** 1 large
- [ ] **RED ONION** 1 medium
- [ ] **PEPPERS**, green 4
- [ ] **PEPPERS**, red 4 (*or substitute 2 red peppers with 2 small zucchini*)
- [ ] **POTATOES** 8 medium
- [ ] **POTATOES,** red 8 medium
- [ ] **SPROUTS**, alfalfa or mixed 2 pkgs
- [ ] **TOMATOES** 10 medium
- [ ] **ROMA TOMATOES** 14
- [ ] **ZUCCHINI** 1 small
- [ ] **VEGETABLES FOR SNACKS**, assorted (*see side panel page 67*)

GROCERIES

- [ ] **ALMONDS**, slivered ½ cup (125 mL)
- [ ] **EVAPORATED SKIM MILK** 1-14 oz (385 mL) can
- [ ] **TACO SEASONING** 1-1.5 oz (35 g) pkg
- [ ] **FRUIT OF CHOICE**, in juice 4-14 oz (398 mL) cans
- [ ] **MANDARIN ORANGE SEGMENTS**, in juice 1-10 oz (284 mL) can
- [ ] **PEACHES**, sliced, in juice 2-14 oz (398 mL) cans
- [ ] **PINEAPPLE,** crushed, in juice 1-14 oz (398 mL) can
- [ ] **PINEAPPLE TIDBITS**, in juice 1-14 oz (398 mL) can
- [ ] **MUSHROOMS**, sliced 2-10 oz (284 mL) cans
- [ ] **TOMATOES**, diced 1-28 oz (798 mL) can
- [ ] **TOMATO PASTE** 1-14 oz (398 mL) can
- [ ] **TOMATO SAUCE** 1-26 oz (725 mL) can
- [ ] **CAPELLI OR ANGEL HAIR PASTA** 1-12 oz (375 g) pkg
- [ ] **CHICKEN BROTH** 2-10 oz (284 mL) cans
- [ ] **BLACK BEANS** 1-19 oz (540 mL) can
- [ ] **TUNA**, in water 2-7.5 oz (213g) cans
- [ ] **CHILI SAUCE** 1-10 oz (285 mL) bottle
- [ ] **ZESTY ONION RELISH** 1-14 oz (375 mL) jar
- [ ] **WILD RICE** ½ cup (125 mL)

(*continued on reverse*)

MEAT

- ☐ **CHICKEN BREASTS**, boneless, skinless 4
- ☐ **CHICKEN LEGS**, whole (*thigh & drumstick*) 4
- ☐ **CHICKEN THIGHS**, skinless, bone in 8
- ☐ **LEAN GROUND BEEF** 2 lbs (900 g)
- ☐ **SOLE FILLETS**, fresh or frozen
  1-14 oz (400 g) pkg
- ☐ **BLACK FOREST HAM**, sliced ½" (1 cm) thick
  1 lb (450 g)
- ☐ **ROASTED DELI TURKEY BREAST,**
  thinly sliced 8 oz (240 g)

BAKERY

- ☐ **BAGELS**, whole grain 8
- ☐ **BREAD**, whole grain 2 loaves
- ☐ **BUNS**, whole grain 4
- ☐ **FRENCH BREAD** , sliced 1 loaf
- ☐ **PITA BREAD**, whole wheat 4

FROZEN

- ☐ **BLUEBERRIES** 1 cup (250 mL)
- ☐ **GREEN BEANS**, cut 6 cups (1.5 L)
- ☐ **KERNEL CORN** 2 cups (500 mL)
- ☐ **SPINACH**, chopped 1-10 oz (300 g) pkg
- ☐ **ORANGE JUICE CONCENTRATE**
  1-12 oz (355 mL) can

DAIRY

- ☐ **MILK** 13 quarts (13 L)
- ☐ **YOGURT**, vanilla, fat-free ½ cup (125 mL)
- ☐ **SOUR CREAM**, fat-free 2½ cups (625 mL)
- ☐ **COTTAGE CHEESE**, 1% milk fat
  2 cups (500 mL)
- ☐ **CREAM CHEESE**, low-fat ¾ cup (175 mL)
- ☐ **CHEDDAR CHEESE**, low-fat, grated
  1½ cups (375 mL)
- ☐ **FETA CHEESE**, low-fat 4 oz (120 g)
- ☐ **CHEESE SLICES** 1% milk fat 16
- ☐ **MARGARINE**, non hydrogenated
- ☐ **EGGS** 10

PANTRY & OTHER

- ☐ _____
- ☐ _____
- ☐ _____
- ☐ _____
- ☐ _____
- ☐ _____
- ☐ _____
- ☐ _____
- ☐ _____
- ☐ _____
- ☐ _____

BREAKFAST
Garden Scramble, Whole Grain Toast, Fruit Juice of Choice

LUNCH
"Fit to Eat" Grilled Cheese Sandwich, Dill Pickle, Fruit of Choice, Milk

DINNER
Spaghetti with "Salsa di Carné",
Garden Salad

SNACK
Cinnamon Graham Fruit
(see side panel page 65)

NUTRITION INFORMATION
See page 6 for standards used.

MENU ITEMS (single portion)	calories	carbs (grams)	protein (grams)	fat (grams)
Garden Scramble	104.3	3.4	10.2	5.1
Whole Grain Toast — 1	63	12.4	2.7	0.8
Fruit Juice of Choice	80	20	1	0
"Fit to Eat" Grilled Cheese Sandwich	182	29.6	15.6	2
Dill Pickle — 4" (10 cm)	14	2.7	0.7	0.3
Fruit of Choice	81	21	0.2	0.5
Milk	86	11.9	8.3	0.4
"Salsa di Carné"	225.2	21.2	15.5	9.5
Spaghetti	301	63	10	1.2
Garden Salad	77	16.6	3.1	0.5
Cinnamon Graham Fruit	122	28.7	1.5	0.8
Total for day	1336	230.5	68.8	21.1
			percentage fat ▶	14%

REMEMBER, these are the MINIMUM REQUIREMENTS of the Canada and U.S. Food Guides. Some people will need more calories.

GAME PLAN

Again, we assume that you will go grocery shopping before lunch on Saturday, because the organization of your week starts then.

Thaw the leftover tomato paste from Saturday, Week 1 to add to the spaghetti sauce for dinner.

When unpacking the groceries, keep the ground beef for tonight's dinner in the fridge, as well as the chicken legs for tomorrow's dinner. Freeze all remaining meat except for the Black Forest Ham and Deli Turkey. Freeze breads as in Week 1 except for the number of bagels needed for Sunday's brunch, and the whole grain bread for today's lunch. Fill a plastic container with "mouse food" (see pages 21 and 67).

... continued on page 66

GARDEN SCRAMBLE

Throw the extra egg yolk away and save 5.6 g of fat. As Denise's Auntie used to say: "Better it goes to waste than to my waist."

2 tbsp	green onion, chopped	30 mL
2 tbsp	canned mushrooms, sliced *(Use remaining canned mushrooms, if any, in tonight's spaghetti sauce.)*	30 mL
2 tbsp	red pepper, diced	30 mL
1	egg white	1
1	whole egg	1
¼ tsp	Worcestershire sauce	1 mL
pinch	salt	pinch
pinch	black pepper	pinch
2 tbsp	water	30 mL

1. Sauté onion, mushrooms and red pepper for 3 to 5 minutes, over medium heat, in a nonstick skillet coated with cooking spray.

2. Meanwhile, separate yolk from white of <u>one</u> egg over a medium size bowl (*see below*). Discard yolk. Your egg white will have fallen into the bowl.

3. Add the other egg, Worcestershire sauce, salt, black pepper and water to the bowl. Stir gently with a fork (beating will cause watery eggs).

4. Add egg mixture all at once to mushroom mixture. Stir and cook until desired consistency.

5. Serve on toasted whole grain bread.

Makes 1 portion.

To separate egg yolk from egg white if you don't have an egg separator:

- crack raw egg on the side of a bowl;

- holding the egg over the bowl, gently pour yolk back and forth into the broken shell halves;

- the egg white will overflow into the bowl until you just have yolk remaining (in the **Garden Scramble** recipe, you will discard this yolk).

"FIT TO EAT" GRILLED CHEESE SANDWICH

Grilling is not always required — just pack as a plain cheese sandwich in a picnic basket for your Saturday hike. To spice up this sandwich, add some thinly sliced red onion and/or jalapeño peppers and/or pickles.

2	slices whole grain bread	2
2	slices 1% milk-fat cheese	2

1. Sandwich 2 slices of cheese between 2 slices of unbuttered bread.

2. Brown each side lightly over medium heat, in a nonstick skillet coated with butter-flavoured cooking spray, until cheese is melted.

Makes 1 portion.

Grilled cheese sandwiches made with regular cheese slices would equal 158 extra calories, because of the extra 17.6 grams of fat! Is it worth it to your arteries when your taste buds won't notice the difference?

GARDEN SALAD

Garden Salad doesn't need to be complicated — toss in any vegetables or fruit and load up on vitamins, minerals and fibre!

1 cup	romaine lettuce, shredded	250 mL
¼ cup	alfalfa sprouts	50 mL
¼ cup	cucumber, sliced	50 mL
¼ cup	carrot, grated	50 mL
2 tbsp	green onion, chopped	30 mL
1	Roma tomato, quartered	1
1 tbsp	fat-free salad dressing	15 mL

1. Toss all ingredients with your favourite fat-free dressing.

Makes 1 portion.

CINNAMON GRAHAM FRUIT

This recipe is ideal for unexpected guests!

1 cup (250 mL) canned fruit of choice, in juice

1 low-fat cinnamon graham wafer

1. Place fruit in a fruit cup.

2. Top with crumbled graham wafer or serve the graham wafer on the side.

Makes 1 portion.

... continued from page 63

Begin cooking dinner by preparing the spaghetti sauce. About 15 minutes before the sauce is done, cook the pasta. While the pasta cooks, make the salad.

Total preparation and cooking time: **50 min.**

Make only enough pasta for the portions you need today. To measure spaghetti: 1 portion (3 oz [85 g]) is a bundle about 1" (2.5 cm) in diameter.

Freeze leftover meat sauce in portions of 2 or 4 cups. When you need a quick meal, the sauce reheats well in the microwave while you cook some pasta.

SPAGHETTI WITH "SALSA DI CARNÉ"

Submitted by Germaine Couture, Windsor, Quebec. This recipe is part of Chantal's heritage; her mom served it every Friday night.

2 lbs	**lean ground beef, browned, fat drained**	900 g
1	**large onion, diced**	1
3	**cloves garlic, minced**	3
4	**stalks celery, diced**	4
2	**green peppers, diced**	2
2	**red peppers, diced** (*or 2 small zucchini, grated*)	2
3	**medium carrots, grated**	3
2	**10 oz (284 mL) cans sliced mushrooms, drained**	2
1 tbsp	**oregano**	15 mL
1 tsp	**basil**	5 mL
1 tbsp	**paprika**	15 mL
pinch each	**black pepper & cayenne pepper**	pinch each
2	**bay leaves** (*Remove before serving.*)	2
1	**28 oz (796 mL) can diced tomatoes**	1
1	**26 oz (725 mL) can tomato sauce**	1
1	**14 oz (398 mL) can tomato paste**	1
2 tbsp	**cooking molasses**	30 mL
1 tbsp	**red pepper flakes** (*Optional for those who like it hot!*)	15 mL
	high-fibre spaghetti	

1. Brown beef over medium-high heat in a Dutch oven coated with cooking spray. Drain fat.
2. Reduce heat to medium. Add onion, garlic, celery, green and red peppers, carrots and mushrooms. Sauté for 2 to 3 minutes.
3. Add all remaining ingredients. Stir well. Bring to a boil, stirring frequently. Reduce heat to low and simmer, uncovered, for 30 minutes, stirring occasionally.
4. Meanwhile, boil water in a Dutch oven and cook pasta according to package directions.

Makes about 14 —1 cup (250 mL) portions of meat sauce. *One portion = 1 cup (250 mL) of meat sauce over 1½ cups (375 mL) of cooked spaghetti. Doubles easily. Freezes well.*

Olé Quesadillas
page 104

BRUNCH

Cinnamon Bagel French Toast,
Maple Cream Topping, Half Grapefruit, Milk

DINNER

Veggies and Dip,
Toss and Bake Chicken, **Spinach-Stuffed Potato**,
Garlic-Parmesan Tomato

SNACK

Saucy Apple Pudding, Milk

GAME PLAN

Thaw the fish in the fridge for tomorrow's dinner.

Breakfast is easy — just follow the recipes.

... continued on page 69

If you get the munchies, eat the **Veggies and Dip** in the afternoon.

"MOUSE FOOD"

Many vegetables are good eaten raw (even better with fat-free dip): broccoli, red, orange or yellow peppers, jicama, snow peas, turnip, radishes, etc. Place them in the fridge in a plastic container and bring it out every evening when returning from work. Raw vegetables make a good low-fat, anytime snack.

NUTRITION INFORMATION
See page 6 for standards used.

MENU ITEMS (single portion)	calories	carbs (grams)	protein (grams)	fat (grams)
Cinnamon Bagel French Toast	330.4	62.4	9.8	4.4
Maple Cream Topping	83.3	3	2.9	6.8
Grapefruit — 1/2	38.5	9.7	0.8	0.1
Milk	86	11.9	8.3	0.4
Veggies & Dip	67	15.2	2.4	0.4
Toss & Bake Chicken	195	6	24.2	9.6
Spinach-Stuffed Potato	284	58.5	11.1	1.7
Garlic-Parmesan Tomato	32.3	5.5	2.4	0.6
Saucy Apple Pudding	222.8	46.8	4.9	2.5
Milk	86	11.9	8.3	0.4
Total for day	1425.3	230.9	75.1	26.9
			percentage fat ▶	17%

REMEMBER, these are the MINIMUM REQUIREMENTS of the Canada and U.S. Food Guides. Some people will need more calories.

Extra **Cinnamon Bagel French Toast** can be reheated in the microwave for a quick breakfast any morning.

CINNAMON BAGEL FRENCH TOAST

This is impressive enough and easy enough to be served as Christmas morning brunch: a feast for the eye and the palate!

2	whole grain bagels, sliced in half to form circles	2
1	egg	1
¼ cup	skim milk	50 mL
1 tsp	sugar	5 mL
½ tsp	vanilla extract	2 mL
½ tsp	cinnamon	2 mL
½ tsp	non hydrogenated margarine	2 mL
¼ cup	light maple-flavoured syrup	50 mL
pinch	cinnamon	pinch

1. Whisk together egg, milk, sugar, vanilla and cinnamon in a medium bowl. Pour into a 9" x 13" (22 cm x 33 cm) baking dish.

2. Add bagels cut side down. Allow to soak for 15 minutes. (While bagels are soaking, prepare **Maple Cream Topping**.)

3. Cook bagels (cut side down), until golden brown, over medium-low heat on a griddle or a nonstick skillet coated with cooking spray and margarine.

4. Place 2 bagel halves on each plate. Drizzle 1 tbsp (15 mL) of maple - flavoured syrup on each. Top with **Maple Cream Topping**. Sprinkle with cinnamon.

Makes 2 portions. *Doubles easily. Freezes well.*

MAPLE CREAM TOPPING

This topping is also great on toasted bagels!

¼ cup	low-fat cream cheese	50 mL
1 tbsp	fat-free sour cream	15 mL
1 tsp	icing sugar	5 mL
½ tsp	vanilla extract	2 mL
¼ tsp	maple extract	1 mL

1. Whisk all ingredients together.

Makes 2 portions. *Doubles easily*

VEGGIES AND DIP

Eat as much as you want, anytime you want. Mix and match veggies of your own choosing. This fast, healthy snack can and should be prepared weekly when you return from grocery shopping.

2	**medium carrots, cut into sticks**	2
2	**celery stalks, cut into sticks**	2
1	**green pepper, cut into sticks**	1
1 cup	**cauliflower, cut into small pieces**	250 mL
¼ cup	**fat-free Ranch dressing**	50 mL

1. Serve with fat-free Ranch Dressing or ***Homemade Vegetable Dip** (page 177).

Makes 4 portions. *Doubles easily.*

 For family of four, make an extra portion per person for tomorrow's dinner.

SPINACH-STUFFED POTATOES

Popeye would have been proud of this dish. This recipe freezes well, so if you wish, double this recipe and use as a fast food.

4	**medium baking potatoes, washed & pierced**	4
¼ cup	**green onion, chopped**	50 mL
1	**10 oz (300 g) pkg chopped frozen spinach, thawed**	1
½ cup	**fat-free sour cream**	125 mL
½ tsp each	**salt & black pepper**	2 mL each
½ cup	**low-fat cheddar cheese, grated**	125 mL

1. Bake potatoes at 350°F (180°C) for 45 to 60 minutes, or until fork-tender.

2. Remove from oven. Slice each potato in half lengthwise. Set aside to cool for 15 minutes.

3. Scoop pulp into a medium bowl, leaving ½" (1 cm) of potato pulp inside the skin. To potato pulp, add green onion, spinach, sour cream, salt and black pepper. Mash well and divide mixture equally into potato skins. Top each with 1 tbsp (15 mL) cheese.

4. Bake at 400°F (200°C) for 30 minutes.

Makes 4 portions. *Doubles easily. Freezes well.*

...continued from page 67

Begin cooking dinner by preparing the potatoes. While the potatoes bake, prepare the **Saucy Apple Pudding**.

Place the pudding in the oven along with the potatoes; they should both be ready at the same time.

While the potatoes and pudding bake, prepare **Coating Mix for Meat** and **Garlic-Parmesan Tomatoes**.

While the potatoes cool, coat the chicken and prepare the ingredients for the potato stuffing. Stuff the potatoes.

At this point the chicken, potatoes and tomatoes can be refrigerated for several hours. The meal cooks together in the oven for 30 carefree minutes!

Total preparation and cooking time: **90 min.**

Don't forget to make tomorrow's lunch.

Saucy Apple Pudding leftovers freeze well, or better yet, invite a friend over for coffee and pudding!

SAUCY APPLE PUDDING

Tastes like apple pie and magically makes its own sauce!

4	medium apples, peeled, cored & thinly sliced.	4
2 tsp	cinnamon	10 mL
1 cup	all-purpose flour	250 mL
2 tsp	baking powder	10 mL
¼ tsp	salt	1 mL
½ cup	fat-free sour cream	125 mL
¼ cup	sugar	50 mL
1	egg, beaten	1
½ cup	skim milk	125 mL
½ cup	brown sugar, packed	125 mL
1 tbsp	all-purpose flour	15 mL
1 tsp	vanilla extract	5 mL
1 tbsp	non hydrogenated margarine	15 mL
1½ cups	boiling water	375 mL
½ cup	fat-free vanilla yogurt	125 mL

1. Set water to boil.

2. Meanwhile, place apple slices in a 12 cup (3 L) casserole dish coated with cooking spray. Sprinkle apples with cinnamon.

3. Mix the 1cup (250 mL) of flour, baking powder and salt together. Add sour cream, sugar, egg and milk. Mix well. Spoon dough with a large spoon onto the apples.

4. Mix brown sugar and the 1 tbsp (15 mL) of flour thoroughly in a glass measuring cup or a small bowl that holds at least 2cups (500 mL). Stir in vanilla, margarine and boiling water. Pour this gently on top of cake batter.

5. Bake at 350˚F (180˚C) for 45 to 50 minutes or until a toothpick inserted in the centre comes out clean.

6. Top each portion with 1 tablespoon (15 mL) of fat-free vanilla yogurt.

Makes 8 portions. *Doubles easily. Freezes well.*

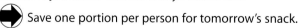 Save one portion per person for tomorrow's snack.

COATING MIX FOR MEAT

This mixture is a multi-purpose life saver. Keep it in a dry, tightly-sealed container. It will be used in several of the recipes in this book. It is less expensive and tastes better than a commercial product.

2 cups	all-purpose flour	500 mL
1 cup	oat bran	250 mL
1 cup	fine dry bread crumbs	250 mL
¼ cup	paprika	50 mL
1 tbsp	seasoning salt	15 mL
1 tbsp	black pepper	15 mL
2 tbsp	dry mustard	30 mL
2 tbsp	garlic powder	30 mL
2 tbsp	onion powder	30 mL
1 tsp	ginger	5 mL
½ tsp	thyme	2 mL
½ tsp	basil	2 mL
½ tsp	oregano	2 mL

1. Mix all ingredients together.

2. Put in a dry container and label it "**Coating Mix for Meat**".

Makes 4 cups.

If you need a motivator, walk to the video store. Because all the little walks add up, return the movie on foot as well.

FIRST TIME WALKING:

Please review walking technique on page 90. Be gentle with your body and choose a flat area rather than a hill, at least for starters. Start walking slowly for 3 to 5 minutes, then increase your pace for 10 minutes. You should be slightly winded, but still able to carry on a conversation. Return home at a slower pace to cool down.

You got off the couch – good for you!

... continued on page 78

TOSS AND BAKE CHICKEN

It doesn't get any easier than this!

1	**whole chicken leg** (*thigh and drumstick*), **skinless, all visible fat removed**	1
2 tbsp	**"Coating Mix for Meat"** (*see page 71*)	30 mL

1. Put **Coating Mix for Meat** in a plastic bag.

2. Dip chicken in water to moisten. Shake off excess water and place chicken in the bag. Toss to cover meat with coating mix. Discard plastic bag.

3. Place chicken on a baking sheet coated with cooking spray.

4. Bake for 30 minutes at 400°F (200°C).

Makes 1 portion.

GARLIC-PARMESAN TOMATO

The Parmesan gets crunchy and brown. Delicious!

1	**medium tomato**	1
pinch	**garlic powder**	pinch
1 tsp	**low-fat Parmesan cheese, grated**	5 mL

1. Cut ½" (1 cm) off top of tomato.

2. Place tomato in a shallow baking dish coated with cooking spray.

3. Sprinkle tomato with garlic powder and top with Parmesan cheese.

4. Bake at 400°F (200°C) for 30 minutes.

Makes 1 portion.

BREAKFAST
Whole Grain Cereal of Choice, Banana, Fruit Juice of Choice, Milk

LUNCH
Vegetarian Pita Pocket, Fruit of Choice, Vegetable Juice of Choice

DINNER
Fillet of Sole Veronique, **Le Riz Vert**, **Broccoli "Noël"**,
Veggies & Dip, Milk

SNACK
Saucy Apple Pudding

GAME PLAN

Thaw chicken breasts for tomorrow's dinner, in the fridge, before leaving for work.

"Monday, Monday..."

06:00 (a.m.) — If you didn't make your lunch last night, now is a good time.

... continued on page 75

Remember to choose whole grain cereal more often.

Leave the refined, sugary "pink and blue" cereal on the shelf. With the money saved, you can buy your kids better "prizes" than those out of a cereal box!

NUTRITION INFORMATION
See page 6 for standards used.

MENU ITEMS (single portion)	calories	carbs (grams)	protein (grams)	fat (grams)
Whole Grain Cereal of Choice	126	20.3	2.6	4.4
Banana	109	27.6	1.2	0.5
Fruit Juice of Choice	80	20	1	0
Milk	86	11.9	8.3	0.4
Vegetarian Pita Pocket	241.5	39.1	19.6	1.7
Fruit of Choice	81	21	0.2	0.5
Vegetable Juice of Choice	43	8.7	1.3	0.4
Fillet of Sole Veronique	144.4	6.3	22	1.3
Le Riz Vert	309.3	66.1	6.6	1.6
Broccoli "Noël"	120.3	9.9	8.6	6.5
Veggies & Dip	67	15.2	2.4	0.4
Milk	86	11.9	8.3	0.4
Saucy Apple Pudding	222.8	46.8	4.9	2.5
Total for day	1716.3	304.8	87	20.6
percentage fat ▶ 11%				

REMEMBER, these are the MINIMUM REQUIREMENTS of the Canada and U.S. Food Guides. Some people will need more calories.

VEGETARIAN PITA POCKET

Doubling the thickness of the pita bread makes the sandwich more sturdy.

1	**whole wheat pita bread**	1
2	**slices 1% milk fat cheese**	2
1 tbsp	**fat-free Ranch dressing**	15 mL
½ cup	**romaine lettuce, shredded**	125 mL
1	**medium tomato, sliced**	1
2 tbsp	**alfalfa or mixed sprouts**	30 mL
4	**slices cucumber**	4

1. Cut pita in half. Slip one half of pita inside the other.

2. Coat inner sides of pita with dressing.

3. Add lettuce and cheese slices. Wrap if brown-bagging.

4. Place tomato slices into a tightly sealed container. Add tomato to sandwich immediately before eating.

Makes 1 portion.

 A great motivator is to invite a friend to walk with you – you won't want to lag behind.

LE RIZ VERT (GREEN RICE)

If you are in a hurry, replace the long grain brown rice with converted rice to save 25 minutes of cooking time. Be aware, though— you will sacrifice some nutrients.

1½ cups	**long grain brown rice**	**375 mL**
3 cups	**cold water**	**750 mL**
1 tbsp	**dry parsley**	**15 mL**
¼ cup	**green onion, thinly sliced lengthwise**	**50 mL**

1. Place rice, water and parsley in a large saucepan. Bring to a boil over medium-high heat.
2. Immediately reduce heat to low and simmer, covered, for 45 minutes or until rice is tender and liquid is absorbed. Remove from heat.
3. Garnish with slivers of thinly sliced green onion.

Makes 4 —1 cup (250 mL) portions. *Doubles easily. Freezes well.*

BROCCOLI "NOËL"

Looks like Christmas.

4	**stalks broccoli, cut into florets**	**4**
½ cup	**red pepper, diced**	**125 mL**
4 oz	**Feta cheese, crumbled**	**120 g**
pinch	**black pepper**	**pinch**

1. Place broccoli in the steamer insert of a medium saucepan. Add water to bottom of saucepan. Bring to a boil over medium-high heat.
2. Reduce heat to medium-low. Cover. Steam for 5 minutes or until crisp-tender. Drain.
3. Toss broccoli with all remaining ingredients.

Makes 4 portions. *Halves or doubles easily. Freezes well.*

...continued from page 73

Begin cooking tonight's dinner by cooking the rice.

Then, wash and chop the vegetables. Place the broccoli in a steamer. Set aside.

10 minutes before the rice is cooked, steam the broccoli.

Meanwhile, prepare **Fillets of Sole Veronique**. During step 6, (while the fish is reheating), finish preparing the broccoli. *Fini!*

Total preparation and cooking time: **50 min.**

Before cleaning the kitchen, you might as well prepare tomorrow's lunch. Don't panic, the soup is simple and quick to make.

FILLETS OF SOLE VERONIQUE

If you really don't like fish, you can use 4 boneless, skinless chicken breasts, but do try this recipe —sole is very mild-tasting.

1	**14 oz (400 g) pkg fillet of sole, thawed**	1
¼ **tsp**	**white pepper**	1 mL
¼ **tsp**	**onion powder**	1 mL
½ **cup**	**undiluted chicken broth, fat removed** *(Save leftover undiluted broth for tomorrow's soup.)*	125 mL
½ **cup**	**white wine**, **dry** (*or apple juice*)	125 mL
2	**whole bay leaves**	2
4	**whole allspice** (*or a pinch of ground allspice*)	4
1½ **tbsp**	**all-purpose flour**	22 mL
¼ **cup**	**cold water**	50 mL
½ **cup**	**canned evaporated skim milk** *(Save leftover canned skim milk for tomorrow's soup.)*	125 mL
¼ **tsp**	**paprika**	1 mL
optional	**green grapes**, **seedless**	**optional**

1. Sprinkle one side of each fish fillet with white pepper and onion powder. Fold each fillet in half with the spices on the inside.

2. Place in a deep skillet coated with cooking spray.

3. Pour chicken broth and wine over fish. Bring to a boil over medium-high heat. Add bay leaves and allspice. Reduce heat to medium-low and simmer for 8 to 10 minutes.

4. Remove fillets to a covered plate. Bring the liquid in the skillet to a boil over medium-high heat. Lower heat to medium and simmer for 5 minutes to reduce the liquid.

5. Meanwhile, in a small jar with a tight-fitting lid, shake flour and water vigorously until there are no lumps.

6. Remove bay leaves and whole allspice. Whisk flour mixture into liquid, stirring constantly for 2 to 3 minutes or until thickened. Reduce heat to medium-low. Add milk. Stir. Return fish to skillet. Reheat on medium-low for 1 to 2 minutes. Add grapes (optional).

7. Serve with rice. Sprinkle with paprika.

Makes 4 portions. *Doubles easily. Freezes well.*

BREAKFAST

Toasted Whole Grain Bagel, Fat-Free Cream Cheese (use leftovers from week 1),
Fruit-Only Jam, Fruit Juice of Choice

LUNCH

Golden Cream of Carrot Soup, **Turkey Bunwich**,
Fruit of Choice

DINNER

Southwestern Black Bean Chicken Salad, **Garlic Toast**, Milk

SNACK

Fruit of Choice

GAME PLAN

If you don't have a microwave oven at work, reheat your soup for lunch and carry it in a thermos container.

You can make your **Turkey Bunwich** while the soup reheats if you didn't make it last night.

... continued on page 79

NUTRITION INFORMATION
See page 6 for standards used.

MENU ITEMS (single portion)	calories	carbs (grams)	protein (grams)	fat (grams)
Whole Grain Bagel — 1	152	31.5	5.5	0.6
Fat-Free Cream Cheese — 1 tbsp (15 mL)	11.9	2	0.9	0
Fruit-Only Jam	43	11	0.1	0
Fruit Juice of Choice	80	20	1	0
Golden Cream of Carrot Soup	129.3	21.1	9.2	0.6
Turkey Bunwich	233.5	21.7	19.5	8.1
Fruit of Choice	81	21	0.2	0.5
Southwestern Black Bean Chicken Salad	311	31.1	36.1	4.7
Garlic Toast	132.7	15	4.6	6.1
Milk	86	11.9	8.3	0.4
Fruit of Choice	81	21	0.2	0.5
Total for day	1357	210.7	86.8	21.5
percentage fat ▶ 14%				

REMEMBER, these are the MINIMUM REQUIREMENTS of the Canada and U.S. Food Guides. Some people will need more calories.

Exercise program by

SECOND TIME WALKING:

Don't forget to warm up then stretch your leg muscles. Walk for 10 minutes, or until you are slightly winded, before you return home. If need be, slow your pace on the way back.

... continued on page 89

GOLDEN CREAM OF CARROT SOUP

Folks used to say,

> *"Eat your carrots, you'll see far away."*

Now health nuts say,

> *"Beta carotene chases illness away."*

Same advice, different day;

> *This poetry is not great — O.K.?*

2 cups	**carrots, peeled & thinly sliced** (*about 6 medium*)	500 mL
½ cup	**undiluted chicken broth** (*leftover from yesterday*)	125 mL
1 tbsp	**lemon juice**	15 mL
½ tsp	**onion powder**	2 mL
pinch	**black pepper**	pinch
1 cup	**canned evaporated skim milk** (*leftover from yesterday*)	250 mL
1 cup	**skim milk**	250 mL
2 tbsp	**all-purpose flour**	30 mL
¼ cup	**cold water**	50 mL

1. Place carrots, broth, lemon juice, onion powder and black pepper in a medium saucepan. Bring to a boil over medium-high heat. Reduce heat to medium-low. Cover and simmer for 15 to 20 minutes, or until fork-tender.

2. Purée carrot mixture in a blender or food processor (or use a hand-held blender).

3. Return to saucepan. Add canned milk and skim milk.

4. Meanwhile, in a small jar with a tight-fitting lid, shake flour and water vigorously until there are no lumps. Whisk into soup.

5. While stirring **constantly**, bring to the boiling point over medium-high heat, then simmer 2 to 3 minutes over medium-low heat. Watch carefully, as milk burns easily, so use an underpot wire.

Makes 4 —1 cup (250 mL) portions. *Doubles easily. Freezes well.*

TURKEY BUNWICH

Who says relish is only for hot dogs?

1	whole grain bun, cut in half	1
2 oz	roasted deli turkey breast	60 g
½ cup	alfalfa sprouts	125 mL
1 tbsp	Zesty Onion Relish	15 mL
¼ cup	low-fat cheddar cheese, grated	50 mL

1. Spread relish on bun.

2. Layer turkey slices, sprouts and cheese. Close sandwich and wrap if brown-bagging.

Makes 1 portion.

GARLIC TOAST

There is no such thing as a little bit of garlic so you can use a whole clove — the smell is the same!

1	slice 1 " (2.5 cm) thick French bread	1
1 tsp	non hydrogenated margarine	5 mL
1 tbsp	Parmesan cheese, grated	15 mL
1/2	clove garlic, minced	1/2

1. Place oven rack 6 " (15 cm) from top element. Turn oven to broil.

2. Mix margarine, Parmesan cheese and garlic together in a small bowl. Spread evenly on bread.

3. Place bread on a baking sheet. Broil for 1 or 2 minutes or until lightly brown. Burns quickly, so watch carefully.

Makes 1 portion.

...continued from page 77

Dinner tonight is a 30 minute affair. While the chicken cooks, prepare and toss the salad; divide and place on serving plates.

Prepare the garlic toast.

Total preparation and cooking time: **30 min.**

If you have plans for this evening or tomorrow evening, decide which of the two days you will do a workout and which day you will bake the **Banana-Pineapple Muffins** for tomorrow's snack.

Life is full of choices!

Your cooking time was so short that you **MUST** want more time in the kitchen, so prepare tomorrow's lunch now.

SOUTHWESTERN BLACK BEAN CHICKEN SALAD

This is a nice change from chicken Caesar salad and it saves mega calories.

2	chicken breasts, skinless, boneless, all visible fat removed	2
2 tbsp	packaged taco seasoning **OR**	30 mL
2 tbsp	"Homemade Taco Seasoning" *(page 178)*	30 mL
2 cups	red or green leaf lettuce, torn into bite-size pieces	500 mL
1/2	19 oz (540 mL) can black beans, rinsed & drained *(If making 2 portions only, freeze the leftover black beans and add them to the vegetarian burritos on Thursday, Week 3.)*	1/2
½ cup	jicama, diced *(Add leftovers to your "mouse food".)*	125 mL
1/2	red pepper, cut in strips	1/2
½ cup	fresh tomato, diced	125 mL
1/4	red onion, diced	1/4
DRESSING:		
2 tbsp	vegetable juice cocktail	30 mL
1 tbsp	fat-free sour cream	15 mL
1 tbsp	lime juice *(fresh is best)*	15 mL
¼ tsp	cumin	1 mL

1. Put taco seasoning in a plastic bag.

2. Dip chicken in water to moisten. Shake off excess water and place chicken in the bag. Toss to cover meat with taco seasoning. Place on a baking sheet coated with cooking spray. Discard plastic bag.

3. Bake chicken for 20 to 25 minutes at 400°F (200°C).

4. While chicken bakes, toss lettuce, black beans, jicama, red pepper, tomato and red onion in a large bowl. Set aside.

5. Shake vegetable juice, fat-free sour cream, lime juice and cumin in a small jar with a tight-fitting lid. Set aside.

6. When ready to serve, toss salad with dressing. Top with chicken. Serve with **Garlic Toast**.

Makes 2 portions. *Doubles easily.*

BREAKFAST
Apple-Cinnamon Oatmeal (see side panel), Fruit Juice of Choice, Milk

LUNCH
Tuna Sandwich, **Orange-Almond Salad**,
Fruit of Choice

DINNER
Black Forest Potatoes, **Garlic Green Beans**

SNACK
Banana-Pineapple Muffin, Milk

GAME PLAN

This morning, thaw the chicken in the fridge for tomorrow's dinner. Don't forget your lunch!

...continued on page 83

APPLE-CINNAMON OATMEAL

⅓ cup (75 mL) quick oats

pinch salt

¼ apple, diced

⅔ cup (150 mL) water

⅓ cup (75 mL) skim milk

¼ tsp (1 mL) cinnamon

½ tsp (2 mL) vanilla extract

2 tsp (10 mL) brown sugar

1. If you have forgotten the cooking instructions, see page 46.

Makes 1 portion.

NUTRITION INFORMATION
See page 6 for standards used.

MENU ITEMS (single portion)	calories	carbs (grams)	protein (grams)	fat (grams)
Apple-Cinnamon Oatmeal	148.4	26.3	7.1	1.8
Fruit Juice of Choice	80	20	1	0
Milk	86	11.9	8.3	0.4
Tuna Sandwich	314	34.2	35.6	4.4
Orange-Almond Salad	159.5	23.2	3.8	7.2
Fruit of Choice	81	21	0.2	0.5
Black Forest Potatoes	361.8	52.6	25	7.7
Garlic Green Beans	66.9	11.1	2.8	2.3
Banana-Pineapple Muffin	185.7	39.8	7.2	0.5
Milk	86	11.9	8.3	0.4
Total for day	1569.3	252	99.3	25.2
percentage fat ➧				15%

REMEMBER, these are the MINIMUM REQUIREMENTS of the Canada and U.S. Food Guides. Some people will need more calories.

Tuna is not sold in single portion cans. The amount of tuna in a 7.5 oz (213 g) can is perfect for two sandwiches. Didn't you want to invite a date for lunch anyway?

TUNA SANDWICHES

Mama Mia! These are "gooood"!

1	7.5 oz (213 g) can tuna (*in water*), drained	1
1	medium carrot, grated	1
½ cup	zucchini, finely diced	125 mL
2	green onions, finely chopped	2
2 tbsp	fat-free Italian dressing	30 mL
2 tbsp	fat-free sour cream	30 mL
4	slices whole grain bread	4

1. Mix all ingredients (except bread) together. Spread on bread and wrap if brown-bagging.

Makes 2 portions. *Doubles easily.*

ORANGE-ALMOND SALAD

A taste delight! Leftover Mandarin oranges can be eaten as a snack (free calories!), and the juice can be added to your morning fruit juice.

2 cups	romaine or red leaf lettuce, torn (*bite size pieces*)	500 mL
1/4	medium red onion, sliced, separated into rings	1/4
2 tbsp	slivered almonds, toasted (*see side panel*)	30 mL
DRESSING:		
1 tbsp each	white wine vinegar, orange juice & lemon juice	15 mL each
½ tsp	dried orange peel	2 mL
1 tsp	sugar	5 mL
pinch each	dry mustard & salt	pinch each
1 tsp	olive or canola oil	5 mL
1/2	10 oz (284 mL) can Mandarin orange segments, in juice, drained	1/2

1. Mix all dressing ingredients together. Toss with salad just before eating.

2. If brown-bagging, divide salad ingredients and dressing into individual portions. Seal in separate containers.

Makes 2 portions. *Doubles easily.*

To toast slivered almonds, place on a baking sheet and brown in oven at 350°F (180°C) for 5 to 10 minutes. Stir every 1 or 2 minutes.

OR

Place almonds on a microwaveable dish. Microwave on high until golden brown, stirring every 20 to 30 seconds.

Consommé au Sherry
page 135

Bruschetta Submarine
page 136

Fruits au Rum
page 135

BLACK FOREST POTATOES

Tell the kids to set the table now — no time for video games tonight!

3 cups	red potatoes, washed and diced in ½" (1 cm) cubes	750 mL
1 cup	water	250 mL
1½ tsp	prepared mustard	7 mL
1 tbsp	red wine vinegar	15 mL
1½ tsp	olive oil	7 mL
2 tbsp	fat-free sour cream	30 mL
8 oz	Black Forest ham, cut in ½" (1 cm) cubes	225 g
pinch	black pepper	pinch
2	green onions, chopped	2

1. Place potatoes and water in a large saucepan. Bring to a boil over medium-high heat. Reduce heat to medium and simmer for 5 minutes or until fork-tender. Drain. Discard water. (To preserve nutrients, cook the potatoes in a steamer, either on the stove or in the microwave.)

2. Add all remaining ingredients except black pepper and green onions. Toss well. Return to saucepan, cover and continue to cook over low heat for 10 minutes.

3. Sprinkle with black pepper and green onions immediately before serving.

Makes 2 portions. *Doubles easily.*

GARLIC GREEN BEANS

Use the leftovers as a snack (free calories!).

2 cups	cut green beans, cooked and drained	500 mL
1 tsp	non hydrogenated margarine	5 mL
1	clove garlic, minced	1
1 tsp	chicken bouillon concentrate	5 mL

1. Melt margarine in a large saucepan over medium heat. Add garlic. Sauté for one minute.

2. Add chicken bouillon and beans. Stir. Reduce heat to medium-low. Cover and reheat for 3 to 5 minutes.

Makes 2 -1 cup (250 mL) portions. *Doubles easily.*

... continued from page 81

Tonight's dinner is so quick to prepare that reading the instructions takes longer than cooking the whole meal!

Prepare and cook the potatoes. While they cook, prepare the ham, green onions and garlic (for the green beans).

While the **Black Forest Potatoes** cook, prepare and cook the green beans. Finish the potato and green bean recipes. Dinner is ready. It's really that easy!

Total preparation and cooking time: **20 min.**

Black Forest Potatoes can also be cooked entirely in the microwave for an even more carefree dinner. Be sure to use red potatoes— they hold their shape.

If you didn't bake the muffins last night, bake them immediately after dinner.

You'll just have time to clean the kitchen and make your lunch while they bake.

Note to Sports Parents — a muffin and milk combo makes a quick breakfast, or snack, for those "short-of-time" road trips and early morning practices (you won't have to stop for a greasy snack).

BANANA-PINEAPPLE MUFFINS

Wrap cooled leftover muffins individually and freeze for use as a snack or breakfast-on-the-go!

1 cup	**banana, mashed** (*about 2 medium*)	250 mL
½ cup	**brown sugar, packed**	125 mL
¾ cup	**natural wheat bran**	175 mL
1 cup	**crushed pineapple in juice, undrained** (*Use the leftovers on* **Fruity Cottage Cheese** *in tomorrow's lunch.*)	250 mL
½ cup	**fat-free sour cream**	125 mL
1½ tsp	**dried orange peel**	7 mL
1½ tsp	**vanilla extract**	7 mL
3	**egg whites**	3
¾ cup	**skim milk powder**	175 mL
2 cups	**all-purpose flour**	500 mL
1 tbsp	**baking powder**	15 mL
1 tsp	**baking soda**	5 mL
¼ tsp	**salt**	1 mL

1. Mix banana, brown sugar, bran, pineapple, sour cream, orange peel, vanilla, egg whites and milk powder in a large bowl. Stir well. Set aside.

2. Mix flour, baking powder, baking soda and salt in a small bowl.

3. Add flour mixture all at once to banana mixture. Mix only until moistened.

4. Divide mixture evenly among 12 muffin tins coated with cooking spray.

5. Bake at 375°F (190°C) for 15 to 20 minutes. (Do the toothpick test: insert a toothpick into the centre of a few muffins — if it comes out clean, they are done.)

Makes 12 portions. *Freezes well.*

 Save one portion per person for tomorrow's lunch.

BREAKFAST

Whole Grain Toast, Reduced-Fat Peanut Butter, Fruit-Only Jam,
Fruit of Choice, Milk

LUNCH

Fruity Cottage Cheese Salad (*see side panel*),
Banana-Pineapple Muffin

DINNER

Wild Oriental Chicken, Fruit of Choice, Milk

SNACK

Saucy Apple Pudding <u>or</u> a Fig Bar and an Apple

FRUITY COTTAGE CHEESE SALAD

Quick, easy and delicious!

¹⁄₂ cup (125 mL) 1% cottage cheese

¹⁄₂ cup (125 mL) canned fruit of choice, in juice

1. Top cottage cheese with fruit.

Makes 1 portion.

NUTRITION INFORMATION

See page 6 for standards used.

MENU ITEMS (single portion)	calories	carbs (grams)	protein (grams)	fat (grams)
Whole Grain Toast — 2	126	24.8	5.4	1.6
Reduced-Fat Peanut Butter	82	5.2	2.7	5.6
Fruit-Only Jam	43	11	0.1	0
Fruit of Choice	81	21	0.2	0.5
Milk	86	11.9	8.3	0.4
Fruity Cottage Cheese Salad	139	17.7	14.6	1.2
Banana-Pineapple Muffin	185.7	39.8	7.2	0.5
Wild Oriental Chicken	460.1	56.3	34.6	10.7
Fruit of Choice	81	21	0.2	0.5
Milk	86	11.9	8.3	0.4
Saucy Apple Pudding	222.8	46.8	4.9	2.5
Total for day	1593	262.3	86.5	23.9
percentage fat ➤				14%

REMEMBER, these are the MINIMUM REQUIREMENTS of the Canada and U.S. Food Guides. Some people will need more calories.

GAME PLAN

Dinner tonight cooks in one pot.

While the chicken and rice mixture cooks, prepare the broccoli, carrots and cauliflower, then make the sauce. You don't even need to stir, so put your feet up! Oops! We forgot, you have to get up once to add the vegetables, so set your timer.

Total preparation and cooking time: **75 min.**

If you choose not to eat lunch out tomorrow, check your freezer for leftovers. Each member of the family can choose a favourite —just like in a restaurant!

WILD ORIENTAL CHICKEN

*This meal cooks by itself. You'll have time to put your feet up for at least **40 min.***

8	chicken thighs, skinless, bone in, visible fat removed	8
1 tsp	oil	5 mL
1	medium onion, diced	1
1 1 cup	10 oz (284 mL) can chicken broth, fat removed water (*Reserve ¼ cup [50 mL] reconstituted broth for the sauce.*) <u>OR</u>	1 250 mL
2¼ cups	Homemade Chicken Broth (*page 176*)	550 mL
½ cup	wild rice	125 mL
½ cup	brown rice	125 mL
2 tbsp	chicken bouillon concentrate	30 mL
2 cups	broccoli florets & stems, chopped	500 mL
1 cup	carrots, thinly sliced on the diagonal	250 mL
1 cup	cauliflower, chopped	250 mL
SAUCE: (*Serve at room temperature.*)		
3	green onions, chopped	3
2 to 4	cloves garlic, minced	2 to 4
2 tbsp	salt-reduced soy sauce	30 mL
¼ cup each	chili sauce & chicken broth	50 mL each
3 or 4 drops	Tabasco sauce (*optional*)	3 or 4 drops

1. Heat oil over medium heat in a Dutch oven coated with cooking spray.

2. Add chicken. Sauté 2 to 3 minutes on each side until lightly browned. Add onion. Sauté 2 to 3 minutes, or until translucent.

4. Add canned broth, water, wild rice, brown rice and chicken bouillon concentrate. Bring to a boil. Reduce heat to medium-low. Cover. Simmer for 40 minutes.

6. Meanwhile, mix sauce ingredients together. Set aside.

7. After 40 minutes, add broccoli, carrots and cauliflower on top of chicken mixture. **Do not stir.** Cover and simmer for another 20 minutes.

8. Serve with 2 tbsp (30 mL) sauce on top of each portion.

Makes 4 portions. *Doubles easily. Freezes well.*

BREAKFAST

Whole Grain Cereal of Choice topped with Canned Peach Slices,
Fruit Juice of Choice, Milk

LUNCH

T.G.I.F. *(Use up leftovers or buy a lunch.)*

DINNER

Capelli Medley with Roasted Tomatoes, **Fruit and Crème Brulé**, Milk

SNACK

Your favourite treat is calling your name!
(How about popcorn and a video tonight?)

CONGRATULATIONS!
You have achieved a **full 2 weeks** of following the Canadian and U.S. Food Guides!

NUTRITION INFORMATION
See page 6 for standards used.

MENU ITEMS (single portion)	calories	carbs (grams)	protein (grams)	fat (grams)
Whole Grain Cereal of Choice	126	20.3	2.6	4.4
Canned Peach Slices — 1/2 cup (125 mL)	55	14.3	0.8	0
Fruit Juice of Choice	80	20	1	0
Milk	86	11.9	8.3	0.4
Capelli Medley with Roasted Tomatoes	439.3	74.1	15.8	12
Fruit & Crème Brulé	167.3	44.6	3.3	2.4
Milk	86	11.9	8.3	0.4
Total for day	1039.6	197.1	40.1	19.6
percentage fat ▶				17%

REMEMBER, these are the MINIMUM REQUIREMENTS of the Canada and U.S. Food Guides. Some people will need more calories.

GAME PLAN

For dinner, follow the capelli recipe as is. Right after step 4, prepare steps 1, 2 and 3 of **Fruit and Crème Brulé**. Set aside.

Finish the capelli recipe and enjoy dinner. At dessert time, complete steps 4 and 5 of the fruit recipe.

Total preparation and cooking time: **40 min.**

Dinner can be served in a bowl, so it can be eaten in front of "the tube" or wherever!

CAPELLI MEDLEY WITH ROASTED TOMATOES

In the Fall you can easily replace the corn and green beans with yellow squash and zucchini. Roast them with the green onions and tomatoes.

4 to 6	cloves garlic, crushed	4 to 6
1	bunch green onions, cut in 1 " (2.5 cm) pieces	1
1 tbsp	olive oil	15 mL
10	Roma tomatoes, diced	10
2 cups	frozen kernel corn	500 mL
2 cups	frozen cut green beans	500 mL
4 oz	low-fat Feta cheese, crumbled	120 g
1 tsp	black pepper	5 mL
1/2	12 oz (375 g) pkg capelli *(angel hair pasta)*	1/2

1. Boil water in a Dutch oven.
2. Toss garlic, green onions, tomatoes and oil in a large uncovered roasting pan. Roast for 25 to 30 minutes at 400°F (200°C). Stir occasionally.
3. Meanwhile, cook pasta according to package instructions. Drain well and set aside.
4. Place corn and green beans in a microwaveable dish with 1tbsp (15 mL) water. Cook on high for approximately 8 minutes*. Drain.
5. When tomato mixture is roasted, toss all ingredients together.

Makes 4 —2 cup (500 mL) portions. *Halves or doubles easily. Freezes well.*

*Microwave cooking times may vary, depending on the wattage of the oven.

FRUIT AND CRÈME BRULÉ

If there are leftovers, use them anytime you need an extra snack... like NOW! Add the leftover pineapple juice to your morning fruit juice.

1	14 oz (398 mL) can pineapple tidbits, in juice, drained	1
1 cup	blueberries, fresh or frozen	250 mL
4	kiwi fruit, peeled and cut into slices ¼" (.5 cm) thick	4
¼ cup	brown sugar	50 mL
¼ cup	fat-free sour cream	50 mL
2 tbsp	low-fat cream cheese	30 mL
¼ tsp	cinnamon	1 mL

1. Combine all fruits in a medium bowl.

2. Divide into 4 oven-proof custard cups placed on a baking sheet <u>or</u> place in an 8" x 8" (20 cm x 20 cm) square baking dish. Set aside.

3. Whisk together sour cream and cream cheese. Spoon over fruit. Sprinkle with brown sugar.

4. Broil 6" (15 cm) from top element for 2 minutes or until lightly browned. Watch closely as this could burn very quickly!

5. Sprinkle with cinnamon and serve immediately.

Makes 4 portions. *Doubles easily.*

If you are tired of feeling tired, follow this proverb:

Sit less, move more,
Eat less, chew more,
Talk less, say more,
Breathe deeper, drink more (water that is),
and better health will be yours.

Exercise program by

THIRD EXERCISE SESSION IN WEEK 2

Give yourself a homemade spa treatment today. Do a warm-up, then stretch your whole body before slipping into a scented bubble bath. Ahhh...

...continued on page 107

HEART AND LUNG FITNESS

Please have water handy and sip regularly while exercising. Ideally, you should do some form of cardio-vascular exercise for a minimum of 10 to 20 minutes at least 3 times each week. If you are a beginner, 5 minutes of stair walking within your heart rate target zone is a good start. Your goal is to strengthen your heart and lungs. Please remember to breathe deeply when you are exercising. In this book, you will learn correct walking technique because walking benefits the heart and lungs, requires only minimum equipment, can be done in every season in any geographic location, can be done at any age and is easy on the joints. Enjoy your walk!

WALKING TECHNIQUE

Perhaps it's time to slip into something more sneaker-like? A brisk walk for 5 minutes each day over 3 months can burn off the caloric energy of more than 3/4 of a pound (340 g) of fat. In one year, that equals a 2 1/4 pound (1 kg) fat loss. Suddenly, walking sounds like a great idea but research has proved that there is a correct way to walk, so please concentrate on your form.

1. Stand tall, shoulders and head back.

2. Place your heel down first, then roll through to the ball of your foot. Use a comfortable stride because over-striding can stress the hip and the knee joints.

3. Move your arms naturally by your side. Please work within your heart rate target zone (see page 14).

4. Now that you are walking "posture-correctly", try with each stride to maintain a soft spring in your knee joint as you squeeze your buttock muscles. This, in time, will help work against the force of gravity that invariably has everything moving south. Note, too, that hills are particularly good for toning the hamstrings and the bottom.

WATER AND EXERCISE

Regular exercise is healthy but exercising in the heat of the sun increases the risk of heat exhaustion or heat stroke, especially in adults 50 to 60 plus. The body's dehydration monitor does not function well throughout our lives and gets worse as we age. Many times we are dehydrated before our bodies notify us! So, when exercising in the heat (or even in cool weather), please carry a bottle of spring water with you and sip, sip, sip.

There are two reasons for drinking <u>spring water</u> rather than distilled water:

1. **Distilled water has no minerals.** Therefore, the digestion and absorption of distilled water deplete the minerals already in your body. Some schools of thought believe that if you drink distilled water, you are drinking "dead" water.

2. **Drinking spring water with its natural minerals actually feeds the body.** Please be aware, though, that when it comes to reading labels, words can be misleading. For example, glacier water may come from a tap, which may also account for its cheaper price. Legally, the label on spring water must state the spring source. Aim for 6 to 8—8 oz glasses a day. For every cup of caffeinated coffees and/or teas you drink (which dehydrate you), you need to drink two cups of spring water to replace your body's water loss.

Upper Body Stretches

SHOULDER ROTATIONS

When no one is there to give you a pat on the back, a few of these shoulder rolls will do just that. To stretch and warm up the shoulder and neck region from a standing or seated position:

1. Simply push your shoulders back and circle them around in one direction, very slowly, 5 times.

2. Repeat in the opposite direction for 5 times also. Please keep your arms down by your sides and stretch. Breathe slowly and deeply all the while.

NECK STRETCH

This stretch is particularly good for anyone who suffers from a stiff neck or shoulder. If you avoid shallow breathing (when your shoulders rise and fall) and breathe deeply (when your belly moves in and out), you may avoid neck stiffness altogether.

1. Seated or standing, clasp the wrist of your right hand as pictured.

2. Pull your right arm across your body while your head tilts toward your left shoulder. Once you have stretched as far as you can, hold the stretch for a slow count of 20 to 30. Return to centre and repeat on the same side. You will feel the stretch in the side of your neck.

3. Repeat in the opposite direction twice as well. Please remember to breathe slowly and deeply while you stretch.

PECTORAL STRETCH

Smiling during any exercise is highly recommended, but optional.

1. Stand as pictured, clasping the wrist of your right hand behind your back. Pull your right arm down and across your lower back region, pulling your right arm as far as you comfortably can.

2. Tilt your left ear toward your left shoulder as in the neck stretch. Hold the entire stretch for a slow count of 20 to 30. You should feel the stretch in your chest region, from your shoulder to your breast.

3. Please stretch twice on each side.

UPPER **B**ODY **S**TRETCHES

SPINE STRETCH

You can attempt this spine stretch while sitting, but you will get a better stretch while standing.

1. As pictured, rest your hands mid-thigh. Bend your shock absorbers (knees).

2. Drop your chin to your chest as you round your shoulders and spine. Tighten your tummy muscles as though you are trying to push your belly button to touch your spine, (this tones the abdominal muscles at the same time). Hold for a slow A, B, C, D. You will feel the stretch from your tail bone right up to your neck. Keep breathing.

3. Slowly release the stretch, flattening your back. Unlike yours truly in the photo, keep your neck in line with your spine and your eyes down. Please think long with this spine stretch. Hold for a slow A, B, C, D.

4. Repeat this stretch twice.

LOWER BACK STRETCH

Let me see, there's Angie, Joni, Pauline, Paul, Ray, Claudette, Darin—just to name a few of the millions who suffer from back pain. They should be doing this stretch and so should you.

1. Lie on your back on a floor mat or towel. Bend your knees, placing your feet flat on the floor. Keep your feet together and relax briefly.

2. To stretch your lower back, push your spine flat so there is no space between your back and the floor. Slowly, bring your right knee then your left knee toward your chest.

3. Place your hands behind your bent knees. Keeping your back flat and in full contact with the floor, hold this stretch and ponder why it is that when you put French bread in the toaster it does not come out as French toast!

4. Repeat this stretch twice.

UPPER BODY STRETCHES

SIDE STRETCH

A simple side stretch before you exercise can actually help to prevent side cramps during exercise.

1. Cross your right leg over your left leg as pictured, or stand with your feet shoulder width apart if you have trouble with balance. Please think soft with your knee joints; keep them slightly bent.

2. Lean to your right side and reach for your ankle with your right hand. Ensure that your leaning shoulder remains in line with the side of your knee and ankle.

3. Stretch as far as you comfortably can, allowing your left hand to slide up to your waist. If it is more comfortable, just rest your left arm along the side of your body.

4. Allow your head to move into a natural, relaxed position. Hold each stretch for a slow count of 20 to 30. You should feel the stretch from your waist to your arm pit.

5. Do this stretch twice on the right side, then repeat on the other side.

6. **More advanced people:** bring your left arm up over your head, as pictured, to increase the stretch at your waist. Try it—you'll feel the difference.

WEEK 3 MENU

Recipes are provided in this chapter for menu items in **BOLD** on the day they are first prepared.

DAY	BREAKFAST	LUNCH	DINNER	SNACK
S SAT pg. 101	*Seasoned Hash Browns, Egg "Your Way", Whole Grain Toast, Fruit Juice of Choice	Olé Quesadillas with Avocado Slices, Salsa & Sour Cream, Milk	*Pork Roast Dinner, *Marinated Vegetable Salad, *Blueberry Bubbly➡ with 1% Vanilla Ice Cream	*Cherry Pie Yogurt
S SUN pg. 107	**BRUNCH** *So-Easy Oatmeal Pancakes with *Peach Sauce & Vanilla Cream, Fruit Juice of Choice, Vanilla Coffee		Jambalaya, Lettuce and Carrot Slaw, Whole Grain Baguette, Milk	*Rice Crisp Square➡ Milk
M MON pg. 115	Whole Grain Cereal of Choice, Fruit of Choice, Milk	*P.T.L.C., Vegetable Juice of Choice, Rice Crisp Square	*Salmon in a Nest, *Creamy Peas, *Orange-Romaine Salad	Fat-Free Fruit Yogurt of Choice
T TUE pg. 119	Whole Grain English Muffin, Reduced-Fat Peanut Butter, Fruit-Only Jam, Fruit of Choice, Milk	*Cream of Mushroom Soup, Whole Grain Bun, Fat-Free Monterey Jack Cheese Slice, Fruit of Choice	*Salisbury Steak, *Slight Smashed Spuds, French Cut Green Beans	Blueberry Bubbly, Milk
W WED pg. 123	Whole Grain Cereal of Choice, Banana, Milk	*Tuna Salad in Whole Wheat Pita, Vegetable Juice of Choice, Fruit of Choice	*Chicken Fingers, *Potato and Yam Fries, *Tomato Basil Salad➡	Sunshine Bar➡ Milk
T THU pg. 129	Sunshine Bar, Fruit of Choice, Hot Chocolate	*Nutty Banana Raisin Bread Sandwich, Fat-Free Fruit Yogurt	Vegetarian Burrito, *Apple-Carrot Salad, Low-Fat Cinnamon Graham Wafers, Milk	Fruit of Choice
F FRI pg. 133	*Maple-Sugar Oatmeal, Fruit of Choice, Milk	T.G.I.F. (Use up leftovers or buy a lunch.)	*Bruschetta Submarine, *Consommé au Sherry, *Fruits au Rum, Milk	Wine anyone? (The kids can have white or purple grape juice.)

✳ These recipes provide **EXACT MINIMUM PORTIONS** and may need to be adjusted for extra portions.

➡ This symbol will remind you to save portions of this recipe for use later this week.

PANTRY NEEDS

These items might be in your pantry now.

If not, add them to your shopping list on the following pages, as well as any personal preferences such as shampoo, toothpaste, cleaning supplies and so on.

Please note: ground spices and dried herbs are used in recipes unless otherwise specified.

- [ ] **BASIL**
- [ ] **BAY LEAVES**
- [ ] **CHILI POWDER**
- [ ] **CUMIN**
- [ ] **LEMON PEEL**, dried
- [ ] **NUTMEG**
- [ ] **OREGANO**
- [ ] **PAPRIKA**
- [ ] **PEPPER**, black
- [ ] **RED PEPPER FLAKES**
- [ ] **SALT**
- [ ] **SEASONING SALT**
- [ ] **THYME**
- [ ] **ALMOND EXTRACT**
- [ ] **LEMON EXTRACT**
- [ ] **MAPLE EXTRACT**
- [ ] **VANILLA EXTRACT**
- [ ] **BOUILLON CONCENTRATE**, chicken
- [ ] **BAKING POWDER**
- [ ] **BAKING SODA**
- [ ] **COCONUT**, finely shredded, unsweetened
- [ ] **CORNSTARCH**
- [ ] **DATES**, pitted
- [ ] **FLOUR**, all-purpose
- [ ] **FLOUR**, whole wheat
- [ ] **QUICK-COOKING TAPIOCA**
- [ ] **SKIM MILK POWDER**
- [ ] **SUGAR**, brown
- [ ] **SUGAR**, icing
- [ ] **SUGAR**, white
- [ ] **CEREALS**, whole grain, breakfast
- [ ] **NATURAL WHEAT BRAN**

- [ ] **OAT BRAN**
- [ ] **QUICK OATS**
- [ ] **WHEAT GERM**
- [ ] **CINNAMON GRAHAM WAFERS**, low-fat
- [ ] **JAMS**, fruit-only
- [ ] **PEANUT BUTTER**, reduced-fat
- [ ] **LIQUID HONEY**
- [ ] **COFFEE**
- [ ] **HOT CHOCOLATE**, skim milk
- [ ] **JUICES**, fruit, assorted
- [ ] **JUICES**, vegetable, assorted
- [ ] **LEMON JUICE**, bottled or fresh
- [ ] **LIME JUICE**, bottled or fresh
- [ ] **TEAS**, assorted
- [ ] **WINE**, red or white, dry
- [ ] **WHITE RUM** (optional)
- [ ] **COOKING SPRAY**, plain
- [ ] **MUSTARD**, prepared
- [ ] **OIL**, olive and/or canola
- [ ] **SALAD DRESSINGS**, assorted, fat-free
- [ ] **SALAD DRESSING**, Italian, fat-free
- [ ] **SALAD DRESSING**, Ranch, fat-free
- [ ] **TABASCO SAUCE**
- [ ] **VINEGAR**, apple cider
- [ ] **VINEGAR**, balsamic
- [ ] **VINEGAR**, red wine
- [ ] **SOY SAUCE**, salt-reduced
- [ ] **RICE**, brown, long grain
- [ ] **PARMESAN CHEESE**, low-fat, grated
- [ ] **ALUMINUM FOIL**

SHOPPING LIST

Review all recipes for portion requirements (see page 22). Add any missing pantry items to your grocery list.

PRODUCE

- [ ] **APPLES** 2
- [ ] **BANANAS** 4
- [ ] **FRUIT**, assorted 12 portions
- [ ] **GRAPES**, seedless (*of choice*) 1 cup (250 mL)
- [ ] **LEMON** 1
- [ ] **ORANGES** 2
- [ ] **AVOCADOS** 2
- [ ] **BROCCOLI** 2 stalks
- [ ] **CARROTS** 1-3 lb (1.4 kg) bag
- [ ] **CAULIFLOWER** 1 head
- [ ] **CELERY** 4 stalks
- [ ] **CUCUMBER** 1 small
- [ ] **GARLIC** 1 head
- [ ] **LETTUCE**, iceberg 1 head
- [ ] **LETTUCE**, romaine 1 head
- [ ] **MUSHROOMS** 1 lb (450 g)
- [ ] **GREEN ONIONS** 2 bunches
- [ ] **ONIONS** 4 large
- [ ] **ONION** 1 medium
- [ ] **WHITE ONIONS** 3 small
- [ ] **PEPPERS**, green 4
- [ ] **PEPPERS**, red 3
- [ ] **PEPPERS**, yellow 2
- [ ] **POTATOES** 10 medium
- [ ] **RADISHES** 1 bunch
- [ ] **SPROUTS**, alfalfa (*optional*)
- [ ] **TOMATOES** 2 medium
- [ ] **ROMA TOMATOES** 8
- [ ] **TURNIP** 1 small
- [ ] **YAMS** 2 small
- [ ] **VEGETABLES FOR SNACKS**, assorted (*see side panel page 67*)

GROCERIES

- [ ] **CRISPY RICE CEREAL** 6 cups (1.5 L)
- [ ] **EVAPORATED SKIM MILK** 1-14 oz (385 mL) can
- [ ] **MARSHMALLOWS** 1-8 oz (250 g) bag
- [ ] **MESQUITE SEASONING** 1 pkg (*hint: look in spice aisle*)
- [ ] **PECANS**, chopped ½ cup (125 mL)
- [ ] **APPLE SAUCE**, sweetened 1-14 oz (398 mL) can
- [ ] **PINEAPPLE TIDBITS**, in juice 1-14 oz (398 mL) can
- [ ] **TOMATOES**, diced 1-28 oz (796 mL) can
- [ ] **TOMATO SAUCE** 1-19 oz (540 mL) can
- [ ] **NOODLES**, fine, yolk-free 1-12 oz (340 g) bag
- [ ] **CHICKEN BROTH** 2-10 oz (284 mL) cans
- [ ] **CONSOMMÉ** 1-10 oz (284 mL) can
- [ ] **KIDNEY BEANS** 1-14 oz (398 mL) can
- [ ] **SALMON** 1-7.5 oz (213 g) can
- [ ] **TUNA**, in water 1-7.5 oz (213 g) can
- [ ] **VEGETABLE JUICE COCKTAIL** 1 cup (250 mL)
- [ ] **MARASCHINO CHERRIES** 1 jar (*optional*)
- [ ] **REFRIED BEANS**, reduced-fat 1-14 oz (398 mL) can
- [ ] **SALSA** 1-5 cup (1.36 L) jar

(continued on reverse)

FAMILY OF 2

MEAT

- [ ] **CHICKEN BREASTS**, boneless, skinless 4
- [ ] **EXTRA LEAN GROUND BEEF** 1 lb (450 g)
- [ ] **PORK TENDERLOIN** (*or boneless pork leg*) 1 lb (450 g)
- [ ] **SHRIMP**, uncooked, peeled 8 oz (225 g)
- [ ] **BLACK FOREST HAM**, sliced ½" (1 cm) thick 8 oz (225 g)
- [ ] **LEAN HAM**, sliced 1 small air-tight pkg

BAKERY

- [ ] **BUNS**, whole grain 2
- [ ] **ENGLISH MUFFINS**, whole grain 2
- [ ] **BAGUETTE**, whole grain 1 small
- [ ] **PITA BREAD**, whole wheat 4
- [ ] **RAISIN BREAD** 1 loaf
- [ ] **SUBMARINE BUNS**, whole grain 2 small
- [ ] **TORTILLAS**, whole wheat 14-8" (20 cm)

FROZEN

- [ ] **BLUEBERRIES** 2 cups (500 mL)
- [ ] **PEACHES**, sliced, unsweetened 2 cups (500 mL)
- [ ] **GREEN BEANS**, French cut 2 cups (500 mL)
- [ ] **KERNEL CORN** 1 cup (250 mL)
- [ ] **PEAS** 2 cups (500 mL)
- [ ] **ORANGE JUICE CONCENTRATE** 1-12 oz (355 mL) can
- [ ] **VANILLA ICE CREAM**, 1% milk fat 2 cups (500 mL)

DAIRY

- [ ] **BUTTERMILK**, 1% milk fat 1 quart (1 L)
- [ ] **MILK** 6 quarts (6 L)
- [ ] **YOGURT**, with fruit, fat-free 4 - ¾ cup (175 g) containers
- [ ] **YOGURT**, plain, fat-free 3 cups (750 mL)
- [ ] **SOUR CREAM**, fat-free 4 cups (1 L)
- [ ] **CREAM CHEESE**, low-fat ¼ cup (50 mL)
- [ ] **CHEDDAR CHEESE**, low-fat 1 lb (454 g)
- [ ] **CHEESE SLICES**, Monterey Jack, fat-free 6
- [ ] **MARGARINE**, non hydrogenated
- [ ] **EGGS** 8

PANTRY & OTHER

- [ ] _____
- [ ] _____
- [ ] _____
- [ ] _____
- [ ] _____
- [ ] _____
- [ ] _____
- [ ] _____
- [ ] _____
- [ ] _____
- [ ] _____
- [ ] _____
- [ ] _____
- [ ] _____
- [ ] _____
- [ ] _____
- [ ] _____
- [ ] _____

SHOPPING LIST

Review all recipes for portion requirements (see page 22). Add any missing pantry items to your grocery list.

PRODUCE

☐ **APPLES** 2

☐ **BANANAS** 4

☐ **FRUIT**, assorted 12 portions

☐ **GRAPES**, seedless (*of choice*) 1 cup (250 mL)

☐ **LEMON** 1

☐ **ORANGES** 2

☐ **AVOCADOS** 2

☐ **BROCCOLI** 2 stalks

☐ **CARROTS** 1-3 lb (1.4 kg) bag

☐ **CAULIFLOWER** 1 head

☐ **CELERY** 4 stalks

☐ **CUCUMBER** 1 small

☐ **GARLIC** 1 head

☐ **LETTUCE**, iceberg 1 head

☐ **LETTUCE**, romaine 1 head

☐ **MUSHROOMS** 1 lb (450 g)

☐ **GREEN ONIONS** 2 bunches

☐ **ONIONS** 4 large

☐ **ONION** 1 medium

☐ **WHITE ONIONS** 3 small

☐ **PEPPERS**, green 4

☐ **PEPPERS**, red 3

☐ **PEPPERS**, yellow 2

☐ **POTATOES** 10 medium

☐ **RADISHES** 1 bunch

☐ **SPROUTS**, alfalfa (*optional*)

☐ **TOMATOES** 2 medium

☐ **ROMA TOMATOES** 8

☐ **TURNIP** 1 small

☐ **YAMS** 2 small

☐ **VEGETABLES FOR SNACKS**, assorted
(*see side panel page 67*)

GROCERIES

☐ **CRISPY RICE CEREAL** 6 cups (1.5 L)

☐ **EVAPORATED SKIM MILK**
1-14 oz (385 mL) can

☐ **MARSHMALLOWS** 1-8 oz (250 g) bag

☐ **MESQUITE SEASONING** 1 pkg
(*hint: look in spice aisle*)

☐ **PECANS**, chopped ½ cup (125 mL)

☐ **APPLE SAUCE**, sweetened
1-14 oz (398 mL) can

☐ **PINEAPPLE TIDBITS**, in juice
1-14 oz (398 mL) can

☐ **TOMATOES**, diced 1-28 oz (796 mL) can

☐ **TOMATO SAUCE** 1-19 oz (540 mL) can

☐ **NOODLES**, fine, yolk-free
1-12 oz (340 g) bag

☐ **CHICKEN BROTH** 2-10 oz (284 mL) cans

☐ **CONSOMMÉ** 1-10 oz (284 mL) can

☐ **KIDNEY BEANS** 1-14 oz (398 mL) can

☐ **SALMON** 1-7.5 oz (213 g) can

☐ **TUNA**, in water 1-7.5 oz (213 g) can

☐ **VEGETABLE JUICE COCKTAIL** 1 cup (250 mL)

☐ **MARASCHINO CHERRIES** 1 jar (*optional*)

☐ **REFRIED BEANS**, reduced-fat
1-14 oz (398 mL) can

☐ **SALSA** 1-5 cup (1.36 L) jar

(*continued on reverse*)

Family of 2

MEAT

- [ ] **CHICKEN BREASTS**, boneless, skinless 4
- [ ] **EXTRA LEAN GROUND BEEF** 1 lb (450 g)
- [ ] **PORK TENDERLOIN** (*or boneless pork leg*) 1 lb (450 g)
- [ ] **SHRIMP**, uncooked, peeled 8 oz (225 g)
- [ ] **BLACK FOREST HAM**, sliced ½" (1 cm) thick 8 oz (225 g)
- [ ] **LEAN HAM**, sliced 1 small air-tight pkg

BAKERY

- [ ] **BUNS**, whole grain 2
- [ ] **ENGLISH MUFFINS**, whole grain 2
- [ ] **BAGUETTE**, whole grain 1 small
- [ ] **PITA BREAD**, whole wheat 4
- [ ] **RAISIN BREAD** 1 loaf
- [ ] **SUBMARINE BUNS**, whole grain 2 small
- [ ] **TORTILLAS**, whole wheat 14-8" (20 cm)

FROZEN

- [ ] **BLUEBERRIES** 2 cups (500 mL)
- [ ] **PEACHES**, sliced, unsweetened 2 cups (500 mL)
- [ ] **GREEN BEANS**, French cut 2 cups (500 mL)
- [ ] **KERNEL CORN** 1 cup (250 mL)
- [ ] **PEAS** 2 cups (500 mL)
- [ ] **ORANGE JUICE CONCENTRATE** 1-12 oz (355 mL) can
- [ ] **VANILLA ICE CREAM**, 1% milk fat 2 cups (500 mL)

DAIRY

- [ ] **BUTTERMILK**, 1% milk fat 1 quart (1 L)
- [ ] **MILK** 6 quarts (6 L)
- [ ] **YOGURT**, with fruit, fat-free 4 - ¾ cup (175 g) containers
- [ ] **YOGURT**, plain, fat-free 3 cups (750 mL)
- [ ] **SOUR CREAM**, fat-free 4 cups (1 L)
- [ ] **CREAM CHEESE**, low-fat ¼ cup (50 mL)
- [ ] **CHEDDAR CHEESE**, low-fat 1 lb (454 g)
- [ ] **CHEESE SLICES**, Monterey Jack, fat-free 6
- [ ] **MARGARINE**, non hydrogenated
- [ ] **EGGS** 8

PANTRY & OTHER

- [ ] _____
- [ ] _____
- [ ] _____
- [ ] _____
- [ ] _____
- [ ] _____
- [ ] _____
- [ ] _____
- [ ] _____
- [ ] _____
- [ ] _____
- [ ] _____
- [ ] _____
- [ ] _____
- [ ] _____
- [ ] _____
- [ ] _____
- [ ] _____

SHOPPING LIST

Review all recipes for portion requirements (see page 22). Add any missing pantry items to your grocery list.

PRODUCE

☐ **APPLES** 3
☐ **BANANAS** 8
☐ **FRUIT**, assorted 24 portions
☐ **GRAPES**, seedless (*of choice*) 1 cup (250 mL)
☐ **LEMON** 1
☐ **ORANGES** 3
☐ **AVOCADOS** 2
☐ **BROCCOLI** 2 stalks
☐ **CARROTS** 1-5 lb (2.3 kg) bag
☐ **CAULIFLOWER** 1 head
☐ **CELERY** 5 stalks
☐ **CUCUMBERS** 2 small
☐ **GARLIC** 1 head
☐ **LETTUCE**, iceberg 2 heads
☐ **LETTUCE**, romaine 2 heads
☐ **MUSHROOMS** 1 lb (450 g)
☐ **GREEN ONIONS** 2 bunches
☐ **ONIONS** 4 large
☐ **ONION** 1 medium
☐ **WHITE ONIONS** 3 small
☐ **PEPPERS**, green 4
☐ **PEPPERS**, red 3
☐ **PEPPERS**, yellow 2
☐ **POTATOES** 12 medium
☐ **RADISHES** 1 bunch
☐ **SPROUTS**, alfalfa (optional)
☐ **TOMATOES** 3 medium
☐ **ROMA TOMATOES** 8
☐ **TURNIP** 1 small
☐ **YAMS** 3 small
☐ **VEGETABLES FOR SNACKS**, assorted
(*see side panel page 67*)

GROCERIES

☐ **CRISPY RICE CEREAL** 6 cups (1.5 L)
☐ **EVAPORATED SKIM MILK**
2-14 oz (385 mL) cans
☐ **MARSHMALLOWS** 1-8 oz (250 g) bag
☐ **MESQUITE SEASONING** 1 pkg
(*hint: look in spice aisle*)
☐ **PECANS**, chopped ½ cup (125 mL)
☐ **APPLE SAUCE**, sweetened
1-14 oz (398 mL) can
☐ **PINEAPPLE TIDBITS**, in juice
1-14 oz (398 mL) can
☐ **TOMATOES**, diced 1-28 oz (796 mL) can
☐ **TOMATO SAUCE** 1-19 oz (540 mL) can
☐ **NOODLES**, fine, yolk-free
1-12 oz (340 g) bag
☐ **CHICKEN BROTH** 2-10 oz (284 mL) cans
☐ **CONSOMMÉ** 1-10 oz (284 mL) can
☐ **KIDNEY BEANS** 1-14 oz (398 mL) can
☐ **SALMON** 2-7.5 oz (213 g) cans
☐ **TUNA**, in water 2-7.5 oz (213 g) cans
☐ **VEGETABLE JUICE COCKTAIL**
1 cup (250 mL)
☐ **MARASCHINO CHERRIES** 1 jar (*optional*)
☐ **REFRIED BEANS**, reduced-fat
1-14 oz (398 mL) can
☐ **SALSA** 1-5 cup (1.36 L) jar

(*continued on reverse*)

MEAT

- [ ] **CHICKEN BREASTS**, boneless, skinless 6
- [ ] **EXTRA LEAN GROUND BEEF** 1 lb (450 g)
- [ ] **PORK TENDERLOIN** (*or boneless pork leg*) 1 lb (450 g)
- [ ] **SHRIMP**, uncooked, peeled 8 oz (225 g)
- [ ] **BLACK FOREST HAM**, sliced ½" (1 cm) thick 8 oz (225 g)
- [ ] **LEAN HAM**, sliced 1 small air-tight pkg

BAKERY

- [ ] **BUNS**, whole grain 4
- [ ] **ENGLISH MUFFINS**, whole grain 4
- [ ] **BAGUETTE**, whole grain 1 large
- [ ] **PITA BREAD**, whole wheat 8
- [ ] **RAISIN BREAD** 1 loaf
- [ ] **SUBMARINE BUNS**, whole grain 4 small
- [ ] **TORTILLAS**, whole wheat 14-8" (20 cm)

FROZEN

- [ ] **BLUEBERRIES** 2 cups (500 mL)
- [ ] **PEACHES**, sliced (*unsweetened*) 2 cups (500 mL)
- [ ] **GREEN BEANS**, French cut 4 cups (1 L)
- [ ] **KERNEL CORN** 1 cup (250 mL)
- [ ] **PEAS** 4 cups (1 L)
- [ ] **ORANGE JUICE CONCENTRATE** 1-12 oz (355 mL) can
- [ ] **VANILLA ICE CREAM**, 1% milk fat 2 cups (500 mL)

DAIRY

- [ ] **BUTTERMILK**, 1% milk fat 1 quart (1 L)
- [ ] **MILK** 12 quarts (12 L)
- [ ] **YOGURT,** with fruit, fat-free 8 - ¾ cup (175 g) containers
- [ ] **YOGURT**, plain, fat-free 6 cups (1.5 L)
- [ ] **SOUR CREAM**, fat-free 4 cups (1 L)
- [ ] **CREAM CHEESE**, low-fat ¼ cup (50 mL)
- [ ] **CHEDDAR CHEESE**, low-fat 1 lb (454 g)
- [ ] **CHEESE SLICES**, Monterey Jack, fat-free 12
- [ ] **MARGARINE**, non hydrogenated
- [ ] **EGGS** 11

PANTRY & OTHER

- [ ] _____
- [ ] _____
- [ ] _____
- [ ] _____
- [ ] _____
- [ ] _____
- [ ] _____
- [ ] _____
- [ ] _____
- [ ] _____
- [ ] _____
- [ ] _____
- [ ] _____
- [ ] _____
- [ ] _____
- [ ] _____

SHOPPING LIST

Review all recipes for portion requirements (see page 22). Add any missing pantry items to your grocery list.

PRODUCE

- [ ] **APPLES** 3
- [ ] **BANANAS** 8
- [ ] **FRUIT**, assorted 24 portions
- [ ] **GRAPES**, seedless (*of choice*) 1 cup (250 mL)
- [ ] **LEMON** 1
- [ ] **ORANGES** 3
- [ ] **AVOCADOS** 2
- [ ] **BROCCOLI** 2 stalks
- [ ] **CARROTS** 1-5 lb (2.3 kg) bag
- [ ] **CAULIFLOWER** 1 head
- [ ] **CELERY** 5 stalks
- [ ] **CUCUMBERS** 2 small
- [ ] **GARLIC** 1 head
- [ ] **LETTUCE**, iceberg 2 heads
- [ ] **LETTUCE**, romaine 2 heads
- [ ] **MUSHROOMS** 1 lb (450 g)
- [ ] **GREEN ONIONS** 2 bunches
- [ ] **ONIONS** 4 large
- [ ] **ONION** 1 medium
- [ ] **WHITE ONIONS** 3 small
- [ ] **PEPPERS**, green 4
- [ ] **PEPPERS**, red 3
- [ ] **PEPPERS**, yellow 2
- [ ] **POTATOES** 12 medium
- [ ] **RADISHES** 1 bunch
- [ ] **SPROUTS**, alfalfa (optional)
- [ ] **TOMATOES** 3 medium
- [ ] **ROMA TOMATOES** 8
- [ ] **TURNIP** 1 small
- [ ] **YAMS** 3 small
- [ ] **VEGETABLES FOR SNACKS**, assorted (*see side panel page 67*)

GROCERIES

- [ ] **CRISPY RICE CEREAL** 6 cups (1.5 L)
- [ ] **EVAPORATED SKIM MILK** 2-14 oz (385 mL) cans
- [ ] **MARSHMALLOWS** 1-8 oz (250 g) bag
- [ ] **MESQUITE SEASONING** 1 pkg (*hint: look in spice aisle*)
- [ ] **PECANS**, chopped ½ cup (125 mL)
- [ ] **APPLE SAUCE**, sweetened 1-14 oz (398 mL) can
- [ ] **PINEAPPLE TIDBITS**, in juice 1-14 oz (398 mL) can
- [ ] **TOMATOES**, diced 1-28 oz (796 mL) can
- [ ] **TOMATO SAUCE** 1-19 oz (540 mL) can
- [ ] **NOODLES**, fine, yolk-free 1-12 oz (340 g) bag
- [ ] **CHICKEN BROTH** 2-10 oz (284 mL) cans
- [ ] **CONSOMMÉ** 1-10 oz (284 mL) can
- [ ] **KIDNEY BEANS** 1-14 oz (398 mL) can
- [ ] **SALMON** 2-7.5 oz (213 g) cans
- [ ] **TUNA**, in water 2-7.5 oz (213 g) cans
- [ ] **VEGETABLE JUICE COCKTAIL** 1 cup (250 mL)
- [ ] **MARASCHINO CHERRIES** 1 jar (*optional*)
- [ ] **REFRIED BEANS**, reduced-fat 1-14 oz (398 mL) can
- [ ] **SALSA** 1-5 cup (1.36 L) jar

(continued on reverse)

MEAT

- [ ] **CHICKEN BREASTS**, boneless, skinless 6
- [ ] **EXTRA LEAN GROUND BEEF** 1 lb (450 g)
- [ ] **PORK TENDERLOIN** (*or boneless pork leg*)
  1 lb (450 g)
- [ ] **SHRIMP**, uncooked, peeled 8 oz (225 g)
- [ ] **BLACK FOREST HAM**, sliced ½″ (1 cm) thick
  8 oz (225 g)
- [ ] **LEAN HAM**, sliced 1 small air-tight pkg

BAKERY

- [ ] **BUNS**, whole grain 4
- [ ] **ENGLISH MUFFINS**, whole grain 4
- [ ] **BAGUETTE**, whole grain 1 large
- [ ] **PITA BREAD**, whole wheat 8
- [ ] **RAISIN BREAD** 1 loaf
- [ ] **SUBMARINE BUNS**, whole grain 4 small
- [ ] **TORTILLAS**, whole wheat 14-8″ (20 cm)

FROZEN

- [ ] **BLUEBERRIES** 2 cups (500 mL)
- [ ] **PEACHES**, sliced (*unsweetened*)
  2 cups (500 mL)
- [ ] **GREEN BEANS**, French cut 4 cups (1 L)
- [ ] **KERNEL CORN** 1 cup (250 mL)
- [ ] **PEAS** 4 cups (1 L)
- [ ] **ORANGE JUICE CONCENTRATE**
  1-12 oz (355 mL) can
- [ ] **VANILLA ICE CREAM**, 1% milk fat
  2 cups (500 mL)

DAIRY

- [ ] **BUTTERMILK**, 1% milk fat 1 quart (1 L)
- [ ] **MILK** 12 quarts (12 L)
- [ ] **YOGURT,** with fruit, fat-free
  8 - ¾ cup (175 g) containers
- [ ] **YOGURT**, plain, fat-free 6 cups (1.5 L)
- [ ] **SOUR CREAM**, fat-free 4 cups (1 L)
- [ ] **CREAM CHEESE**, low-fat ¼ cup (50 mL)
- [ ] **CHEDDAR CHEESE**, low-fat 1 lb (454 g)
- [ ] **CHEESE SLICES**, Monterey Jack, fat-free 12
- [ ] **MARGARINE**, non hydrogenated
- [ ] **EGGS** 11

PANTRY & OTHER

- [ ] _____
- [ ] _____
- [ ] _____
- [ ] _____
- [ ] _____
- [ ] _____
- [ ] _____
- [ ] _____
- [ ] _____
- [ ] _____
- [ ] _____
- [ ] _____
- [ ] _____
- [ ] _____
- [ ] _____
- [ ] _____
- [ ] _____

BREAKFAST

Seasoned Hash Browns, Egg "Your Way", Whole Grain Toast, Fruit Juice of Choice

LUNCH

Olé Quesadillas with Avocado Slices, Salsa and Sour Cream, Milk

DINNER

Pork Roast Dinner, **Marinated Vegetable Salad**,
Blueberry Bubbly with 1% Vanilla Ice Cream

SNACK

Cherry Pie Yogurt (see side panel, page 103)

NUTRITION INFORMATION
See page 6 for standards used.

MENU ITEMS (single portion)	calories	carbs (grams)	protein (grams)	fat (grams)
Seasoned Hash Browns	76	17.1	2.1	0.1
Egg "Your Way"	75	0.6	6.4	5.1
Whole Grain Toast — 1	63	12.4	2.7	0.8
Fruit Juice of Choice	80	20	1	0
Olé Quesadilla	208.9	32	9.4	5.1
Avocado	80.5	7.4	1	7.7
Salsa	12	2	0.4	0
Fat-Free Sour Cream	18	3	2	0
Milk	86	11.9	8.3	0.4
Pork Roast Dinner	390.8	48.5	29.6	8.1
Marinated Vegetable Salad	94	12.8	3.1	3.9
Blueberry Bubbly	153.6	32.7	3.9	1.1
1% Vanilla Ice Cream — 1/4 cup (50 mL)	57.5	10	2	0.4
Cherry Pie Yogurt	131.3	22.3	9.8	0.3
Total for day	1527	232.7	81.7	33
		percentage fat ▶		19%

REMEMBER, these are the MINIMUM REQUIREMENTS of the Canada and U.S. Food Guides. Some people will need more calories.

GAME PLAN

Check your groceries on hand against the menu for today's breakfast: the ingredients were included in the Week 2 shopping list.

Thaw the cherry pie filling from Thursday, Week 1 for tonight's snack. As in Week 1, freeze the bread items, except for the tortillas and the baguette. Tortillas keep well in the fridge. True connoisseurs of baguettes prefer to eat them fresh— you may want to buy yours tomorrow.

Fill a plastic container with raw vegetable pieces ("mouse food", see pages 21 and 67), and refrigerate. Make the **Marinated Vegetable Salad** for tonight's dinner and refrigerate. Thaw the chicken breasts and shrimp in the fridge for tomorrow's dinner. Keep the pork roast and all of the ham in the fridge. Freeze the remaining meat.

... continued on page 105

By using cooking spray instead of 1 tbsp (15 mL) butter or oil, you save at least 11.5 g of fat and 102 calories.

SEASONED HASH BROWNS

*From **scratch***, hash browns take only slightly longer to prepare than the commercial varieties, but the taste and the nutritional value are not even comparable.*

1	medium potato, washed & cut in ½ " (1.5 cm) cubes	1
¼ tsp	seasoning salt	1 mL
½ tsp	dry parsley	2 mL

1. Place potatoes in a microwaveable covered dish and cook on high for 4 minutes, stirring once at half time. (Potatoes will be partially cooked and appear translucent.)
   OR
   Steam for 5 minutes as in steps 1 and 2 on page 103.

2. Transfer potatoes to a nonstick skillet coated with butter-flavoured cooking spray.

3. Add spices and cook over medium heat until crispy and lightly browned (about 10 to 15 minutes), stirring frequently.

Makes 1 portion. *Doubles or quadruples easily, just increase the microwave cooking time. Freezes well.*

*I have combed this entire recipe book and can not find one recipe that calls for "scratch"! My Mom, probably yours too, cooked and baked everything from scratch. I guess because it is soooo difficult to find in the stores, no recipes call for it anymore!

Was that a chuckle I heard? Well, you just exercised your abdominal muscles! If your back aches regularly it could be that you need to exercise those abdominal muscles. Here are your choices: read this story 15 times (laughing each time) OR tighten your tummy muscles as though someone is about to punch you there (hold this while you chuckle "*Tee Hee Hee Hee*" and repeat 10 times).

Marinated Vegetable Salad

This recipe originated with Denise's friend Janet, and has been enjoyed by Denise's guests for many years.

2 cups	broccoli florets & peeled stems, cut in 2 " (5 cm) pieces	500 mL
2 cups	cauliflower, cut in 2 " (5 cm) pieces	500 mL
1 cup	carrots, thinly sliced	250 mL
1	red pepper, thinly sliced	1
1	small white onion, thinly sliced into rings	1
¼ cup	red wine vinegar	50 mL
1 tbsp	olive oil	15 mL
½ tsp	prepared mustard	2 mL
1	clove garlic, minced	1
1½ tsp	sugar	7 mL
½ tsp	salt	2 mL
¼ tsp	black pepper	1 mL

1. Place broccoli, cauliflower and carrots in the steamer insert of a large saucepan. Add water to bottom of saucepan. Bring to a boil over medium-high heat.
2. Steam for 10 minutes or until fork-tender. Set aside to cool.
3. Mix vinegar, oil, mustard, garlic, sugar, salt and pepper together. Set aside.
4. Add red pepper and onion to cooled steamed vegetables.
5. Toss <u>all</u> vegetables with vinegar mixture in a container with a tight-sealing lid.
6. Let marinate for 3 to 4 hours, tossing occasionally.

Makes 4 portions. *Doubles easily.*

Marinated Vegetable Salad keeps for one week in the fridge. Use any time as a snack.

Cherry Pie Yogurt

If you don't have any cherry pie filling leftover, use any fresh or canned fruit. Leftover cherry pie filling would taste great on your English muffin tomorrow — it's a good substitute for jam.

³⁄₄ **cup (175 mL) fat-free plain yogurt**

2 tbsp (30 mL) cherry pie filling
(Use the leftovers from Thursday, Week 1.)

1. Stir ingredients together and enjoy!

Makes 1 portion.

OLÉ QUESADILLAS

Freeze leftover quesadillas and avocado. They reheat well in the microwave or oven. You'll have your own fast food on hand — as quick as you can say "OLÉ"!

2	**medium avocados, peeled & sliced into eighths**	2
2 tsp	**lemon juice**	10 mL
2	**red peppers, diced**	2
2	**yellow peppers, diced**	2
1	**large onion, diced**	1
1	**14 oz (398 mL) can reduced-fat refried beans**	1
3 cups	**salsa, divided**	750 mL
1 cup	**low-fat cheddar cheese, grated**	250 mL
8	**8" (20 cm) whole wheat tortillas**	8
1 cup	**fat-free sour cream**	250 mL

1. Toss avocado slices in lemon juice to prevent browning. Set aside.

2. Stir-fry peppers and onion for 2 to 3 minutes over medium-high heat in a nonstick skillet coated with cooking spray. Set aside.

3. Mix refried beans and pepper mixture with 1 cup (250 mL) of salsa and the grated cheese in a medium bowl. Divide mixture into 8 equal portions. Spread one portion over half of each tortilla.

4. Fold tortillas in half. Lightly brown tortillas on each side over medium heat in a nonstick skillet coated with cooking spray.

5. To serve, cut each tortilla into 4 wedges.

Makes 8 portions. *One portion = 1 quesadilla topped with ¼ cup (50 mL) salsa, 2 tbsp (30 mL) fat-free sour cream and 2 slices avocado. Doubles easily. Freezes well.*

By using fat-free sour cream instead of regular sour cream, you save 5 g of fat per 2 tbsp (30 mL) portion.

A Workout for the Chops (*not the pork variety*)**:**

"Zeal, zebra, zero, zest, zinc, zoo, zone, zen, zany, zip."
This is actually an exercise designed to warm the mouth and jaw area. It will help prevent getting your "mords wixed" and having "trouth moubles" before giving a speech or before any other speaking event.

PORK ROAST DINNER

Be trendy! Do try balsamic vinegar, the new kid on the block— your taste buds will tell you it's worth every penny. Besides, you'll use it again later in this book.

2 tbsp	chicken bouillon concentrate	30 mL
3 tbsp	balsamic vinegar	45 mL
1 tbsp	canola oil	15 mL
1	clove garlic , minced	1
2 tbsp	red wine or apple juice	30 mL
1 lb	pork tenderloin or boneless pork leg, cut in 4 pieces, visible fat removed	450 g
4	medium potatoes, washed & cut into 1½ " (4 cm) pieces	4
1	large onion, diced in 1½ " (4 cm) pieces	1
4	medium carrots, peeled & cut into 1½ " (4 cm) pieces	4
1	small turnip, peeled & cut into 1½ " (4 cm) pieces	1
1 cup	apple sauce, canned, sweetened **OR**	250 mL
1 cup	"Homemade Spiced Apple Sauce" *(page 177)*	250 mL

1. Mix bouillon, balsamic vinegar, oil, garlic and red wine in a large mixing bowl. Add pork and vegetable pieces. Coat well.

2. Transfer pork and vegetables to a large roasting pan coated with cooking spray.

3. Bake uncovered for 30 minutes at 400°F (200°C). Stir. Add 2 to 3 tbsp (30 to 45 mL) water if dry.

4. Cover and bake another 20 to 30 minutes. Serve with apple sauce.

Makes 4 portions. *One portion = 1/4 of the pork roast, 1/4 of the vegetables and ¼ cup (50 mL) of apple sauce. Doubles easily. Freezes well.*

...continued from page 101

About 75 minutes before you plan to eat, prepare and bake the **Pork Roast Dinner**. While it is in the oven, prepare and cook the **Blueberry Bubbly**.

Total Preparation and cooking time: **75min.**

If you are entertaining, steps 1 and 2 of **Pork Roast Dinner** can be prepared ahead of time and refrigerated. One hour before you plan to eat, place the roaster in the oven and follow steps 3 and 4.

Family of two:
freeze leftover
Blueberry Bubbly
in single portions.
Use 2 portions for
your snack on
Tuesday and use the
remaining 4 portions
anytime you
need a treat!

BLUEBERRY BUBBLY

When unexpected guests arrive, you need never be caught without baking on hand. This recipe can be made with any fruit (peaches, raspberries, rhubarb, sour cherries, etc.).

2 cups	blueberries, fresh or frozen	500 mL
1½ tbsp	quick-cooking tapioca	22 mL
¼ tsp	almond extract	1 mL
1 cup	water	250 mL
½ cup	sugar	125 mL
1 tbsp	lemon juice	15 mL
¼ cup	quick oats	50 mL
¾ cup	all-purpose flour	175 mL
1 tsp	baking powder	5 mL
¼ tsp	salt	1 mL
1 tsp	dried lemon peel	5 mL
1 tbsp	brown sugar	15 mL
½ cup	canned evaporated skim milk	125 mL
1	egg, lightly beaten	1
2 cups	1% vanilla ice cream	500 mL

1. In a large saucepan, combine berries, tapioca, almond extract, water, sugar, and lemon juice. Bring to a boil over medium-high heat. **Reduce heat** to medium-low and cook for 5 to 10 minutes, stirring frequently.

2. Meanwhile, in a medium mixing bowl, combine quick oats, all-purpose flour, baking powder and salt. Set aside.

3. In a small bowl, combine lemon peel, brown sugar, milk, and egg. Add all at once to dry ingredients. Mix to moisten only.

4. Drop dough from a spoon onto the simmering berry syrup. **Do not stir**.

5. Cover and cook undisturbed for 15 to 20 minutes. If a toothpick inserted into centre of dough comes out clean, they are done. If not, cover and cook 5 to 10 minutes longer. Serve warm with ¼ cup (50 mL) ice cream per portion.

Makes 8 portions. *Freezes well.*

 Freeze one portion per person for your snack on Tuesday.

BRUNCH
So-Easy Oatmeal Pancakes
with
Peach Sauce and **Vanilla Cream**, Fruit Juice of Choice, **Vanilla Coffee**

DINNER
Jambalaya, Lettuce and Carrot Slaw, Whole Grain Baguette, Milk

SNACK
Rice Crisp Square, Milk

Exercise program by

FIRST TIME TONING:

Toning is the third component of your fitness program. In Week 1 you learned stretching for flexibility, in Week 2 you learned correct walking technique for circulation and now in Week 3 you will learn toning for your beach look. Today concentrate on your lower body. First, warm up, then do **Lower Body Stretches** (pages 36 to 40) before you do the **Lower Body Toners** (pages 112 to 114). While you do these exercises carefully and deliberately, remember to breathe deeply and slowly. Don't forget to do the **Cool Down** on page 40 and repeat the stretches of those hard-working muscles.

...continued on page 116

NUTRITION INFORMATION
See page 6 for standards used.

MENU ITEMS (single portion)	calories	carbs (grams)	protein (grams)	fat (grams)
So-Easy Oatmeal Pancakes	408.2	62.7	22.9	8.5
Peach Sauce	93.5	23.4	0.5	0
Vanilla Cream	41.7	1.5	1.5	3.4
Fruit Juice of Choice	80	20	1	0
Vanilla Coffee	2	0	0	0
Jambalaya	432.6	69	38.8	6
Lettuce & Carrot Slaw	65.4	12.4	4.1	0.4
Whole Grain Baguette	95	18.8	3.1	0.8
Milk	86	11.9	8.3	0.4
Rice Crisp Square	142.3	26.8	0.7	2.9
Milk	86	11.9	8.3	0.4
Total for day	1532.7	258.4	89.2	22.8
percentage fat ▶				13%

REMEMBER, these are the MINIMUM REQUIREMENTS of the Canada and U.S. Food Guides. Some people will need more calories.

Leftover pancakes can be frozen to have on hand for a quick breakfast.

Note to Sports Parents — for convenient "Breakfasts-on-the-Go", double the **So-Easy Oatmeal Pancakes** recipe. Spread the extra pancakes with peanut butter and place ½ of a banana on one side — roll, wrap and freeze.

Extra buttermilk mixed half and half with tomato juice makes a great beverage — just ask Denise's Mom and her brothers!

SO-EASY OATMEAL PANCAKES

Denise's nephew could not understand how so few pancakes could be so filling, but he didn't know he was eating "porridge in disguise".

1 cup	quick oats	250 mL
1 cup	whole wheat flour	250 mL
½ cup	oat bran	125 mL
¼ cup	skim milk powder	50 mL
¼ cup	wheat germ	50 mL
1 tsp	baking soda	5 mL
½ tsp	baking powder	2 mL
¼ tsp	salt	1 mL
2	eggs	2
2½ cups	1% buttermilk	625 mL
2 tbsp	brown sugar	30 mL
1 tsp	vanilla extract	5 mL

1. Mix all dry ingredients in a large bowl. Set aside.

2. Mix eggs, buttermilk, brown sugar and vanilla in a small bowl.

3. Add egg mixture all at once to dry ingredients. Stir briefly — a few lumps won't matter.

4. Let batter rest for 15 minutes. Batter will be thick.

5. Spoon ⅓ cup (75 mL) batter per pancake onto a hot griddle coated with cooking spray. Gently spread batter into 5" (12 cm) circles. Flip pancakes when tops are bubbled and edges appear cooked. Continue cooking for another 2 to 3 minutes. (If you do not have a griddle, cook over medium heat in a nonstick pan coated with cooking spray.)

Makes 12 pancakes. *One portion = 3 pancakes topped with ½ cup (125 mL)* **Peach Sauce** *and 1 tbsp (15 mL)* **Vanilla Cream**. *Doubles easily. Freezes well.*

PEACH SAUCE

2 cups	peaches, fresh or frozen, peeled, sliced, unsweetened	500 mL
¼ cup	sugar	50 mL
¼ cup	water	50 mL
2 tbsp	cornstarch	30 mL
pinch	salt	pinch
1 tsp	vanilla extract	5 mL
½ tsp	almond extract	2 mL

1. Mix all ingredients in a medium saucepan. Bring to a boil over medium-high heat, stirring constantly.

2. Reduce heat to medium. Cook 2 to 3 minutes, stirring constantly. Serve hot.

Makes 4 - ½ cup (125 mL) portions. *Doubles easily. Freezes well.*

VANILLA CREAM

This is "Cloud 9". You won't miss whipped cream!

¼ cup	low-fat cream cheese	50 mL
1 tbsp	fat-free sour cream	15 mL
1 tsp	icing sugar	5 mL
½ tsp	vanilla extract	2 mL

1. Whisk together and serve.

Makes 4 portions. *Doubles easily. Freezes well.*

VANILLA COFFEE

	Coffee grounds, vanilla extract	

1. Add 1 tsp (5 mL) vanilla (for each 2 cups [500 mL] coffee) into the glass carafe before brewing.

Make as many cups as you need.

GAME PLAN

Begin preparing brunch by mixing the pancake batter.

While the batter rests (everyone needs to rest on Sunday!), prepare the **Peach Sauce**, **Vanilla Cream** and **Vanilla Coffee**.

After brunch, prepare the **Rice Crisp Squares** so they are ready when you need your snack.

...continued on page 110

... continued from page 109

Because the **Jambalaya** for dinner must cook undisturbed for 40 to 50 minutes, there is plenty of time to prepare the salad during the cooking time.

Total preparation and cooking time: **75 min.**

If you work quickly, you'll even have time to pack your lunch for tomorrow before the **Jambalaya** is ready!

JAMBALAYA

This recipe will transport you to the deep South. Be aware that cayenne pepper is much hotter than red pepper flakes, so do not substitute in equal amounts unless you like it HOT!

1 tsp	olive or canola oil	5 mL
2	chicken breasts, skinless, boneless, cut in 1 " (2.5 cm) cubes	2
1	large onion, diced	1
4	cloves garlic, minced	4
8 oz	Black Forest ham, cut into ½ " (1 cm) cubes	225 g
3	stalks celery, diced	3
2	green peppers, diced	2
1½ tsp	thyme	7 mL
½ tsp each	red pepper flakes & black pepper	2 mL each
2	bay leaves (*Remove before serving.*)	2
1 tsp each	oregano & basil	5 mL each
1	26 oz (725 mL) can tomato sauce	1
1	28 oz (796 mL) can tomatoes, diced	1
1½ cups	brown rice, long grain (*You can substitute ½ cup [125 mL] wild rice for ½ cup [125 mL] brown rice.*)	375 mL
8 oz	shrimp, uncooked, peeled & deveined (*You can replace shrimp with 2 chicken breasts, cubed.*)	225 g

1. Heat oil over medium-high heat in a Dutch oven coated with cooking spray. Add chicken and brown for 5 minutes, stirring frequently.

2. Add onion, garlic and ham. Cook another 3 minutes, stirring constantly.

3. Add celery, peppers and spices. Continue to cook over medium heat for 5 minutes, stirring occasionally.

4. Add tomato sauce and tomatoes. Bring to a boil, stirring occasionally. Once liquid is boiling, add rice and shrimp. Stir well. Return to boiling point, then reduce heat to low. Cover and let simmer, undisturbed, for 45 to 50 minutes or until rice is tender and liquid is absorbed.

Makes 6 portions. *Doubles easily. Freezes well.*

Roast Beef Gyro
page 47

LETTUCE AND CARROT SLAW

If you need only 1 portion, use 1/2 of the vegetable quantities but make the full recipe of dressing, which can be used anytime you need a fat-free salad dressing.

4 cups	**iceberg lettuce, shredded**	**1 L**
½ cup	**radishes, sliced**	**125 mL**
1 cup	**carrot, grated**	**250 mL**
2 tbsp	**green onion, chopped**	**30 mL**
Dressing:		
¼ cup	**fat-free sour cream**	**50 mL**
1 tbsp	**fat-free plain yogurt**	**15 mL**
1 tsp	**prepared mustard**	**5 mL**
1 tsp	**lemon juice**	**5 mL**
1 tsp	**sugar**	**5 mL**
pinch each	**salt & black pepper**	**pinch each**
1 or 2 drops	**Tabasco sauce**	**1 or 2 drops**

1. Mix dressing ingredients in a small bowl. Set aside.

2. Mix lettuce, radishes, carrot and green onion in a medium bowl.

3. Just before serving, pour dressing over lettuce. Toss well and serve.

Makes 2 portions salad & 4 portions dressing. *Doubles or quadruples easily.*

RICE CRISP SQUARES

¼ cup	**non hydrogenated margarine**	**50 mL**
1	**8 oz (250 g) bag marshmallows** (*40 regular*)	**1**
1 tsp	**vanilla extract**	**5 mL**
6 cups	**crispy rice cereal**	**1.5 L**

1. Melt margarine over low heat in a Dutch oven. Add marshmallows and stir constantly until melted.

2. Remove from heat. Stir in vanilla. Add cereal and stir until coated.

3. Press into a 9" x 13" (23 cm x 33 cm) pan coated with cooking spray.

Makes 16 —2" x 3" (7cm x 10 cm) portions.

 Save one portion per person for tomorrow's lunch.

To avoid "pigging out" on **Rice Crisp Squares** (and who can resist?), take the leftovers to work and share them.

LOWER BODY TONERS

Should you tone the same muscles every day? My answer is "No". Every other day is best because your muscles need to rest a bit. You run a higher risk of injury doing the same exercise day after day, so toss the guilt out the window (please open it first). Mix and match your workouts. Daily movement is what will keep you moving yearly.

SQUAT

You may actually feel the burn of this most effective calorie-consuming exercise since you are using your two largest muscle groups. The burning sensation that you may or may not experience could be due to low potassium so to put out the fire, eat a banana. If you see smoke, call 911!

1. Sit on the edge of a chair, feet shoulder-width apart, 6 to 8 inches (15 to 20 cm) from the chair. Make sure your heels are directly beneath your knees. Place your hands on your thighs, fingers pointed inward.

2. Lift your toes to prevent your knees from moving past your toes. As you stand, do a small pause, slowly pushing your heels down and squeezing your buttocks.

3. Slowly return to a sitting position, again doing a small pause just before sitting. Lean forward slightly. To prevent straining your knee joints, do not allow your knees to move past your toes. Who knows—you might develop "kneesles"?

4. Try 5 and work your way up to 20. You should feel your bottom and your quadricep muscles (front of legs) working.

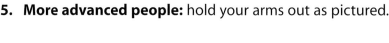
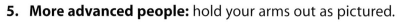

5. **More advanced people:** hold your arms out as pictured.

Just read sentence by sentence and do step by step. Don't get discouraged!

*L*OWER BODY TONERS

REAR LEG LIFT

This is one of my all time favourite exercises because it is safe, easy to do and gets results!

1. Stand as pictured, feet shoulder width apart. Hold the back of a chair, using both hands for support. Think tall with your spine.

2. Please ensure that the knee of your left (supporting) leg is slightly bent (think of the knee joint as a spring). At a 45° angle from your body, point the toes of your right foot to the back. Keep your hips and eyes forward. Balance yourself on your left leg, using your right hand for support. Please don't lean onto your left leg, forcing it to take all the weight.

3. Now slowly squeeze your right buttock and hamstring muscles so that your right foot lifts 3 to 6 inches (7 to 15 cm) above the floor. Hold for a quick A, B, C, D, then slowly release and lower. Try it again. In fact, start with 10 lifts. Remember to maintain good posture and avoid leaning forward.

4. Repeat on the other side. You should feel the muscles in your bottom working. Tomorrow you will feel the difference; soon you will see the difference.

ADDUCTOR TONER

This movement tones your inner thigh muscles by making them work against the force of gravity.

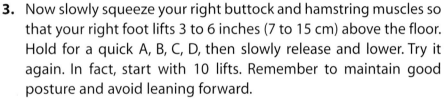

1. As pictured, lie on your back on a floor mat or towel. Place your hands beneath the lower part of your buttocks. Push your spine flat so there is no space between your lower back and the mat.

2. With your knees bent or with your legs extended, slowly lower your legs to the sides as pictured, up to 18 inches (45 cm) apart. Just as slowly, bring your legs back to the start position. You should feel your inner thighs working.

3. Try 10 and work up to 30.

LOWER BODY TONERS

LYING ABDUCTOR TONER

If you don't feel that this exercise is tightening (toning) your outer thighs, try the Standing Abductor Toner as described below.

1. Please come join me. Lie on your side as pictured. Bend your lower leg to take any potential strain off your lower back muscles and spine. Get comfy.

2. Stretch your upper leg out, keeping it in line with the side of your body. Please keep your knee joint relaxed and breathe deeply.

3. Slowly lift your upper leg approximately 2 feet (60 cm) above the floor. Just as slowly, lower your leg either to rest or simply to touch the floor and immediately repeat. You should feel your outer thigh working.

4. Try 10 and work your way up to 30. Don't forget to repeat on your other side.

STANDING ABDUCTOR TONER

NEWS FLASH: recently reported new research confirms that you do not have to jiggle when you wiggle. If you jiggle when you wiggle, try this exercise, don't just giggle.

1. Stand as straight and tall as possible, using a chair or wall for support (if need be).

2. Place your feet shoulder width apart. Slightly bend your left knee. Always think soft with the knee joints. Keep your hips square, ensuring your left hip is above your left foot. Avoid leaning. Lift your right leg to the side no more than 12" (30 cm) from your body. You should feel this in the outer part of your right thigh. If you feel this in your left leg, you are doing a great impression of the Leaning Tower of Pisa (not a good thing). Alternating legs, repeat this exercise 10 to 15 times on each side. Use very controlled, very slow motions. Don't let momentum do this exercise for you.

3. **More advanced people:** instead of alternating legs, repeat on the same side 10 to 15 times before changing legs.

BREAKFAST
Whole Grain Cereal of Choice, Fruit of Choice, Milk

LUNCH
P.T.L.C., Vegetable Juice of Choice, Rice Crisp Square

DINNER
Salmon in a Nest, **Creamy Peas**, **Orange-Romaine Salad**

SNACK
Fat-Free Fruit Yogurt of Choice

GAME PLAN

Before breakfast, place the ground beef for tomorrow's dinner and the English muffins for tomorrow's breakfast into the fridge to thaw.

...continued on page 117

NUTRITION INFORMATION
See page 6 for standards used.

MENU ITEMS (single portion)	calories	carbs (grams)	protein (grams)	fat (grams)
Whole Grain Cereal of Choice	126	20.3	2.6	4.4
Fruit of Choice	81	21	0.2	0.5
Milk	86	11.9	8.3	0.4
P.T.L.C.	244	46.3	13	1.7
Vegetable Juice of Choice	43	8.7	1.3	0.4
Rice Crisp Square	142.3	26.8	0.7	2.9
Salmon in a Nest	453.8	43	40.8	12.3
Creamy Peas	166.5	29.4	10.9	0.4
Orange-Romaine Salad	106	26.8	1.7	0.2
Fat-Free Fruit Yogurt	130	25	6.9	0.1
Total for day	1578.6	259.2	86.4	23.3
			percentage fat ▶	13%

REMEMBER, these are the MINIMUM REQUIREMENTS of the Canada and U.S. Food Guides. Some people will need more calories.

Exercise program by

THIRD TIME WALKING:

Ready for a slight incline? Your bottom is telling me by its decline that it **is** inclined. All the more reason to warm up and stretch your leg muscles, because they will work a bit harder today. Locate a gradual slope of one block or more and walk up the hill until you are winded but can still speak. Turn around and descend at a slower pace. Remember to squeeze your gluteal (buttock) muscles with each step. Do this uphill walk twice if you can before returning home to do those great-feeling leg stretches.

... continued on page 123

P.T.L.C. (Pita/Tomato/Lettuce/Cheese)

Nurses can't resist providing T.L.C.!

1	**pita bread, whole wheat** (*cut in half*)	1
1	**slice fat-free Monterey Jack cheese**	1
1/2	**medium tomato, sliced**	1/2
6	**slices cucumber**	6
½ cup	**lettuce, shredded** (*or alfalfa sprouts for the adventurous*)	125 mL
1/4	**green pepper, sliced**	1/4
¼ cup	**carrot, grated**	50 mL
1 tbsp	**fat-free dressing of choice**	15 mL

1. Slip one half of pita inside the other. Spread with dressing.
2. Add cheese slice. Wrap if brown-bagging.
3. Place vegetables in a lunch container.   Add to sandwich just before eating.

Makes 1 portion.

Orange-Romaine Salad

The round, smooth flavour of balsamic vinegar makes this salad dressing so divine that the addition of oil is unnecessary.

1 cup	**romaine lettuce, torn in bite-size pieces**	250 mL
1/2	**orange, peeled & sectioned**	1/2
1 tbsp	**green onion, sliced**	15 mL
1 tbsp	**liquid honey**	15 mL
1 tbsp	**balsamic vinegar**	15 mL
pinch	**salt**	pinch

1. Top lettuce with orange sections and green onion in a serving bowl.
2. Blend honey, vinegar and salt in a small bowl. Pour over salad just before serving.

Makes 1 portion.

SALMON IN A NEST

This is an adaptation of Denise's Mom's recipe — a childhood favourite.

1½ **cups**	**fine yolk-free noodles**	375 mL
1	**small onion, diced**	1
½ **cup**	**canned evaporated skim milk**	125 mL
¼ **tsp**	**black pepper**	1 mL
1	**7.5 oz (213 g) can salmon, undrained**	1
2 **tbsp**	**all-purpose flour**	30 mL
¼ **cup**	**cold water**	50 mL
½ **tsp**	**paprika**	2 mL

1. Cook noodles according to package instructions. Drain well. Set aside.

2. Meanwhile, sauté onion for 1 to 2 minutes over medium heat in a nonstick skillet coated with cooking spray. Add milk and black pepper.

3. In a small jar with a tight-fitting lid, shake flour and water vigorously until there are no lumps. Whisk into milk mixture. Bring to a boil over medium heat, stirring constantly. Cook for 1 minute.

4. Add salmon and continue to cook over low heat for 3 minutes, stirring frequently.

5. Place half of the noodles on each of the 2 serving plates, making an indentation in the centre. Fill each indentation with half of the salmon mixture.

6. Sprinkle with paprika and serve.

Makes 2 portions. *Doubles or triples easily. Freezes well.*

Being dense is a good thing... when it comes to your bones. Did you know that the average woman's bone mass begins to decrease after age 35? That's why calcium is important daily (men need calcium too). It can be found in high amounts in low-fat dairy products as well as in sesame seeds, almonds, sardines, **salmon**, broccoli and collards — to list a few.

... continued from page 115

To prepare dinner, begin by making the salad and dressing; place them in the fridge.

Set water to boil for the noodles. Meanwhile, begin cooking the peas and dice the onion for the salmon mixture.

Finish preparing the peas and set them aside over low heat.

Sauté the onions. While they cook, add the noodles to the boiling water. Finish preparing the salmon sauce.

Total preparation and cooking time: **30 min.**

Don't forget... your salad and dressing are in the fridge!

If you work away from home, you should prepare the soup for tomorrow's lunch and pack the rest of your lunch now, before doing the kitchen clean-up .

CREAMY PEAS

What a nice change from plain peas!

2 cups	frozen peas	500 mL
4	shallots, chopped	4
1 tsp	chicken bouillon concentrate	5 mL
½ cup	water	125 mL
¼ cup	canned evaporated skim milk	50 mL
1½ tsp	cornstarch	7 mL
pinch	black pepper	pinch

1. Combine peas, shallots, chicken bouillon concentrate and water in a medium saucepan. Bring to a boil over medium-high heat. Reduce heat to medium-low. Cover and cook for 5 minutes.

2. Mix cornstarch with milk. Add to peas while stirring. Keep stirring over medium-low heat until thickened. Keep warm over low heat until the **Salmon in a Nest** dish is ready.

3. Sprinkle with pepper and serve.

Makes 2 portions. *Doubles or quadruples easily. Freezes well.*

If looking great and feeling good are not sufficient motivators for your regular walk, leave the kitchen clean up to someone else. That should get you out the door!

BREAKFAST
Whole Grain English Muffin, Reduced-Fat Peanut Butter, Fruit-Only Jam
(*or leftover cherry pie filling from yesterday*), Fruit of Choice, Milk

LUNCH
Cream of Mushroom Soup, Whole Grain Bun,
Fat-Free Monterey Jack Cheese Slice, Fruit of Choice

DINNER
Salisbury Steak, **Slight Smashed Spuds**, French Cut Green Beans

SNACK
Blueberry Bubbly, Milk

GAME PLAN

Place these items in the fridge to thaw:

- **Blueberry Bubbly** (for today's snack);
- pitas (for tomorrow's lunch);
- chicken (for tomorrow's dinner);
- orange juice concentrate (for tomorrow's **Sunshine Bars**).

If the English muffins for today's breakfast are still in the freezer, just pop them into the toaster.

...continued on page 120

NUTRITION INFORMATION
See page 6 for standards used.

MENU ITEMS (single portion)	calories	carbs (grams)	protein (grams)	fat (grams)
Whole Grain English Muffin — 1	132	25.3	4.6	1.2
Reduced-Fat Peanut Butter	82	5.2	2.7	5.6
Fruit-Only Jam	43	11	0.1	0
Fruit of Choice	81	21	0.2	0.5
Milk	86	11.9	8.3	0.4
Cream of Mushroom Soup	160	19.4	12.5	3.7
Whole Grain Bun — 1	93	18.8	3.6	1
Fat-Free Monterey Jack Cheese — 1 slice	31	2.6	4.6	0.2
Fruit of Choice	81	21	0.2	0.5
Salisbury Steak	270.9	10.9	22.5	14.1
Slight Smashed Spuds	114	22.6	5.9	0.2
French Green Beans — 1 cup (250 mL)	44	9.8	2.4	0.4
Blueberry Bubbly	153.6	32.7	3.9	1.1
Milk	86	11.9	8.3	0.4
Total for day	1458	224.1	79.8	29.3
percentage fat ▶				18%

REMEMBER, these are the MINIMUM REQUIREMENTS of the Canada and U.S. Food Guides. Some people will need more calories.

...continued from page 119

Begin preparing dinner by cooking the potatoes (see the **Slight Smashed Spuds** recipe on page 31 for cooking instructions). While the potatoes cook, prepare and broil the beef patties. While the patties cook, finish the **Salisbury Steak** recipe. By now the potatoes and meat should be done. Add the meat to the gravy and simmer.

Cook the beans in a microwave or steamer, then mash the potatoes—*easy!*

Total preparation and cooking time: **45 min.**

After dinner, remember to prepare tomorrow's lunch.

CREAM OF MUSHROOM SOUP

You won't need to hunt for the mushrooms in this soup!

1 lb	**fresh mushrooms, diced or sliced**	450 g
	(¼ cup [50 mL] reserved for garnish)	
1	**small onion, diced**	1
1½ tsp	**non hydrogenated margarine**	7 mL
⅓ cup	**all-purpose flour**	75 mL
2	**10 oz (284 mL) cans chicken broth, fat removed**	2
1½ cups	**water**	375 mL
	OR	
4 cups	**Homemade Chicken Broth** *(page 176)*	1 L
½ cup	**canned evaporated skim milk**	125 mL
pinch	**nutmeg**	pinch
pinch	**black pepper**	pinch
¼ cup	**green onion, chopped** *(garnish)*	50 mL

1. Lightly brown mushrooms (except those reserved for garnish) and onion in margarine over medium heat for 5 minutes in a Dutch oven, stirring frequently.

2. Add flour and stir vigorously. Add canned broth and water. Cook over medium heat until thickened, stirring constantly. Remove from heat for 5 minutes (slight cooling will prevent milk from curdling).

3. Add milk, nutmeg and pepper. Reheat uncovered over low heat for 5 minutes. Do not boil. Stir frequently.

4. Serve in soup bowls. Top with green onions and sliced mushrooms.

Makes 4 —1½ cup (375 mL) portions. *Doubles easily. Freezes well.*

SALISBURY STEAK

Meat, potatoes and gravy—what more do you need? Your favourite vegetable, of course. We suggest French green beans, but it's really your choice!

1 lb	extra lean ground beef	450 g
½ tsp	salt	2 mL
¼ tsp	black pepper	1 mL
1	large onion, sliced	1
1 tsp	sugar	5 mL
2 tbsp	cornstarch	30 mL
2 cups	water	500 mL
3 tbsp	salt-reduced soy sauce	45 mL
4	medium potatoes, peeled & quartered	4

1. Mix ground beef, salt and pepper together. Shape into 4 — 1" (2.5 cm) thick, oblong patties.

2. Arrange patties on a rack in a broiler pan. Cover bottom of pan with hot water to prevent splattering. Broil 6" (15 cm) from heat for 5 to 10 minutes. Turn patties and broil an additional 5 minutes. Remove from oven.

3. Meanwhile, brown onion over medium-high heat in a skillet coated with cooking spray. Stir frequently.

4. Mix water, cornstarch, sugar and soy sauce in a small bowl. Add to onions. Reduce heat to medium. Cook until thickened, stirring constantly.

5. Add beef patties. Cover and simmer over medium-low heat for 15 minutes.

6. Serve over **Slight Smashed Spuds** (*see page 31*).

Makes 4 portions. *One portion = 1 cup (250 mL)* **Slight Smashed Spuds**, *1 beef patty, ½ cup (125 mL) gravy and 1 cup (250 mL) French cut green beans. Doubles easily. Freezes well.*

Don't let fat collect in **your** pipes — let it drip into the pan by broiling your meat.

If you have leftovers tonight, create single portion "TV Dinners" by placing mashed potatoes in the bottom of a freezer container. Cover with meat and top with gravy to prevent drying. You can place green beans to one side of the meat.

Cover the "TV Dinners" with plastic wrap so that it touches the surface of the food— this prevents "freezer burn". Place a lid on the container. Label and freeze.

HEALTHY SNACKS FOR KIDS

FRUITS

Banana Bites: roll small chunks of ripe banana in grated semi-sweet chocolate, then freeze. Serve frozen.

Toppers: fill small containers with assorted dried fruits, ready for topping hot or cold cereals, nut butter sandwiches, pudding, etc.

Kebobs: place assorted pieces of fresh fruit and a few pieces of cheese on a straw. Munch.

Kaitie's Frozen Tears: spread washed green grapes on a cookie sheet. Freeze. Eat like frozen candy.

VEGETABLES

Lettuce Wraps: mix any combination of grated or julienned vegetables, cheese and/or fruits in a bowl. Toss with low-fat dressing. Wrap in clean, dry lettuce leaves to form small rolls. Eat immediately.

Veggies & Dip: keep clean, cut-up vegetables and assorted low-fat dips in separate containers in the fridge. Eat any time.

Pita Pockets: buy mini whole grain pita breads and fill them with chopped tomato and cucumber. Add sprouts and a low-fat dressing. The pita breads can be kept in the freezer and thawed in the microwave as needed.

Marinated Cauliflower: toss cauliflower pieces with low-fat Italian dressing. Let marinate in the fridge for 24 hours. Keeps for one week in the fridge.

Salsa & Chips: serve your favourite vegetable or fruit salsa with baked tortilla chips.

THESE SNACKS ARE GOOD FOR BIG KIDS TOO!

DAIRY PRODUCTS

Dustin's Yogipops: blend any 100% pure fruit juice with an equal amount of low-fat vanilla yogurt. Freeze in popsicle makers.

Cheese & Fruit: serve fruit chunks with assorted cheese.

Fruit Smoothies: blend a banana or any other fresh or frozen fruit with your favourite yogurt. Serve with a straw!

Cheese Fondue: mix 1 cup (250 mL) skim milk, 1/2 cup (125 mL) grated sharp cheese, pinch each of onion and garlic powder and a dash of Worcestershire sauce. Heat in microwave until cheese is melted, stirring occasionally. Use as a dip for whole grain bread sticks or bread cubes.

WHOLE GRAINS

Muffin Tops: you do need a special pan, but the kids will eat the whole muffin.

Crunchy Bites: serve dry, unsweetened cereals with pieces of dried fruits.

Nuttery Sticks: fill a celery stick with nut butter. Add a topping such as grated carrot or apple, dried apricots, raisins, etc.

Pinwheels: spread low-fat cream cheese on a whole grain tortilla. Add a topping of chopped fruit or julienned vegetables. Roll and cut into bite-size portions.

Ian's Pudding: crush 4 graham wafers into a cup. Add milk to desired "mushy" consistency. Trust us, kids love it!

DON'T MISTAKE DEHYDRATION FOR HUNGER!

The body's thirst mechanism is very unreliable. Sometimes children think they are hungry, but what they are lacking is water. Children also need at least 6 to 8 glasses of water each day.

BREAKFAST
Whole Grain Cereal of Choice, Banana, Milk

LUNCH
Tuna Salad in Whole Wheat Pita,
Vegetable Juice of Choice, Fruit of Choice

DINNER
Chicken Fingers, **Potato and Yam Fries**, **Tomato Basil Salad**

SNACK
Sunshine Bar, Milk

NUTRITION INFORMATION
See page 6 for standards used.

MENU ITEMS (single portion)	calories	carbs (grams)	protein (grams)	fat (grams)
Whole Grain Cereal of Choice	126	20.3	2.6	4.4
Banana	109	27.6	1.2	0.5
Milk	86	11.9	8.3	0.4
Tuna Salad in Whole Wheat Pita	284.2	32.7	33.6	1.7
Vegetable Juice of Choice	43	8.7	1.3	0.4
Fruit of Choice	81	21	0.2	0.5
Chicken Fingers	163	3	27.1	4.8
Potato & Yam Fries	242	54.9	5.7	0.3
Tomato Basil Salad	83.8	9.1	3.7	4.6
Sunshine Bar	195.7	34.7	5.7	5.3
Milk	86	11.9	8.3	0.4
Total for day	1499.7	235.8	97.7	23.3
percentage fat ▶				14%

REMEMBER, these are the MINIMUM REQUIREMENTS of the Canada and U.S. Food Guides. Some people will need more calories.

SECOND TIME TONING:
Today you start toning your upper body. Why? If you do these exercises often enough, you won't have to flex your muscles at the beach—they'll already look great. If the thought of marching makes you moan, try warming up with your favourite dance step, then do the **Upper Body Stretches** starting on page 92. Now you're ready for the **Upper Body Toners** on page 148. You may want to try the **"Groaners"** on page 156 as well. Don't forget your cool down before you repeat the upper body stretches.

...continued on page 130

Fish is an excellent source of easily digestible protein.

Fish is also a good source of omega-3 essential fatty acids, which are considered heart-healthy.

TUNA SALAD IN WHOLE WHEAT PITA

This is not the catch of the day, but it is a favourite seafood delight.

1	**7.5 oz (213 g) can tuna, in water**	1
1	**medium carrot, grated**	1
1	**stalk celery, diced**	1
2	**green onions, thinly sliced**	2
2 tbsp	**fat-free sour cream**	30 mL
2 tbsp	**fat-free Ranch dressing**	30 mL
¼ tsp	**black pepper**	1 mL
2	**leaves lettuce** (*optional if brown-bagging*)	2
2	**whole wheat pita breads, cut in half**	2

1. Mix all ingredients, except lettuce and pita, in a medium bowl.
2. Slip one half of pita inside the other. Wrap if brown-bagging. Repeat for the other pita.
3. Place tuna mixture in a lunch container. Add to pita pocket just before eating.

Makes 2 portions. *Doubles easily.*

TOMATO BASIL SALAD

This is so good, you'll have to hide it if you want leftovers. To impress guests, you can also serve this salad as a "bruschetta" appetizer over toasted baguette slices.

1 tbsp	olive or canola oil	15 mL
2 tbsp	apple cider vinegar	30 mL
1	clove garlic, minced	1
½ tsp	basil	2 mL
pinch	salt	pinch
pinch	black pepper	pinch
2 tbsp	low-fat Parmesan cheese, grated	30 mL
8	Roma tomatoes, cut in ½" (1 cm) cubes	8
2	green onions, thinly sliced	2

1. Mix all ingredients (except green onion) in a medium glass or plastic bowl.
2. Marinate for one hour. Serve topped with green onion.

Makes 4 portions. *Halves or doubles easily.*

POTATO AND YAM FRIES

If you didn't like yams before, you will now!

2	medium potatoes, washed, cut into 8 wedges	2
2 cups	yam, peeled & cut into wedges about the same size as the potatoes	500 mL
1	egg white, lightly beaten	1
½ tsp	seasoning salt	2 mL

1. Put all ingredients in a large plastic bag. Shake well to coat all wedges with seasoning and egg white. Discard the bag and excess seasoning.

2. Place potatoes and yams in a large roasting pan coated with cooking spray. Bake for 40 minutes at 350°F (180°C), stirring every 10 minutes. Bake for an extra 10 to 15 minutes if you want your fries extra crispy.

Makes 2 portions. *Doubles easily.*

GAME PLAN

Begin preparing dinner by making the **Tomato Basil Salad**; set aside to marinate.

Meanwhile, prepare the **Potato and Yam Fries** and place in the oven. Prepare the chicken and place it in the oven. While the fries and chicken bake, make the **Sunshine Bars**— they will bake while you eat dinner.

Tonight you will spend 1 hour in the kitchen but your baking will be done.

Total preparation and cooking time: **60 min.**

After dinner, place the tortillas and two slices of raisin bread per person into the fridge to thaw. Leftover raisin bread will be used on Saturday, Week 4.

Tomorrow's sandwich is best prepared in the morning.

Breakfast is portable if you sleep in.

Do not re-use plastic bags that have contained raw egg or raw meat because of the high risk of food poisoning.

Also, be sure to thoroughly clean all utensils and surfaces that have been in contact with raw meat (*see side panel, page 30*).

CHICKEN FINGERS

These tasty morsels give you barbecue flavour right out of the oven.

2	chicken breasts, boneless, skinless, visible fat removed	2
2 tbsp	packaged Mesquite seasoning **OR**	30 mL
2 tbsp	"Homemade Mesquite Seasoning" *(page 178)*	30 mL

1. Cut each chicken breast into 4 or 5 strips. Dip in water to moisten. Shake off excess water.

2. Place chicken pieces into a plastic bag. Add seasoning. Shake to coat all pieces. Discard bag and excess seasoning.

3. Place in a baking pan coated with cooking spray.

4. Bake for 20 to 30 minutes at 350˚F (180˚C).

Makes 2 portions. *Doubles easily. Freezes well.*

GINGER TEA

Ginger has been known to help reduce pain and inflammation. You may find it helps your creaky joints. I make ginger tea from the root, add a little honey while it's hot, and keep it in the fridge for days. It's good cold or warm. Ginger has also been known to help motion sickness.

Red Sky in the Morning
page 151

Citrus Salad
page 150

SUNSHINE BARS

Keep these on hand for the days when you hit the snooze button more than the allowed three times. They even taste good right out of the freezer if you're late for the Monday morning meeting.

½ cup	frozen orange juice concentrate, thawed, undiluted	125 mL
¼ cup	dates, chopped	50 mL
¼ cup	unsweetened coconut, finely shredded	50 mL
½ cup	pecans, chopped	125 mL
1 cup	whole wheat flour	250 mL
½ cup	oat bran	125 mL
¾ cup	natural wheat bran	175 mL
½ cup	quick oats	125 mL
1 tsp	baking powder	5 mL
¼ tsp	baking soda	1 mL
¼ tsp	salt	1 mL
1 cup	fat-free sour cream	250 mL
¾ cup	brown sugar, packed	175 mL
2	egg whites	2
¼ tsp	lemon extract	1 mL

1. Mix orange juice concentrate, dates, coconut and pecans in a medium bowl. Set aside.

2. Mix flour, oat bran, wheat bran, oats, baking powder, baking soda and salt in a large bowl. Set aside.

3. Mix sour cream, brown sugar, egg whites and lemon extract together in a medium bowl. Add to flour mixture and stir to moisten. Using a spatula, press half of the dough to cover the bottom of a 9" x 9" (23 cm x 23 cm) baking pan coated with cooking spray.

4. Spread orange juice mixture evenly over first layer.

5. Using your fingers, crumble remaining dough evenly over orange mixture.

6. Bake for 20 to 30 minutes at 350°F (180°C) or until lightly browned.

Makes 12 portions. *Doubles easily. Freezes well.*

➡ Save one portion per person for tomorrow's breakfast.

By using fat-free sour cream, you avoid using oil or butter.

By using orange juice instead of white sugar, you replace empty calories with nutrient-dense calories.

For ease of handling this sticky dough, coat the spatula *and* your fingers with cooking spray.

Extra **Sunshine Bars** can be individually wrapped and frozen for use as a fast food.

Add grated carrot or zucchini to spaghetti sauce, chili, meat loaf, meatballs, hamburger patties, etc. You can also add wheat germ, wheat bran or oat bran.

Hide raisins by processing them in a blender before adding them to baked goods.

Add wheat germ to cooked cereals, muffins, cookies, meatloaf, hamburger patties, "coating mix for meat", etc.

Add extra skim milk powder to baked goods, milk soups, puddings, milkshakes, coffee, hot chocolate, hot cereals, etc.

Replace soda pop with 100% pure fruit juice mixed with carbonated mineral water.

Make low-fat desserts that have a fruit or a vegetable base, for example, carrot cake, apple cake, zucchini chocolate cake, pumpkin muffins, date loaf, etc.

Replace regular pastas with wholewheat or high fibre pastas.

How to Hide Vitamins, Minerals and Fibre from your Picky Eaters

(BIG AND SMALL!)

Increase fruit portions by topping pudding, cake or hot and cold cereal with fruit.

Add finely chopped vegetables to sandwich fillings, for example, chopped tomato to salmon salad, grated carrot to tuna salad and grated zucchini to chicken salad.

Eliminate all-purpose flour in muffins and cookies. Replace it with equal amounts of whole wheat and/or barley flour. They won't even notice. *P.S. cut the sugar by at least one third; they won't notice that either!*

Cook brown rice in chicken broth instead of white rice in water.

Replace the egg yolk and 1/2 of the oil in Caesar salad dressing with fat-free sour cream.

Replace 1/2 of the margarine or butter in cake and muffin recipes with fat-free sour cream or applesauce.

Replace high calorie desserts with Fruit Smoothies (see page 122 or 144).

... Happy Sneaky Cooking!

BREAKFAST
Sunshine Bar, Fruit of Choice, Hot Chocolate

LUNCH
Nutty Banana Raisin Bread Sandwich,
Fat-Free Fruit Yogurt

DINNER
Vegetarian Burrito, Apple-Carrot Salad,
Low-Fat Cinnamon Graham Wafers, Milk

SNACK
Fruit of Choice

GAME PLAN

Organize
your lunch
this morning.

... continued page 131

NUTRITION INFORMATION
See page 6 for standards used.

MENU ITEMS (single portion)	calories	carbs (grams)	protein (grams)	fat (grams)
Sunshine Bar	195.7	34.7	5.7	5.3
Fruit of Choice	81	21	0.2	0.5
Hot Chocolate	41	5.6	3.9	0.4
Nutty Banana Raisin Bread Sandwich	293.8	52.4	6.7	7.3
Fat-Free Fruit Yogurt — 3/4 cup (175 mL)	130	25	6.9	0.1
Vegetarian Burrito	288.6	56.4	10.5	3.8
Apple-Carrot Salad	152	25.8	6	4.5
Low-Fat Cinnamon Graham Wafers — 3	94	16	1.5	2.5
Milk	86	11.9	8.3	0.4
Fruit of Choice	81	21	0.2	0.5
Total for day	1461	272.8	51.9	25.3
percentage fat ▶				16%

REMEMBER, these are the MINIMUM REQUIREMENTS of the Canada and U.S. Food Guides. Some people will need more calories.

Exercise program by

FOURTH TIME WALKING

As usual, do your warm-up and leg stretches which by now should feel natural to you. Today when walking, include your upper body by pumping your arms forward and back, keeping your arms close to your body. Please do not clench your fists as this may create tension. Since this is the first time you include upper body movements while walking, choose a flat area so that you can concentrate fully on your form. Walk posture-correctly for 15 to 20 minutes— challenge yourself before you return home. Remember to cool down and to add **Upper Body Stretches** to your usual routine.

... continued on page 145

NUTTY BANANA RAISIN BREAD SANDWICH

Using raisin bread is a nice way to dress up a peanut butter and banana sandwich.

2	slices raisin bread	2
1/2	banana, mashed	1/2
1 tsp	honey	5 mL
1 tbsp	reduced-fat peanut butter	15 mL

1. Mix banana, honey and peanut butter together.

2. Spread on bread and close sandwich.

Makes 1 portion.

Deep breathing and potassium (found in such foods as tomatoes and bananas) also help fuel muscles for exercise.

You're doing very well with your walking program; you're very dedicated.

Now you're ready to involve more energy-consuming muscles into your workout. However, I cannot recommend using hand-held weights while you are walking because they alter your posture.

Vegetarian Burritos

Meat is not necessary in this burrito: all of the building blocks for a complete protein are present when a legume (kidney beans) is combined with whole grains (corn and whole wheat tortillas). Those Mexicans are smart hombres!

2 cups	**yam, peeled, diced in ½ " (1 cm) cubes**	**500 mL**
1 cup	**frozen kernel corn**	**250 mL**
1	**medium onion, diced**	**1**
2	**cloves garlic, minced**	**2**
2 tsp	**chili powder**	**10 mL**
1 tsp	**oregano**	**5 mL**
1 tsp	**cumin**	**5 mL**
1	**14 oz (398 mL) can kidney beans, drained** *(If you have black beans in the freezer from Tuesday, Week 2, thaw them in the microwave and add them to the kidney beans.)*	**1**
1	**green pepper, diced**	**1**
1½ cups	**salsa**	**375 mL**
1 tbsp	**lime juice**	**15 mL**
6	**8" (20 cm) whole wheat tortillas**	**6**
¾ cup	**fat-free sour cream**	**175 mL**

1. Place yam and corn in the steamer insert of a medium saucepan. Add water to bottom of saucepan. Bring to a boil over medium-high heat.

2. Reduce heat to medium-low. Cover. Steam for 10 minutes or until yam is fork-tender. Drain.

3. Add onion, garlic, spices, beans, green pepper, salsa and lime juice to yam mixture.

4. Place 1 cup (250 mL) of yam mixture on each tortilla. Roll tortillas and place seam-side down in a 9" x 13" (23 cm x 33 cm) baking dish coated with cooking spray. Cover with foil.

5. Bake at 350°F (180°C) for 30 minutes.

Makes 6 portions. *One portion = 1 burrito topped with 2 tbsp (30 mL) fat-free sour cream and extra salsa if desired. Doubles easily. Freezes well.*

... continued from page 129

Tonight, prepare the **Vegetarian Burritos** first. There is plenty of time to make the salad and put your feet up while the burritos bake for 30 minutes.

Total preparation and cooking time: **45 min.**

This meal is short and sweet, so don't miss Cynthia's workout!

You can prepare the burritos from Steps 1 to 3, then refrigerate or freeze and bake when you are ready.

If you aren't going to eat lunch out tomorrow, thaw your favourite leftovers tonight.

APPLE-CARROT SALAD

Fruit adds interest to a salad — you can also use kiwi, strawberries, grapes ....

1 cup	**lettuce, torn** (*any variety*)	250 mL
1/2	**apple, cored & diced**	1/2
¼ cup	**carrot, grated**	50 mL
¼ cup	**low-fat cheddar cheese, cubed**	50 mL
1 tbsp	**fat-free salad dressing of choice**	15 mL
optional	**alfalfa sprouts**	optional

1. Toss together and enjoy!

Makes 1 portion.

You may think that stretching is frivolous, but every action requires an equal and opposite reaction.

Walking, just like any other form of exercise, causes your muscles to flex (tighten). Therefore, those muscles must stretch (loosen). Well-balanced muscles keep your body in good alignment so you can walk tall and feel good.

BREAKFAST

Maple-Sugar Oatmeal, Fruit of Choice, Milk

LUNCH

T.G.I.F. (Use up leftovers or buy a lunch.)

DINNER

**Bruschetta Submarine, Consommé au Sherry,
Fruits au Rum**, Milk

SNACK

Wine, anyone?

GAME PLAN

Thaw the submarine buns in the fridge for tonight's dinner, then make your oatmeal.

Be sure to eat your breakfast to prevent binging at lunch time.

... continued on page 136

NUTRITION INFORMATION
See page 6 for standards used.

MENU ITEMS (single portion)	calories	carbs (grams)	protein (grams)	fat (grams)
Maple-Sugar Oatmeal	148.4	26.3	7.1	1.8
Fruit of Choice	81	21	0.2	0.5
Milk	86	11.9	8.3	0.4
Bruschetta Submarine	451.5	64.7	25.8	9.3
Consommé au Sherry	30	3.8	3.7	0.5
Fruits au Rum	132.5	29.7	1	0.4
Milk	86	11.9	8.3	0.4
Total for day	1015.4	169.3	54.4	13.3
	percentage fat ▶			12%

REMEMBER, these are the MINIMUM REQUIREMENTS of the Canada and U.S. Food Guides. Some people will need more calories.

Refer to page 46 for oatmeal cooking time in <u>your</u> microwave.

MAPLE-SUGAR OATMEAL

If you have real maple syrup, you can replace the brown sugar and maple extract with syrup, but if you don't, this is a good substitute.

⅓ cup	quick oats	75 mL
pinch	salt	pinch
1 tsp	brown sugar	5 mL
⅔ cup	water	150 mL
⅓ cup	skim milk	75 mL
½ tsp	maple extract	2 mL

1. Place all ingredients in **uncovered** microwaveable cereal bowl.

2. Microwave on high for 1½ to 2 minutes. Stir. Microwave on medium-low for 2 minutes, stirring after 1 minute.

3. Serve with extra brown sugar and milk if desired (these will be additional calories).

Makes 1 portion.

Will that be one lump of sugar or two? Before you answer that question, ask yourself, "Will I walk for about 10 minutes today?"

Brisk walking with your heart rate elevated until you are winded (not gasping for air) for 10 minutes burns the calories found in 2 lumps or 2 tsp (10 mL) of sugar.

CONSOMMÉ AU SHERRY

Dust flour on your face to look like you cooked all day — they'll never know the difference.

1	**10 oz (284 mL) can consommé, undiluted**	1
1 cup	**vegetable cocktail juice**	250 mL
½ **cup**	**water**	125 mL
¼ **cup**	**dry sherry or any dry wine**	125 mL
4	**thin slices lemon**	4

1. Mix consommé, vegetable juice, water and wine in a medium saucepan. Heat on medium-high for 5 to 6 minutes.

2. Garnish with lemon slices. Voilà, la soupe!

Makes 4 portions. *Doubles easily. Leftovers can be used as free calories.*

FRUITS AU RUM

Teetotalers may replace the rum with the same amount of pineapple juice.

1	**orange, peeled & cut in bite size pieces**	1
1	**apple with peel, cored & cut in bite size pieces**	1
1 cup	**seedless grapes**	250 mL
1	**14 oz (398 mL) can pineapple tidbits, drained, juice reserved**	1
optional	**maraschino cherries**	optional
2 tbsp	**white rum**	30 mL
2 tbsp	**pineapple juice**	30 mL

1. Toss all ingredients together in a medium bowl. Voilà, le dessert!

Makes 4 portions. *Doubles easily. Leftovers can be used as free calories.*

JUST HOW MANY CALORIES ARE IN THOSE DRINKS?

Beer:
12 oz (355 mL)   **151**

Light Beer:
12 oz (355 mL)   **101**

Table Wine:
3.5 oz (100 g)   **70**

Dessert Wine:
3.5 oz (100 g)   **153**

Martini:
1 classic   **158**

Margarita:
1 classic   **170**

Rum:
1 oz (42 g)   **97**

Vodka:
1 oz (42 g)   **97**

Gin:
1 oz (42 g)   **110**

Rye Whiskey:
1 oz (42 g)   **105**

... continued from page 133

Before preparing the subs for dinner, mix the fruit salad, then make the soup. You may also want to set the table or a TV tray now, because dinner is very quick to prepare and is best eaten fresh out of the oven.

Total preparation and cooking time: **20 min.** (*including the time spent opening the can and the bottle of wine*).

If you don't want a "mint sandwich" use unflavoured toothpicks (or use meat skewers) to secure the **Bruschetta Submarine**. Toothpicks hold your sandwich together as you move it to and from the oven.

BRUSCHETTA SUBMARINE

Whether you're having a romantic dinner for 2 or entertaining 20, tonight's menu is simple to duplicate, triplicate, quadruple — just have enough ingredients on hand.

1	egg	1
pinch	salt	pinch
pinch	black pepper	pinch
1 tbsp	green onion, sliced	15 mL
1 tbsp	water	15 mL
1	small submarine bun, whole grain, sliced horizontally (*to open book-style*)	1
2	slices tomato	2
1 tbsp	fat-free Italian dressing **OR**	15 mL
2 tbsp	Tomato Basil Salad, (*see page 125*)	30 mL
1	slice lean ham, cut in half	1
1	slice fat-free Monterey Jack cheese, cut in half	1

1. In a small bowl, lightly whisk egg, salt, black pepper, green onion and water. Pour into a small nonstick skillet coated with cooking spray. Cover and cook over medium heat for 2 minutes or until top is set.

2. Set cooked egg aside on a plate. Slice in half to form 2 half moons.

3. Lightly toast cut side of bun under the broiler.

4. Spread tomato mixture on bun to cover both halves, then add egg, ham and cheese slice in layers. Close bun and secure with toothpicks.

5. Place bun on a baking sheet coated with cooking spray. Cover loosely with aluminum foil. Bake at 350°F (180°C) for 10 minutes.

Makes 1 portion.

WEEK 4 MENU

Recipes are provided in this chapter for menu items in **BOLD** on the day they are first prepared.

DAY	BREAKFAST	LUNCH	DINNER	SNACK
S SAT pg. 143	***Peach Frappé**, Raisin Toast with Honey	***Saturday Sandwich**, Raw Vegetable Sticks, Vegetable Juice of Choice	***Salmon Pie**, ***Marinated Cucumber Salad**, Milk	***Angelic Dessert**
S SUN pg. 149	**BRUNCH** ***Red Sky in the Morning**, ***Citrus Salad**, **Mocha Coffee**		***Chicken à L'Orange with Wild Rice**, ***Garlic-Basil Broccoli**, *****Raspberry Orange Trifle ➡**	Fruit of Choice, Milk
M MON pg. 157	Whole Grain Cereal of Choice, Fruit of Choice, Milk	***Cranberry-Cream Cheese Turkey Sandwich**, ***Fruit Cup**, Fruit Juice of Choice	***Green Pepper Steak with Wun Tun Noodles**, ***Red & Green Salad**	Fig Bars, Milk
T TUE pg. 161	***Creamy Apricot Oat Bran**, Fruit Juice of Choice, Milk	***Cinnamon-Cottage Cheese Salad**, Muffin of Choice _or_ Cinnamon Graham Wafers	***Beefy Mushroom Soup ➡** Whole Grain Bun, Fruit of Choice	Raspberry Orange Trifle
W WED pg. 165	Whole Grain Toast, Cheese Slices, Fruit-Only Jam, Fruit Juice of Choice	Beefy Mushroom Soup, Whole Grain Bun, Fruit of Choice	***Fish Sticks with Lemon Sauce**, ***Grains and Greens**, Pickled Beets	**Heavy Artillery Cookie ➡** Milk
T THU pg. 169	Heavy Artillery Cookie, Fruit of Choice, Hot Chocolate	***Peanut Butter-Banana Sandwich**, Carrot Sticks, Milk	**Fusilli with Paprika Chicken**, Steamed Green Beans, Tossed Salad	Frozen Yogurt _or_ 1% Ice Cream
F FRI pg. 171	Whole Grain Cereal of Choice, Fruit of Choice, Fruit Juice of Choice, Milk	T.G.I.F. (Use up leftovers or buy a lunch.)	**Rice and Bean Casserole**, ***Apple-Carrot Slaw**, Milk	Treat Time!

✻ These recipes provide **EXACT MINIMUM PORTIONS** and may need to be adjusted for extra portions.

➡ This symbol will remind you to save portions of this recipe for use later this week.

PANTRY NEEDS

These items might be in your pantry now.

If not, add them to your shopping list on the following pages, as well as any personal preferences such as shampoo, toothpaste, cleaning supplies and so on.

Please note: ground spices and dried herbs are used in recipes unless otherwise specified.

☐ **BASIL**

☐ **BAY LEAVES**

☐ **CINNAMON**

☐ **CAYENNE PEPPER**

☐ **CUMIN**

☐ **CHILI POWDER**

☐ **GARLIC POWDER**

☐ **LEMON PEEL**, dried

☐ **LEMON-PEPPER SEASONING**

☐ **MUSTARD**, dry

☐ **NUTMEG**

☐ **ONION FLAKES**, dried

☐ **PAPRIKA**

☐ **PEPPER**, black

☐ **SALT**

☐ **VANILLA EXTRACT**

☐ **BOUILLON CONCENTRATE**, beef

☐ **BOUILLON CONCENTRATE**, chicken

☐ **BAKING SODA**

☐ **CORNSTARCH**

☐ **FLOUR**, all-purpose

☐ **FLOUR**, whole wheat

☐ **GELATIN**, unflavoured

☐ **RAISINS**

☐ **SKIM MILK POWDER**

☐ **SUGAR**, brown

☐ **SUGAR**, white

☐ **CEREALS**, whole grain, breakfast

☐ **OAT BRAN**

☐ **NATURAL WHEAT BRAN**

☐ **QUICK OATS**

☐ **WHEAT GERM**

☐ **CINNAMON GRAHAM WAFERS**, low-fat

☐ **FIG BARS**

☐ **JAMS**, fruit-only

☐ **LIQUID HONEY**

☐ **PEANUT BUTTER**, reduced-fat

☐ **COFFEE**

☐ **HOT CHOCOLATE**, skim milk

☐ **JUICES**, fruit, assorted

☐ **JUICES**, vegetable, assorted

☐ **LEMON JUICE**, bottled or fresh

☐ **TEAS**, assorted

☐ **WHITE WINE**, dry or white grape juice

☐ **COOKING SPRAY**, plain

☐ **MUSTARD**, prepared

☐ **OIL**, olive and/or canola

☐ **RELISH OF CHOICE**

☐ **VINEGAR**, balsamic

☐ **VINEGAR**, white

☐ **WORCESTERSHIRE SAUCE**

☐ **RICE**, brown, long grain

☐ **SOY SAUCE**, salt-reduced

☐ **PARMESAN CHEESE**, low-fat, grated

☐ **POT BARLEY**

☐ **COATING MIX FOR MEAT** (*see page 71*)

SHOPPING LIST

Review all recipes for portion requirements (see page 22). Add any missing pantry items to your grocery list.

PRODUCE

- [ ] **APPLES** 1
- [ ] **BANANAS** 2
- [ ] **CANTALOUPE** 1/2
- [ ] **FRUIT**, assorted 12 portions
- [ ] **GRAPES**, seedless (*of choice*) 1 cup (250 mL)
- [ ] **LEMON** 1 (*optional*)
- [ ] **ORANGES OR MANDARINS** 4
- [ ] **BROCCOLI** 3 stalks
- [ ] **CABBAGE**, green 1/2 small head
- [ ] **CABBAGE**, red 1/4 small head
- [ ] **CARROTS** 1-2 lb (1 kg) bag
- [ ] **CELERY** 2 stalks
- [ ] **CUCUMBER** 1 large
- [ ] **GARLIC** 1 head
- [ ] **LETTUCE**, green leaf 1 head
- [ ] **LETTUCE** of choice 1 head
- [ ] **MUSHROOMS** 1¼ lbs (575 g)
- [ ] **GREEN ONIONS** 2 bunches
- [ ] **ONIONS** 4 small
- [ ] **ONIONS** 5 medium
- [ ] **RED ONION** 1 medium
- [ ] **PEPPERS**, green 3
- [ ] **PEPPERS**, red 2
- [ ] **POTATOES** 8 medium
- [ ] **TOMATOES** 3 medium
- [ ] **SPRING ROLL SHELLS** (*wraps*) 1-7 oz (200 g) pkg
- [ ] **VEGETABLES FOR SNACKS**, assorted (*see side panel page 67*)

GROCERIES

- [ ] **APRICOTS**, dried 1 small pkg
- [ ] **EVAPORATED SKIM MILK** 1-14 oz (385 mL) can
- [ ] **PRUNES**, pitted 1 small pkg
- [ ] **VANILLA PUDDING**, prepared, low-fat 2-5 oz (142 g) containers
- [ ] **CRANBERRY SAUCE**, whole berry 1-14 oz (398 mL) can
- [ ] **FRUIT COCKTAIL**, in juice 1-14 oz (398 mL) can
- [ ] **FRUIT OF CHOICE**, in juice 1-14 oz (398 mL) can
- [ ] **MANDARIN ORANGE SEGMENTS**, in juice 1-10 oz (284 mL) can
- [ ] **PINEAPPLE TIDBITS**, in juice 1-14 oz (398 mL) can
- [ ] **PINEAPPLE JUICE** 1-32 oz (1 L) box
- [ ] **RASPBERRY COCKTAIL DRINK** 1-32 oz (1 L) box
- [ ] **TOMATO SAUCE** 1-14 oz (398 mL) can
- [ ] **FUSILLI OR CORKSCREW PASTA** 1-12 oz (375 g) pkg
- [ ] **WUN TUN NOODLES** 1-16 oz (454 g) pkg
- [ ] **CHICKEN BROTH** 2-10 oz (284 mL) cans
- [ ] **CONSOMMÉ** 2-10 oz (284 mL) cans
- [ ] **TOMATO SOUP** 1-10 oz (284 mL) can
- [ ] **KIDNEY BEANS** 1-14 oz (398 mL) can
- [ ] **SALMON** 1-7.5 oz (213 g) can
- [ ] **PICKLED BEETS** 1-26 oz (750 mL) jar
- [ ] **WILD RICE** ¼ cup (50 mL)

(*continued on reverse*)

FAMILY OF 2

MEAT

- [ ] **CHICKEN BREASTS**, bone in 2
- [ ] **CHICKEN BREASTS**, boneless, skinless 4
- [ ] **EYE OF ROUND STEAK** 1 lb (450 g)
  (*thinly sliced if available*)
- [ ] **SIRLOIN STEAK** 1 lb (450 g)
  (*thinly sliced if available*)
- [ ] **LEAN HAM SLICES** 4 oz (120 g)
  (*? some left from week 3*)
- [ ] **ROASTED DELI TURKEY BREAST**,
  thinly sliced 4 oz (120 g)

BAKERY

- [ ] **BREAD**, whole grain 2 loaves
- [ ] **BUNS**, whole grain 4
- [ ] **ANGEL FOOD CAKE** 1

FROZEN

- [ ] **PEACHES**, sliced, unsweetened
  1 cup (250 mL)
- [ ] **RASPBERRIES**, unsweetened
  1-10 oz (300 g) pkg
- [ ] **ASPARAGUS**, cut 1-10 oz (300 g) pkg
- [ ] **GREEN BEANS**, whole or cut
  2 cups (500 mL)
- [ ] **SPINACH**, chopped 1-10 oz (300 g) pkg
- [ ] **FISH FILLETS**, frozen
  (*not individually wrapped*) 1-14 oz (400 g) pkg
- [ ] **FROZEN YOGURT OR ICE CREAM**,
  1% milk fat 1 cup (25 mL)

DAIRY

- [ ] **MILK** 5 quarts (5 L)
- [ ] **YOGURT**, plain, fat-free   1½ cups (375 mL)
- [ ] **YOGURT**, vanilla, fat-free   1½ cups (375 mL)
- [ ] **SOUR CREAM**, fat-free 2 cups (500 mL)
- [ ] **COTTAGE CHEESE**, 1% milk fat
  3 cups (750 mL)
- [ ] **CHEDDAR CHEESE**, low-fat, grated
  1 cup (250 mL)
- [ ] **CHEESE SLICES**, 1% milk fat 4
- [ ] **CREAM CHEESE**, low-fat   ¼ cup (50 mL)
- [ ] **EGGS** 9

PANTRY & OTHER

- [ ] _____
- [ ] _____
- [ ] _____
- [ ] _____
- [ ] _____
- [ ] _____
- [ ] _____
- [ ] _____
- [ ] _____
- [ ] _____
- [ ] _____
- [ ] _____
- [ ] _____
- [ ] _____

SHOPPING LIST

Review all recipes for portion requirements (see page 22). Add any missing pantry items to your grocery list.

PRODUCE

- [ ] **APPLES** 1
- [ ] **BANANAS** 2
- [ ] **CANTALOUPE** 1/2
- [ ] **FRUIT**, assorted 12 portions
- [ ] **GRAPES**, seedless (*of choice*) 1 cup (250 mL)
- [ ] **LEMON** 1 (*optional*)
- [ ] **ORANGES OR MANDARINS** 4
- [ ] **BROCCOLI** 3 stalks
- [ ] **CABBAGE**, green 1/2 small head
- [ ] **CABBAGE**, red 1/4 small head
- [ ] **CARROTS** 1-2 lb (1 kg) bag
- [ ] **CELERY** 2 stalks
- [ ] **CUCUMBER** 1 large
- [ ] **GARLIC** 1 head
- [ ] **LETTUCE**, green leaf 1 head
- [ ] **LETTUCE** of choice 1 head
- [ ] **MUSHROOMS** 1¼ lbs (575 g)
- [ ] **GREEN ONIONS** 2 bunches
- [ ] **ONIONS** 4 small
- [ ] **ONIONS** 5 medium
- [ ] **RED ONION** 1 medium
- [ ] **PEPPERS**, green 3
- [ ] **PEPPERS**, red 2
- [ ] **POTATOES** 8 medium
- [ ] **TOMATOES** 3 medium
- [ ] **SPRING ROLL SHELLS** (*wraps*) 1-7 oz (200 g) pkg
- [ ] **VEGETABLES FOR SNACKS**, assorted (*see side panel page 67*)

GROCERIES

- [ ] **APRICOTS**, dried 1 small pkg
- [ ] **EVAPORATED SKIM MILK** 1-14 oz (385 mL) can
- [ ] **PRUNES**, pitted 1 small pkg
- [ ] **VANILLA PUDDING**, prepared, low-fat 2-5 oz (142 g) containers
- [ ] **CRANBERRY SAUCE**, whole berry 1-14 oz (398 mL) can
- [ ] **FRUIT COCKTAIL**, in juice 1-14 oz (398 mL) can
- [ ] **FRUIT OF CHOICE**, in juice 1-14 oz (398 mL) can
- [ ] **MANDARIN ORANGE SEGMENTS**, in juice 1-10 oz (284 mL) can
- [ ] **PINEAPPLE TIDBITS**, in juice 1-14 oz (398 mL) can
- [ ] **PINEAPPLE JUICE** 1-32 oz (1 L) box
- [ ] **RASPBERRY COCKTAIL DRINK** 1-32 oz (1 L) box
- [ ] **TOMATO SAUCE** 1-14 oz (398 mL) can
- [ ] **FUSILLI OR CORKSCREW PASTA** 1-12 oz (375 g) pkg
- [ ] **WUN TUN NOODLES** 1-16 oz (454 g) pkg
- [ ] **CHICKEN BROTH** 2-10 oz (284 mL) cans
- [ ] **CONSOMMÉ** 2-10 oz (284 mL) cans
- [ ] **TOMATO SOUP** 1-10 oz (284 mL) can
- [ ] **KIDNEY BEANS** 1-14 oz (398 mL) can
- [ ] **SALMON** 1-7.5 oz (213 g) can
- [ ] **PICKLED BEETS** 1-26 oz (750 mL) jar
- [ ] **WILD RICE** ¼ cup (50 mL)

(*continued on reverse*)

FAMILY OF 2

MEAT

- [ ] **CHICKEN BREASTS**, bone in 2
- [ ] **CHICKEN BREASTS**, boneless, skinless 4
- [ ] **EYE OF ROUND STEAK** 1 lb (450 g)
  (*thinly sliced if available*)
- [ ] **SIRLOIN STEAK** 1 lb (450 g)
  (*thinly sliced if available*)
- [ ] **LEAN HAM SLICES** 4 oz (120 g)
  (*? some left from week 3*)
- [ ] **ROASTED DELI TURKEY BREAST**,
  thinly sliced 4 oz (120 g)

BAKERY

- [ ] **BREAD**, whole grain 2 loaves
- [ ] **BUNS**, whole grain 4
- [ ] **ANGEL FOOD CAKE** 1

FROZEN

- [ ] **PEACHES**, sliced, unsweetened
  1 cup (250 mL)
- [ ] **RASPBERRIES**, unsweetened
  1-10 oz (300 g) pkg
- [ ] **ASPARAGUS**, cut 1-10 oz (300 g) pkg
- [ ] **GREEN BEANS**, whole or cut
  2 cups (500 mL)
- [ ] **SPINACH**, chopped 1-10 oz (300 g) pkg
- [ ] **FISH FILLETS**, frozen
  (*not individually wrapped*) 1-14 oz (400 g) pkg
- [ ] **FROZEN YOGURT OR ICE CREAM**,
  1% milk fat 1 cup (25 mL)

DAIRY

- [ ] **MILK** 5 quarts (5 L)
- [ ] **YOGURT**, plain, fat-free   1½ cups (375 mL)
- [ ] **YOGURT**, vanilla, fat-free   1½ cups (375 mL)
- [ ] **SOUR CREAM**, fat-free 2 cups (500 mL)
- [ ] **COTTAGE CHEESE**, 1% milk fat
  3 cups (750 mL)
- [ ] **CHEDDAR CHEESE**, low-fat, grated
  1 cup (250 mL)
- [ ] **CHEESE SLICES**, 1% milk fat 4
- [ ] **CREAM CHEESE**, low-fat   ¼ cup (50 mL)
- [ ] **EGGS** 9

PANTRY & OTHER

- [ ] _____
- [ ] _____
- [ ] _____
- [ ] _____
- [ ] _____
- [ ] _____
- [ ] _____
- [ ] _____
- [ ] _____
- [ ] _____
- [ ] _____
- [ ] _____
- [ ] _____

SHOPPING LIST

Review all recipes for portion requirements (see page 22). Add any missing pantry items to your grocery list.

PRODUCE

- ☐ **APPLES** 2
- ☐ **BANANAS** 4
- ☐ **CANTALOUPE** 1
- ☐ **FRUIT**, assorted 24 portions
- ☐ **GRAPES**, seedless (*of choice*) 2 cups (500 mL)
- ☐ **LEMON** 1 (*optional*)
- ☐ **ORANGES OR MANDARINS** 6
- ☐ **BROCCOLI** 6 stalks
- ☐ **CABBAGE**, green 1 small head
- ☐ **CABBAGE**, red 1/2 small head
- ☐ **CARROTS** 1-3 lb (1.5 kg) bag
- ☐ **CELERY** 2 stalks
- ☐ **CUCUMBER** 1 large
- ☐ **GARLIC** 2 heads
- ☐ **LETTUCE**, green leaf 2 heads
- ☐ **LETTUCE** of choice 1 head
- ☐ **MUSHROOMS** 1½ lbs (700 g)
- ☐ **GREEN ONIONS** 3 bunches
- ☐ **ONIONS** 5 small
- ☐ **ONIONS** 6 medium
- ☐ **RED ONION** 1 medium
- ☐ **PEPPERS**, green 3
- ☐ **PEPPERS**, red 3
- ☐ **POTATOES** 8 medium
- ☐ **TOMATOES** 4 medium
- ☐ **SPRING ROLL SHELLS** (*wraps*) 1-7 oz (200 g) pkg
- ☐ **VEGETABLES FOR SNACKS**, assorted (*see side panel page 67*)

GROCERIES

- ☐ **APRICOTS**, dried 1 small pkg
- ☐ **EVAPORATED SKIM MILK** 1-14 oz (385 mL) can
- ☐ **PRUNES**, pitted 1 small pkg
- ☐ **VANILLA PUDDING** (*to be cooked*) 1-6 serving box
- ☐ **CRANBERRY SAUCE**, whole berry 1-14 oz (398 mL) can
- ☐ **FRUIT COCKTAIL**, in juice 1-14 oz (398 mL) can
- ☐ **FRUIT OF CHOICE**, in juice 2-14 oz (398 mL) cans
- ☐ **MANDARIN ORANGE SEGMENTS**, in juice 1-10 oz (284 mL) can
- ☐ **PINEAPPLE TIDBITS**, in juice 1-14 oz (398 mL) can
- ☐ **PINEAPPLE JUICE** 1-32 oz (1 L) box
- ☐ **RASPBERRY COCKTAIL DRINK** 1-32 oz (1 L) box
- ☐ **TOMATO SAUCE** 1-14 oz (398 mL) can
- ☐ **FUSILLI OR CORKSCREW PASTA** 1-12 oz (375 g) pkg
- ☐ **WUN TUN NOODLES** 1-16 oz (454 g) pkg
- ☐ **CHICKEN BROTH** 2-10 oz (284 mL) cans
- ☐ **CONSOMMÉ** 2-10 oz (284 mL) cans
- ☐ **TOMATO SOUP** 1-10 oz (284 mL) can
- ☐ **KIDNEY BEANS** 1-14 oz (398 mL) can
- ☐ **SALMON** 1-7.5 oz (213 g) can
- ☐ **PICKLED BEETS** 1-26 oz (750 mL) jar
- ☐ **WILD RICE** ½ cup (125 mL)

(continued on reverse)

MEAT

- ☐ **CHICKEN BREASTS**, bone in 4
- ☐ **CHICKEN BREASTS**, boneless, skinless 4
- ☐ **EYE OF ROUND STEAK** 1 lb (450 g)
  (*thinly sliced if available*)
- ☐ **SIRLOIN STEAK** 1 lb (450 g)
  (*thinly sliced if available*)
- ☐ **LEAN HAM SLICES** 8 oz (240 g)
  (*? some left from week 3*)
- ☐ **ROASTED DELI TURKEY BREAST**,
  thinly sliced 8 oz (240 g)

BAKERY

- ☐ **BREAD**, whole grain 3 loaves
- ☐ **BUNS**, whole grain 8
- ☐ **ANGEL FOOD CAKE** 1

FROZEN

- ☐ **PEACHES**, sliced, unsweetened
  2 cups (500 mL)
- ☐ **RASPBERRIES**, unsweetened
  1-10 oz (300 g) pkg
- ☐ **ASPARAGUS**, cut 1-10 oz (300 g) pkg
- ☐ **GREEN BEANS**, whole or cut 4 cups (1 L)
- ☐ **SPINACH**, chopped 1-10 oz (300 g) pkg
- ☐ **FISH FILLETS**, frozen
  (*not individually wrapped*) 1-14 oz (400 g) pkg
- ☐ **FROZEN YOGURT OR ICE CREAM**,
  1% milk fat 2 cups (500 mL)

DAIRY

- ☐ **MILK** 10 quarts (10 L)
- ☐ **YOGURT**, plain, fat-free 1½ cups (375 mL)
- ☐ **YOGURT**, vanilla, fat-free 3 cups (750 mL)
- ☐ **SOUR CREAM**, fat-free 2½ cups (625 mL)
- ☐ **COTTAGE CHEESE**, 1% milk fat
  5 cups (1.25 L)
- ☐ **CHEDDAR CHEESE**, low-fat, grated
  1 cup (250 mL)
- ☐ **CHEESE SLICES**, 1% milk fat 8
- ☐ **CREAM CHEESE**, low-fat ½ cup (125 mL)
- ☐ **EGGS** 13

PANTRY & OTHER

- ☐ _____
- ☐ _____
- ☐ _____
- ☐ _____
- ☐ _____
- ☐ _____
- ☐ _____
- ☐ _____
- ☐ _____
- ☐ _____
- ☐ _____
- ☐ _____
- ☐ _____

SHOPPING LIST

Review all recipes for portion requirements (see page 22). Add any missing pantry items to your grocery list.

PRODUCE

- [ ] **APPLES** 2
- [ ] **BANANAS** 4
- [ ] **CANTALOUPE** 1
- [ ] **FRUIT**, assorted 24 portions
- [ ] **GRAPES**, seedless (*of choice*) 2 cups (500 mL)
- [ ] **LEMON** 1 (*optional*)
- [ ] **ORANGES OR MANDARINS** 6
- [ ] **BROCCOLI** 6 stalks
- [ ] **CABBAGE**, green 1 small head
- [ ] **CABBAGE**, red 1/2 small head
- [ ] **CARROTS** 1-3 lb (1.5 kg) bag
- [ ] **CELERY** 2 stalks
- [ ] **CUCUMBER** 1 large
- [ ] **GARLIC** 2 heads
- [ ] **LETTUCE**, green leaf 2 heads
- [ ] **LETTUCE** of choice 1 head
- [ ] **MUSHROOMS** 1½ lbs (700 g)
- [ ] **GREEN ONIONS** 3 bunches
- [ ] **ONIONS** 5 small
- [ ] **ONIONS** 6 medium
- [ ] **RED ONION** 1 medium
- [ ] **PEPPERS**, green 3
- [ ] **PEPPERS**, red 3
- [ ] **POTATOES** 8 medium
- [ ] **TOMATOES** 4 medium
- [ ] **SPRING ROLL SHELLS** (*wraps*) 1-7 oz (200 g) pkg
- [ ] **VEGETABLES FOR SNACKS**, assorted (*see side panel page 67*)

GROCERIES

- [ ] **APRICOTS**, dried 1 small pkg
- [ ] **EVAPORATED SKIM MILK** 1-14 oz (385 mL) can
- [ ] **PRUNES**, pitted 1 small pkg
- [ ] **VANILLA PUDDING** (*to be cooked*) 1-6 serving box
- [ ] **CRANBERRY SAUCE**, whole berry 1-14 oz (398 mL) can
- [ ] **FRUIT COCKTAIL**, in juice 1-14 oz (398 mL) can
- [ ] **FRUIT OF CHOICE**, in juice 2-14 oz (398 mL) cans
- [ ] **MANDARIN ORANGE SEGMENTS**, in juice 1-10 oz (284 mL) can
- [ ] **PINEAPPLE TIDBITS**, in juice 1-14 oz (398 mL) can
- [ ] **PINEAPPLE JUICE** 1-32 oz (1 L) box
- [ ] **RASPBERRY COCKTAIL DRINK** 1-32 oz (1 L) box
- [ ] **TOMATO SAUCE** 1-14 oz (398 mL) can
- [ ] **FUSILLI OR CORKSCREW PASTA** 1-12 oz (375 g) pkg
- [ ] **WUN TUN NOODLES** 1-16 oz (454 g) pkg
- [ ] **CHICKEN BROTH** 2-10 oz (284 mL) cans
- [ ] **CONSOMMÉ** 2-10 oz (284 mL) cans
- [ ] **TOMATO SOUP** 1-10 oz (284 mL) can
- [ ] **KIDNEY BEANS** 1-14 oz (398 mL) can
- [ ] **SALMON** 1-7.5 oz (213 g) can
- [ ] **PICKLED BEETS** 1-26 oz (750 mL) jar
- [ ] **WILD RICE** ½ cup (125 mL)

(continued on reverse)

MEAT

- ☐ **CHICKEN BREASTS**, bone in 4
- ☐ **CHICKEN BREASTS**, boneless, skinless 4
- ☐ **EYE OF ROUND STEAK** 1 lb (450 g)
  (*thinly sliced if available*)
- ☐ **SIRLOIN STEAK** 1 lb (450 g)
  (*thinly sliced if available*)
- ☐ **LEAN HAM SLICES** 8 oz (240 g)
  (*? some left from week 3*)
- ☐ **ROASTED DELI TURKEY BREAST**,
  thinly sliced 8 oz (240 g)

BAKERY

- ☐ **BREAD**, whole grain 3 loaves
- ☐ **BUNS**, whole grain 8
- ☐ **ANGEL FOOD CAKE** 1

FROZEN

- ☐ **PEACHES**, sliced, unsweetened
  2 cups (500 mL)
- ☐ **RASPBERRIES**, unsweetened
  1-10 oz (300 g) pkg
- ☐ **ASPARAGUS**, cut 1-10 oz (300 g) pkg
- ☐ **GREEN BEANS**, whole or cut 4 cups (1 L)
- ☐ **SPINACH**, chopped 1-10 oz (300 g) pkg
- ☐ **FISH FILLETS**, frozen
  (*not individually wrapped*) 1-14 oz (400 g) pkg
- ☐ **FROZEN YOGURT OR ICE CREAM**,
  1% milk fat 2 cups (500 mL)

DAIRY

- ☐ **MILK** 10 quarts (10 L)
- ☐ **YOGURT**, plain, fat-free 1½ cups (375 mL)
- ☐ **YOGURT**, vanilla, fat-free 3 cups (750 mL)
- ☐ **SOUR CREAM**, fat-free 2½ cups (625 mL)
- ☐ **COTTAGE CHEESE**,1% milk fat
  5 cups (1.25 L)
- ☐ **CHEDDAR CHEESE**, low-fat, grated
  1 cup (250 mL)
- ☐ **CHEESE SLICES**,1% milk fat 8
- ☐ **CREAM CHEESE**, low-fat ½ cup (125 mL)
- ☐ **EGGS** 13

PANTRY & OTHER

- ☐ _____
- ☐ _____
- ☐ _____
- ☐ _____
- ☐ _____
- ☐ _____
- ☐ _____
- ☐ _____
- ☐ _____
- ☐ _____
- ☐ _____
- ☐ _____
- ☐ _____
- ☐ _____

BREAKFAST
Peach Frappé,
Raisin Toast with Honey
*(If you don't have raisin bread left from Week 3,
use any type of whole grain bread.)*

LUNCH
Saturday Sandwich, Raw Vegetable Sticks, Vegetable Juice of Choice

DINNER
Salmon Pie, **Marinated Cucumber Salad**, Milk

SNACK
Angelic Dessert

GAME PLAN

When unpacking the groceries, place the chicken breasts, sirloin steak and sliced turkey in the fridge. Freeze the remaining meats, fish and breads, keeping out enough bread for today's lunch and tomorrow's breakfast.

...continued page 146

Remember to prepare raw vegetables for snacking (see pages 21 and 67). While you're at it, prepare the **Marinated Cucumber Salad** for tonight's dinner.

NUTRITION INFORMATION
See page 6 for standards used.

MENU ITEMS (single portion)	calories	carbs (grams)	protein (grams)	fat (grams)
Peach Frappé	222	47.4	8.5	0.8
Raisin Toast — 1	68	13.9	1.7	0.7
Honey — 1 tsp (5 mL)	21.3	5.8	0	0
Saturday Sandwich	191.3	19.9	15.9	6
Raw Vegetable Sticks	43	9.6	2	0.2
Vegetable Juice of Choice	43	8.7	1.3	0.4
Salmon Pie	299.5	33.1	27.5	6.1
Marinated Cucumber Salad	16.5	3.7	0.5	0.1
Milk	86	11.9	8.3	0.4
Angelic Dessert	232	53.1	6.4	0
Total for day	1222.6	207.1	72.1	14.7
percentage fat ▶				**11%**

REMEMBER, these are the MINIMUM REQUIREMENTS of the Canada and U.S. Food Guides. Some people will need more calories.

If you anticipate being busy tomorrow, here are some items that you can prepare in advance and refrigerate:

- **Raspberry Orange Trifle** ;

- rice;

- vegetables for the rice mixture;

- **Garlic Basil Broccoli**.

Peach Frappé

You might have peaches in your freezer from Sunday, Week 3. If you want a real protein boost, add ½ cup (250 mL) of fat-free soy drink.

4	**peach slices, frozen**	**4**
½ cup	**fat-free plain yogurt**	**125 mL**
½ cup	**orange juice**	**125 mL**
1/2	**banana**	**1/2**
1 tsp	**sugar**	**5 mL**
¼ tsp	**almond extract**	**1 mL**
½ tsp	**vanilla extract**	**2 mL**

1. Put all ingredients in a blender.

2. Purée until frothy.

Makes 1 portion.

SATURDAY SANDWICHES

There will be no complaints that the sandwiches are too dry — these are creamy and yummy!

2 tbsp	fat-free sour cream	30 mL
2 tbsp	low-fat cream cheese	30 mL
2	shallots, thinly sliced	2
1	clove garlic, minced	1
¼ tsp	Worcestershire sauce	1 mL
pinch	black pepper	pinch
¼ tsp	dry mustard	1 mL
2 tsp	relish	10 mL
4 oz	lean ham *(There should be ham in the fridge from Week 3.)*	120 g
4	slices tomato	4
4	slices whole grain bread	4

1. Mix sour cream, cream cheese, shallots, garlic, Worcestershire sauce, pepper, mustard and relish in a small bowl. Spread one half of the cream cheese mixture on each sandwich.

2. Place 2 slices of ham and two slices of tomato on each sandwich. Close sandwiches.

3. Brown each side of sandwiches over medium heat in a nonstick skillet coated with butter-flavoured cooking spray.

Makes 2 portions.

Exercise program by

THIRD TIME TONING:

Now let's put it all together. Do a warm-up and a full-body stretch, then go through all seven of the **Toning** exercises and both of the **"Groaners"** before you cool down and stretch again. Notice the improvement— you hardly ever get into pretzel position any more.

...continued on page 151

...continued from page 143

Begin dinner preparations by cooking the potatoes. While the potatoes cook, organize the remaining ingredients for the **Salmon Pie**.

Mash the potatoes, then assemble the pie.

Total preparation and cooking time: **75 min.**

Dinner takes only 20 to 30 minutes to prepare, and then cooks undisturbed for 45 minutes. Start early and enjoy your bubble bath while it cooks!

SALMON PIE

And you thought that making pie was difficult!

4	**medium potatoes, peeled, diced & cooked in 1 cup of water** (*Do not drain.*)	4
¼ **cup**	**skim milk powder**	50 mL
pinch	**salt**	pinch
pinch	**black pepper**	pinch
2 tbsp	**green onion, chopped**	30 mL
2 tbsp	**fat-free sour cream**	30 mL
1	**7.5 oz (213 g) can salmon, undrained**	1
3	**egg whites, lightly beaten**	3
½ cup	**canned evaporated skim milk**	125 mL
1	**small onion, diced**	1
½ tsp	**dry mustard**	2 mL
pinch	**black pepper**	pinch
1 tbsp	**lemon juice, fresh or bottled**	15 mL
1	**10 oz (300 g) pkg frozen asparagus, thawed, cut in 1 " (2.5 cm) pieces**	1
4	**spring roll shells** (*wraps*)	4

1. Mash the potatoes in their cooking water with skim milk powder, salt, black pepper, green onion and sour cream. Set aside.

2. Place the salmon, egg whites, canned skim milk, diced onion, dry mustard, black pepper, lemon juice and asparagus in a large bowl. Mix well. Set aside.

3. Spread the spring roll shells to cover the bottom and sides of a 9" x 9" (23 cm x 23 cm) baking dish coated with cooking spray. Turn the edges of the shells back into the pan so that the sides are covered but the shells do not extend over the top of the pan.

4. Pour the salmon mixture gently into the baking dish. Top with mashed potatoes.

5. Bake at 350°F (180°C) for 45 minutes.

Makes 4 portions. *Doubles easily. Freezes well.*

Family of 2: *Make 2 small pies. Bake one and freeze the other unbaked.*

MARINATED CUCUMBER SALAD

If you have leftovers, consider this an "anytime snack".

2 cups	cucumber, unpeeled, thinly sliced	500 mL
¼ cup	red onion, thinly sliced	50 mL
¼ cup	white vinegar	50 mL
1½ tsp	sugar	7 mL
pinch	black pepper	pinch
pinch	salt	pinch

1. Place cucumber and onion in a shallow bowl.

2. Mix vinegar, sugar, salt and pepper and pour over cucumber slices.

3. Marinate for at least 1 hour in the fridge.

Makes 4 portions. *Doubles easily.*

ANGELIC DESSERT

Enjoy a dessert that is angelic in taste and a blessing as a time-saver!

1	slice (¹⁄₁₂) of an angel food cake	1
	(*There is no financial or taste advantage to baking your own angel food cake, so buy one that is already baked and use the time saved for exercise.*)	
½ cup	canned fruit cocktail, in juice	125 mL
¼ cup	fat-free vanilla yogurt	50 mL

1. Layer on a serving plate in the order given.

Makes 1 portion.

Angelic Dessert™ does not require advance preparations; assemble when you get the growlies.

Upper Body Toners

TRICEP TOUCHES

The tricep is the area that keeps on wiggling and jiggling long after you have stopped clapping. Located on the back of the upper arm, this muscle is not challenged by many daily movements. This exercise is a favourite of mine for toning the tricep.

1. Stand with one foot just ahead of the other, feet parallel and facing forward. This stance will maintain your centre of gravity in the hip rather than in the lower back.

2. Face your palms forward, arms by your sides. Keeping your arms straight, push them back, enjoying a stretch in your chest (pectoral) region. Attempt to touch your baby fingers together, or at least bring them as close to touching as you can. Hold for a quick A, B, C, D. Please relax your neck and don't get discouraged if you can't touch your fingers together yet.

3. Try 5 and work your way up to 20.

POSTURE CORRECTOR

It seems that most of what we do in life has us in the forward, shoulder- rounded position. If you are working at a desk, working on a computer, or caring for and lifting children, this exercise will help you to develop a healthier posture.

1. Sit on the edge of a chair, feet together, 6 to 8 inches (15 to 20 cm) from the chair. Make sure that your heels are directly beneath your knees.

2. Lean forward as pictured, chest to knees. With or without weights (or soup cans) in your hands, bend your elbows and pull them up, forcing your shoulder blades to squeeze together. Hold this squeeze as you recite the alphabet. You will feel this exercise working the latissimus dorsi (upper back) muscles. See, you're already starting to talk like a pro.

3. Try this 3 to 5 times.

BRUNCH
Red Sky in the Morning, **Citrus Salad**,
Mocha Coffee

DINNER
Chicken à l'Orange with Wild Rice,
Garlic-Basil Broccoli, Raspberry Orange Trifle

SNACK
Fruit of Choice, Milk

Be sure
to thoroughly
wash all raw fruits
and vegetables
before eating them.

NUTRITION INFORMATION
See page 6 for standards used.
MENU ITEMS (single portion)

MENU ITEMS (single portion)	calories	carbs (grams)	protein (grams)	fat (grams)
Red Sky in the Morning	286	39.5	16.7	8
Citrus Salad	173.7	37.6	1.5	0.3
Mocha Coffee	41.5	5.6	3.9	0.4
Chicken à l'Orange with Wild Rice	614.8	86.7	39.5	11.7
Garlic-Basil Broccoli	32.4	6.2	3	0.3
Raspberry Orange Trifle (family of 4 recipe)	296.2	66.5	7.7	0.3
Fruit of Choice	81	21	0.2	0.5
Milk	86	11.9	8.3	0.4
Total for day	1612	275	80.8	21.9
percentage fat ▶				12%

REMEMBER, these are the MINIMUM REQUIREMENTS of the Canada and U.S. Food Guides. Some people will need more calories.

GAME PLAN

Begin brunch preparations by making the **Citrus Salad**. Follow the recipes for **Red Sky in the Morning** and **Mocha Coffee**.

Immediately after brunch, prepare the **Raspberry Orange Trifle**, as it needs to set.

...continued on page 154

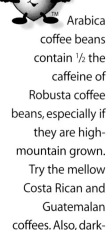

Arabica coffee beans contain ½ the caffeine of Robusta coffee beans, especially if they are high-mountain grown. Try the mellow Costa Rican and Guatemalan coffees. Also, dark-roasting reduces the amount of caffeine.

CITRUS SALAD

Grandma would approve of this dish even though you're popping a wine cork at the crack of dawn!

1	14 oz (398 mL) can pineapple tidbits	1
2	Mandarin or navel oranges, peeled & sectioned	2
8	dry plums, pitted (*Grandma calls them prunes.*)	8
¾ cup	dry white wine **OR**	175 mL
¾ cup	white grape juice	175 mL
1 tbsp	brown sugar, packed	15 mL
½ tsp	cinnamon	2 mL
1 tsp	orange rind, finely grated	5 mL

1. Place fruit in a 9" x 9" (23 cm x 23 cm) baking dish coated with cooking spray.
2. Pour wine (or white grape juice) over fruit. Sprinkle with cinnamon and brown sugar.
3. Bake uncovered at 350˚F (180˚C) for 45 minutes. Stir every 15 minutes. Remove from oven.
4. Serve in individual dessert cups. Sprinkle with grated orange rind.

Makes 4 portions. *Doubles easily. Use leftovers as an anytime snack.*

MOCHA COFFEE

Some people can't decide if they want hot chocolate or coffee, so have it all!

1 portion	skim milk hot chocolate	1 portion
½ cup	boiling water	125 mL
½ cup	strong coffee	125 mL

1. Prepare hot chocolate according to package instructions, using only ½ cup (125 mL) boiling water. Add coffee.

Makes 1 portion.

RED SKY IN THE MORNING

Red sky in the morning, sailors take warning... batten the hatches, your taste buds are in for a ride!

1	**small onion, diced**	1
1/2	**10 oz (284 mL) can tomato soup** *(Leftover soup can be heated with water* *or skim milk for a light snack.)*	1/2
¼ cup	**water**	**50 mL**
1 tsp	**Worcestershire sauce**	**5 mL**
pinch	**black pepper**	**pinch**
2	**large eggs**	**2**
2	**egg whites**	**2**
¼ cup	**water**	**50 mL**
4	**slices whole grain bread**	**4**
garnish	**green onion, chopped**	**garnish**

1. Sauté onion until golden-brown over medium heat in a nonstick skillet coated with cooking spray. Add tomato soup, ¼ cup (50 mL) water, Worcestershire sauce and pepper. Stir well. Set aside over low heat.

2. Whisk eggs and ¼ cup (50 mL) water.

3. Cook egg mixture over medium heat in a nonstick skillet coated with cooking spray, stirring constantly.

4. Serve on toast. Top with tomato soup mixture.

5. Use remaining toast on the side, spread with your favourite topping.

Makes 2 portions. *One portion = 1 slice whole grain toast topped with 1/2 of the egg mixture and 1/2 of the tomato sauce. Doubles easily.*

If you want to feel on top of the world, you have to climb to the summit.

If you walk faster, you'll get to the top faster! You'll know you're exercising your heart and lungs when you become slightly winded.

Exercise program by

FIFTH TIME WALKING:

Don't forget to warm up and stretch before you find a small hill. Get your rear in gear and stride. If you feel that the hill is defeating you, fight back. Pump your arms, breathe deeply and keep in mind that whatever goes up eventually comes down. When you are walking back down the hill, please do so slowly. Bend your knees and lean back slightly. The slower pace will cool you down and you'll be ready for the stretch of your lower body muscles when you get home. Stretch while you catch up on your favourite T.V. program— the distraction will allow you to hold each stretch longer. Who says you can't do two things at once?

...continued on page 163

RASPBERRY ORANGE TRIFLE (FAMILY OF 4)

No need to panic if you don't own a trifle bowl: any large bowl will do (you just won't be able to show-off the pretty layers).

FIRST LAYER:

1/2	**Angel Food cake, cut in 1" (2.5 cm) cubes**	1/2
1	**envelope unflavoured gelatin**	1
¼ **cup**	**raspberry juice**	50 mL
2 cups	**raspberry juice**	500 mL
1	**10 oz (300 g) pkg frozen, unsweetened raspberries**	1

SECOND LAYER:

1	**6 serving box vanilla pudding** (*to be cooked*)	1
1	**10 oz (284 mL) can Mandarin orange segments in juice, drained, juice reserved**	1
2¼ **cups**	**skim milk**	550 mL

THIRD LAYER:

2 cups	**fat-free vanilla yogurt**	500 mL

1. **First layer**: spread cake cubes over bottom of a trifle bowl. Set aside.

2. Place gelatin and ¼ cup (50 mL) raspberry juice in a medium saucepan. Stir well. Dissolve over medium heat, stirring constantly.

3. Add the 2 cups (500 mL) of raspberry juice and the raspberries to the gelatin mixture. Stir just until the raspberries are thawed. Remove from heat. Ladle raspberry mixture gently over cake cubes in the trifle bowl. Refrigerate while preparing second layer.

4. **Second layer**: place vanilla pudding mix, Mandarin orange juice and milk in a medium saucepan. Using an underpot wire, bring to a boil over medium-high heat, stirring constantly (about 10 minutes). Remove from heat.

5. Add orange segments. Stir. Ladle pudding mixture gently over first layer. **Refrigerate for at least 3 hours**.

6. **Third layer**: cover with vanilla yogurt just before serving.

Makes 8—1 cup (250 mL) portions. *Refrigerate leftovers.*

 Save one portion per person for Tuesday's snack.

RASPBERRY ORANGE TRIFLE (FAMILY OF 2)

Trifle for two? Yahoo! It's so nice, let's have it twice.

FIRST LAYER:

1/4	**Angel Food cake, cut in 1" (2.5 cm) cubes**	1/4
1 tsp	**unflavoured gelatin**	5 mL
¼ cup	**raspberry juice**	50 mL
1 cup	**raspberry juice**	250 mL
1/2	**10 oz (300 g) pkg frozen, unsweetened raspberries** *(Use the remainder as a fruit or as a cereal topping.)*	1/2

SECOND LAYER:

1	**10 oz (284 mL) can Mandarin orange segments in juice, drained, juice reserved**	1
1 tsp	**unflavoured gelatin**	5 mL
2	**5 oz (142 g) prepared low-fat vanilla puddings**	2

THIRD LAYER:

1 cup	**fat-free vanilla yogurt**	250 mL

1. **First layer**: spread cake cubes over bottoms of 4 single-serving dessert bowls. Set aside.

2. Place gelatin and ¼ cup (50 mL) raspberry juice in a medium saucepan. Stir well. Dissolve over medium heat, stirring constantly.

3. Add the 1 cup (250 mL) of raspberry juice and the raspberries to the gelatin mixture. Stir just until the raspberries are thawed. Remove from heat. Ladle raspberry mixture gently over cake cubes in the dessert bowls. Refrigerate while preparing second layer.

4. **Second layer**: mix Mandarin orange juice and gelatin in a small saucepan. Stir well. Dissolve over medium heat, stirring constantly.

5. Remove from heat and add puddings. Blend with a whisk. Add orange segments. Stir well. Ladle pudding mixture gently over first layer in each dessert bowl. **Refrigerate for at least 3 hours**.

6. **Third layer**: cover each portion with vanilla yogurt just before serving.

Makes 4 —1cup (250 mL) portions. *Refrigerate leftovers.*

➡ Save one portion per person for Tuesday's snack (there are 301.3 calories and 0.2 grams of fat per portion in this recipe).

... continued from page 150

Approximately 1½ hours before you plan to eat dinner, begin cooking the wild and brown rice, then follow the **Chicken à l'Orange** recipe. While the chicken is baking, make **l'Orange Sauce**. About 20 minutes before dinner time, cook the **Garlic-Basil Broccoli**.

Total preparation and cooking time: **90 min.**

After dinner, make tomorrow's sandwiches.

Use leftover rice mixture, if any, as a side dish or as a snack.

CHICKEN À L'ORANGE WITH WILD RICE

Speechless!

¼ **cup**	wild rice	50 mL
½ **cup**	brown rice, long grain	125 mL
1 tsp	chicken bouillon concentrate	5 mL
1½ cups	water	375 mL
1 tsp	canola or olive oil	5 mL
1	medium onion, diced	1
2	cloves garlic, minced	2
1 cup	fresh mushrooms, diced	250 mL
1	medium red pepper, diced	1
2 tbsp	salt-reduced soy sauce	30 mL
2	chicken breasts, bone in	2

1. Bring the rices, bouillon concentrate and water to a boil over medium-high heat in a medium saucepan.
2. Cover, reduce heat to low and simmer for 40 to 45 minutes or until liquid is absorbed.
3. Meanwhile, heat oil over medium heat in a nonstick skillet. Add onion and garlic and sauté until onion is translucent. Add mushrooms and red pepper. Sauté for another 2 to 3 minutes.
4. Mix rice and vegetable mixtures together. Add soy sauce. Mix. Set aside.
5. Place 1 chicken breast in a roasting pan coated with cooking spray. Cover with 2 cups (500 mL) of the rice mixture. Top with the remaining chicken breast. Seal extra stuffing in aluminum foil coated with cooking spray. Place in the roaster with the chicken.
6. Cover. Bake for 30 to 45 minutes at 400˚F (200˚C) or until chicken is lightly browned.
7. Place on a serving platter. Remove chicken skin. Top each chicken breast with 2tbsp (30 mL) **l'Orange Sauce**.

Makes 2 portions. *Doubles easily. Freezes well.*

MULTI-GRAIN SODA BREAD
page 28

ORANGE-CINNAMON COFFEE
page 29

VANILLA FRUIT SALAD
page 29

L'ORANGE SAUCE

Ooh, la, la!

½ cup	orange juice, freshly squeezed	125 mL
1 tbsp	liquid honey	15 mL
	rind from 1 orange, cut into long thin strips	

1. Bring all ingredients to a boil over medium-high heat in a small saucepan.

2. Reduce heat to medium-low. Simmer, uncovered, until sauce is reduced by half (about 20 minutes).

Makes 2 portions. *Doubles easily. Freezes well.*

If the price of Cornish Hens is not unseasonably high, use them instead of chicken breasts for a more elegant presentation. If using Cornish hens, the rice is placed in the cavity.

GARLIC-BASIL BROCCOLI

You don't need fat for flavour if you use spices!

4	green onions (*scallions only*), sliced	4
1	clove garlic, minced	1
2 cups	broccoli, florets & peeled stems	500 mL
1/4	red pepper, seeded & cut into thin strips	1/4
pinch	salt	pinch
pinch	black pepper	pinch
pinch	cayenne pepper	pinch
½ tsp	basil	2 mL
2 tbsp	water	30 mL

1. Sauté scallions and garlic over medium-low heat in a saucepan coated with cooking spray.

2. Add all remaining ingredients, except water. Stir well.

3. Add water. Cover and cook over low heat for 10-15 minutes.

Makes 2 portions. *Doubles easily. Freezes well.*

EXERCISE

THE "GROANERS"

KNEELING PUSH-UPS

This is not the army! If kneeling push-ups are uncomfortable for your wrists, try using a wall. Standing 18 inches (46 cm) back, place your hands on a wall, slightly lower than chest height and a little further than shoulder width apart. Keep your back flat. Lean into the wall and slowly bring your body toward the wall. Push back to the start position, just as slowly.

1. On a padded surface, in a face down position, support your body weight on your hands and the fleshy part of your knees. Using the fleshy part of your knees takes pressure off your lower back and spine.

2. With your hands shoulder width apart, slowly lower your body to touch your chest to the padded surface below. Equally as slowly, push back to the start position. It is important to think long with your spine as you do this modified push-up, and to keep your head and therefore your neck in a natural position.

3. Try 5 and work your way up to 20. You should feel your pectoral (chest) and bicep (front of upper arm) muscles working. To emphasize the tricep (back of arm) region, push your elbows out at a 45 degree angle from the body.

LOWER ABDOMINAL TONER

You might be tempted to hold your breath while doing this exercise, so please concentrate on deep, slow breathing. Like exercising, deep breathing is a good thing to do on a regular basis.

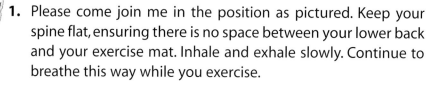

1. Please come join me in the position as pictured. Keep your spine flat, ensuring there is no space between your lower back and your exercise mat. Inhale and exhale slowly. Continue to breathe this way while you exercise.

2. Extend your legs up to be perpendicular to your body, knees soft. Tighten your lower abdominal muscles as though a Sumo wrestler is about to walk on your tummy. Use slow, controlled movements. Contract and hold for a slow count to 3. Release slowly. You should feel this exercise in your lower abdominals (pot belly). This contraction, or tightening, may cause your hips to lift slightly. Please do not rock, allowing momentum to come into play.

3. Repeat 10 times and work your way up to 30.

BREAKFAST
Whole Grain Cereal of Choice, Fruit of Choice, Milk

LUNCH
Cranberry-Cream Cheese Turkey Sandwich, **Fruit Cup**, Fruit Juice of Choice

DINNER
**Green Pepper Steak with Wun Tun Noodles,
Red and Green Salad**

SNACK
Fig Bars, Milk

GAME PLAN

This morning, place the round steak for tomorrow's dinner in the fridge to thaw.

... continued on page 159

NUTRITION INFORMATION
See page 6 for standards used.

MENU ITEMS (single portion)	calories	carbs (grams)	protein (grams)	fat (grams)
Whole Grain Cereal of Choice	126	20.3	2.6	4.4
Fruit of Choice	81	21	0.2	0.5
Milk	86	11.9	8.3	0.4
Cranberry–Cream Cheese Turkey Sandwich	299.5	40	17.1	9.1
Fruit Cup	114	29.2	1.2	0
Fruit Juice of Choice	80	20	1	0
Green Pepper Steak	410	14.6	19.5	28.3
Wun Tun Noodles	180	38.2	6.3	0
Red and Green Salad	88	22.3	1.6	0.3
Fig Bars — 2	120	11	2	2
Milk	86	11.9	8.3	0.4
Total for day	1670.5	240.4	68.1	45.4
			percentage fat ➤	**24%**

REMEMBER, these are the MINIMUM REQUIREMENTS of the Canada and U.S. Food Guides. Some people will need more calories.

Check the calories and fat grams today — eating beef makes both numbers rise dramatically. This is not a bad thing if your overall diet is low in fat.

CRANBERRY-CREAM CHEESE TURKEY SANDWICH

Cranberries aren't just for Christmas — they're a great fat-free flavour enhancer.

2	slices whole grain bread	2
2 oz	roasted deli turkey breast	60 g
1 tbsp	low-fat cream cheese	15 mL
2 tbsp	whole berry cranberry sauce	30 mL
1	lettuce leaf	1

1. Spread one slice of bread with cream cheese and cranberry sauce. Top with turkey and lettuce. Close sandwich with remaining slice of bread.

2. If brown-bagging, omit lettuce, wrap and refrigerate.

Makes 1 portion.

FRUIT CUP

Simple Enough?

1 cup	canned fruit of choice, in juice	250 mL

Makes 1 portion

Green Pepper Steak with Wun Tun Noodles (<u>Not</u> Won Ton Wraps)

We think of pasta dishes as being Italian, but it is actually the Chinese who began using noodles in 1500 B.C. This recipe is a good example of how Chinese culture taught us to enjoy noodles in a sauce.

1 lb	sirloin steak, all visible fat removed, cut in long <u>thin</u> strips	450 g
1	medium onion, diced	1
1	clove garlic, minced	1
2	green peppers, seeded and cut in 1" (2.5 cm) pieces	2
2½ cups	water	625 mL
1 tsp	beef bouillon concentrate	5 mL
3 tbsp	salt-reduced soy sauce	45 mL
3 tbsp	cornstarch, mixed with ¼ cup (50 mL) cold water	45 mL
1/2	16 oz (454 g) pkg wun tun noodles *(looks like thin fettucini)*	1/2
2	medium tomatoes, cut into eighths	2

1. Brown meat over high heat in a nonstick skillet coated with cooking spray.
2. Add onion, garlic and green pepper. Cook for 2 to 3 minutes, or until onion is translucent, stirring constantly.
3. Add water, beef bouillon and soy sauce. Cover and simmer for 20 minutes over medium-low heat.
4. Meanwhile, cook noodles according to package instructions. Drain well. Set aside.
5. Increase heat to medium. Add cornstarch mixture to meat, stirring briskly. Cover and simmer for 5 minutes, stirring frequently.
6. Add tomatoes to meat mixture. Stir gently. Serve with noodles.

Makes 4 portions. *One portion = 1½ cups (375 mL) meat mixture over 1¾ cups (425 mL) noodles. Doubles easily. Freezes well.*

... continued from page 157

Tonight, you will find that the **Green Pepper Steak** is very easy to prepare. While the meat cooks, make the salad then cook the noodles last.

Total preparation and cooking time: **40 min.**

After dinner, prepare the fruit topping for tomorrow's **Cinnamon Cottage Cheese Salad**. Also, check your freezer for leftover muffins. If you have some, place one per person in the fridge to thaw for tomorrow's lunch.

Check the meat section for sirloin or inside round steak that has been pre-cut into thin strips. If you cut your own meat, cut it while it is partially frozen — it's easier.

RED AND GREEN SALAD

You've enjoyed this dressing before. You can see how versatile it is; just change the vegetables for a new taste.

1½ **cups**	**green leaf lettuce, torn**	**375 mL**
½ **cup**	**red cabbage, shredded**	**125 mL**
1 **tbsp**	**green onion, sliced**	**15 mL**
1 **tbsp**	**balsamic vinegar**	**15 mL**
1 **tbsp**	**liquid honey**	**15 mL**
pinch	**black pepper**	**pinch**

1. Mix all ingredients together. Serve.

Makes 1 portion.

BREAKFAST

Creamy Apricot Oat Bran, Fruit Juice of Choice, Milk

LUNCH

Cinnamon-Cottage Cheese Salad,

Muffin of Choice <u>or</u> Cinnamon Graham Wafers

DINNER

Beefy Mushroom Soup, Whole Grain Bun, Fruit of Choice

SNACK

Raspberry Orange Trifle

GAME PLAN

This morning, make sure you try the **Creamy Apricot Oat Bran** — it's another delicious porridge.

Your lunch was prepared last night.

... continue page 164

NUTRITION INFORMATION
See page 6 for standards used.

MENU ITEMS (single portion)	calories	carbs (grams)	protein (grams)	fat (grams)
Creamy Apricot Oat Bran	206.7	36.6	11.2	2.2
Fruit Juice of Choice	80	20	1	0
Milk	86	11.9	8.3	0.4
Cinnamon-Cottage Cheese Salad	314	42.4	30.1	3.4
Cinnamon Graham Wafers — 6	188	32	3	5
Beefy Mushroom Soup	239.1	24.4	16.3	8.1
Whole Grain Bun	93	18.8	3.6	1
Fruit of Choice	81	21	0.2	0.5
Raspberry Orange Trifle	296.2	66.5	7.7	0.3
Total for day	1584	253.6	81.4	20.9
			percentage fat ▶	12%

REMEMBER, these are the MINIMUM REQUIREMENTS of the Canada and U.S. Food Guides. Some people will need more calories.

If brown-bagging
Cinnamon-Cottage Cheese Salad,
pack the fruit and cottage cheese separately.
If you don't have a fridge at work, put an ice pack in your lunch bag.

CREAMY APRICOT OAT BRAN

This hot cereal is a pleasant way to get your fibre.

⅓ **cup**	**oat bran**	75 mL
1⅓ **cups**	**water**	325 mL
pinch	**salt**	**pinch**
2 **tbsp**	**skim milk powder**	30 mL
½ **tsp**	**vanilla extract**	2 mL
2 **tbsp**	**dried apricots, diced**	30 mL
1 **tsp**	**brown sugar**	5 mL

1. Mix all ingredients in a microwaveable, uncovered cereal bowl.

2. Microwave on high for 1½ to 2 minutes. Stir.
   Microwave on medium for 1 minute. Stir.
   Microwave on medium for 30 to 60 seconds.

3. Serve with extra milk and brown sugar if desired (these will be additional calories).

Makes 1 portion.

CINNAMON-COTTAGE CHEESE SALAD

Enjoy your fruit salad with this creamy touch.

1 **cup**	**cantaloupe, diced**	250 mL
½ **cup**	**grapes, seedless, halved**	125 mL
¼ **cup**	**pineapple juice**	50 mL
1 **cup**	**1% milk fat cottage cheese**	250 mL
to taste	**cinnamon** (*We like lots!*)	**to taste**

1. Mix cantaloupe, grapes and pineapple juice.

2. Serve fruit mixture over cottage cheese. Sprinkle with cinnamon.

Makes 1 portion.

Many people have said, "If you do not take time to care for yourself now, you will have to make time to be ill later". If you know of someone who is in the hospital and could use some cheer, read them the following story:

"THE GOWN WITH THE SPLIT DOWN THE BACK"

I was sitting here minding my business, just letting my brain go slack. When in comes a nurse with a smile on her face and a gown split down the back.

"Take a shower", she said, "and get ready, then ease on into the sack".

"We'll need to do some tests", she said.

I wondered, "Will they stretch me out on a rack? With nothing twixt me and the cold cruel world but a gown that's split down the back? In the front I'm barely decent, on the sides there's also a lack. But by far the greatest shortcoming is that doggoned split down the back! The person had some sense of humor who designed this gown of ease. But I fail to see anything funny when it's my fanny that's feeling a breeze! I hear them coming to get me, the wheels going clickety-clack. I'll ride through the halls on a table in a gown with a split down the back. When I get to heaven I won't really care if my robe is white, red or black but I'm down on my knees and praying for one with no split down the back!"

Author Anonymous

Exercise program by

FOURTH TIME TONING:

Same routine as Third time toning (see page 145) and if you feel ready, try to increase the number of repetitions of each **Toning** and **"Groaning"** exercise. I know that you are feeling your muscles, but keep going and soon you will see some firming and less jiggling.

... continued on page 171

... continued from page 161

Dinner is a simple, one bowl meal, quick and easy to prepare. It will be even faster if you enlist a family member to help chop the vegetables.

Total preparation and cooking time: **60 min.**

The leftover soup is tomorrow's lunch, so pack individual portions tonight.

If you will be busy tomorrow evening, you may want to bake the **Heavy Artillery Cookies** tonight, as you have ½ hour to spare while the soup cooks.

BEEFY MUSHROOM SOUP

As Grandpa would say, this will stick to your ribs.

1 lb	**eye of round steak,** cut in ½ " x 2 " (1 cm x 5 cm) strips	450 g
1 tsp	**canola or olive oil**	5 mL
2 tbsp	**lemon juice**	30 mL
1 tbsp	**brown sugar**	15 mL
2 tbsp	**salt-reduced soy sauce**	30 mL
1 tsp	**prepared mustard**	5 mL
2	**cloves garlic, minced**	2
2	**medium onions, diced**	2
4	**medium potatoes, washed & diced**	4
4	**medium carrots, thinly sliced**	4
2	**stalks celery, thinly sliced**	2
1 lb	**mushrooms, sliced**	450 g
2	**10 oz (284 mL) cans consommé**	2
4 cups	**boiling water**	1 L
½ tsp	**black pepper**	2 mL
1	**bay leaf** (*Remove before serving.*)	1
¼ cup	**all-purpose flour**	50 mL
½ cup	**cold water**	125 mL

1. Mix meat, oil, lemon juice, brown sugar, soy sauce, mustard and garlic in a medium bowl. Set aside. Prepare all vegetables.

2. Brown meat over high heat in a Dutch oven coated with cooking spray, stirring constantly. Add vegetables and stir-fry for 3 to 5 minutes.

3. Add consommé, boiling water, black pepper and bay leaf. Bring to a boil. Reduce heat to medium-low. Simmer for 30 minutes.

4. Increase heat to medium-high. In a small jar with a tight-fitting lid, shake flour and **cold** water vigorously until there are no lumps. Gradually stir enough of the flour mixture into the soup, stirring constantly, to achieve the consistency you prefer. Simmer for 10 minutes over medium heat, stirring frequently.

Makes 8 —1½ cup (375 mL) portions. *Doubles easily. Freezes well.*

 Save one portion per person for tomorrow's lunch.

BREAKFAST
Whole Grain Toast, Cheese Slices, Fruit-Only Jam, Fruit Juice of Choice

LUNCH
Beefy Mushroom Soup,
Whole Grain Bun, Fruit of Choice

DINNER
Fish Sticks with Lemon Sauce, Grains and Greens, Pickled Beets

SNACK
Heavy Artillery Cookie, Milk

GAME PLAN

Place the chicken for tomorrow's dinner in the fridge to thaw.

Breakfast and lunch need no instructions.

... continued page 166

NUTRITION INFORMATION
See page 6 for standards used.

MENU ITEMS (single portion)	calories	carbs (grams)	protein (grams)	fat (grams)
Whole Grain Toast — 2	126	24.8	5.4	1.6
1% Cheese Slices — 2	56	4.8	10.2	0.4
Fruit-Only Jam	43	11	0.1	0
Fruit Juice of Choice	80	20	1	0
Beefy Mushroom Soup	239.1	24.4	16.3	8.1
Whole Grain Bun	93	18.8	3.6	1
Fruit of Choice	81	21	0.2	0.5
Fish Sticks with Lemon Sauce	130.7	2.8	23.3	3.4
Grains and Greens	178.3	42.7	9.2	1.2
Pickled Beets — 1/2 cup (125 mL)	74	18.5	0.9	0.1
Heavy Artillery Cookie — 1	168	32.1	5	3.2
Milk	86	11.9	8.3	0.4
Total for day	1355.1	232.8	83.5	19.9
percentage fat ▶				**13%**

REMEMBER, these are the MINIMUM REQUIREMENTS of the Canada and U.S. Food Guides. Some people will need more calories.

Tonight's dinner is a real life-saver, literally. What could be healthier than fish, whole grains and dark green vegetables?

... continued from page 165

Begin dinner preparations by following steps 1 and 2 of **Grains and Greens.** While the barley mixture comes to a boil, prepare the fish and place in the oven. While the barley mixture and fish cook, make the lemon sauce.

Total preparation and cooking time: **55 min.**

This evening, prepare tomorrow's lunch.

You can have a family member mixing the cookie dough so that the cookies bake while you eat dinner.

GRAINS AND GREENS

Oh my, this is good! If you've never eaten barley, this is the best way to start.

1	10 oz (284 mL) can chicken broth	1
10 oz	water	284 mL
1	small onion, diced	1
	OR	
2 tbsp	dried onion flakes	30 mL
1	clove garlic, minced	1
	OR	
½ tsp	garlic powder	2 mL
1	10 oz (300 g) pkg frozen chopped spinach	1
¾ cup	pot barley	175 mL

1. Place all ingredients in a medium saucepan. Bring to a boil over medium-high heat. Stir.

2. Cover and reduce heat to low. Simmer for 45 minutes.

3. Serve.

Makes 4 portions. *Doubles easily. Freezes well.*

If the thought of aerobics makes you ill, biking sounds boring and swimming makes you squirm...

...in other words, if you are not partial to exercising, think of it more as moving. Try not to sit for more than one hour. Find reasons to stretch, bend, reach or walk and your body will respond with fewer aches and pains (you will possibly find yourself moaning and groaning less too).

FISH STICKS WITH LEMON SAUCE

This is not a Cordon Bleu technique, but it works for the 90's cook!

1	**14 oz (400 g) pkg fish fillets, frozen**	1
2 tbsp	**"Coating Mix for Meat"** *(recipe on page 71)*	30 mL
1 tbsp	**lemon-pepper seasoning**	15 mL
Lemon Sauce:		
1	**10 oz (284 mL) can chicken broth, undiluted**	1
1½ tsp	**lemon rind or ½ tsp (2 mL) dried lemon peel**	7 mL
pinch	**nutmeg**	pinch
1 tsp	**sugar**	5 mL
2 tbsp	**fresh or bottled lemon juice**	30 mL
1 tbsp	**cornstarch**	15 mL

1. Unwrap the frozen fish fillets and place on a microwaveable platter. Microwave on defrost for 4 minutes.

2. Place partially thawed fillets on a cutting board and cut in 4 equal sticks.

3. Mix the **Coating Mix for Meat** and lemon-pepper seasoning in a small plastic bag. Shake well.

4. Dip each fish stick in water. Shake off excess water and place one fish stick at a time in the bag. Shake to coat and place on a baking sheet coated with cooking spray. Discard plastic bag and excess seasonings.

5. Bake at 350°F (180°C) for 20 minutes or until fish flakes easily with a fork.

6. Meanwhile, place chicken broth, lemon rind, nutmeg and sugar in a small, uncovered saucepan over medium-high heat. Bring to a boil, stirring frequently.

7. While broth comes to a boil, mix lemon juice and cornstarch in a small bowl. Reduce heat to medium. Slowly add cornstarch mixture to broth while stirring vigorously. Once thickened, serve over fish sticks.

Makes 4 portions. *Doubles easily. Freezes well.*

Any day that you are in a time crunch that  tempts you to buy greasy fast-food, whip up this meal instead.
All of the ingredients are dried, frozen or canned so they can be stocked as emergency supplies.

By now, you have leftovers in your freezer. Use them anytime in the future when you're too busy to cook or bake. These "emergency supplies" will keep you out of the fast-food lane.

Note to Sports Parents — for a great snack or breakfast-on-the-go, **Heavy Artillery Cookies** travel well and provide excellent body fuel.

HEAVY ARTILLERY COOKIES

Napoleon's army wouldn't have starved in the war of 1812 if his cooks had used these cookies as K.P. rations.

½ cup	**fat-free sour cream**	125 mL
½ cup	**reduced-fat peanut butter**	125 mL
¾ cup	**brown sugar**	175 mL
½ cup	**honey**	125 mL
1	**egg**	1
1	**egg white**	1
1 tsp	**vanilla extract**	5 mL
1 cup	**whole wheat flour**	250 mL
½ tsp	**salt**	2 mL
1 tsp	**baking soda**	5 mL
3 cups	**quick oats**	750 mL
1 tsp	**cinnamon**	5 mL
½ cup	**natural wheat bran**	125 mL
¼ cup	**wheat germ**	50 mL
½ cup	**oat bran**	125 mL
1 cup	**raisins**	250 mL

1. Mix sour cream, peanut butter, brown sugar, honey, egg, egg white and vanilla in a large bowl. Beat well. Set aside.

2. Mix all remaining ingredients in a medium bowl. Stir well. Add to peanut butter mixture. Stir until moistened.

3. Drop by heaping tablespoons onto a baking sheet coated with cooking spray.

4. Bake at 350°F (180°C) for 15 to 20 minutes, or until lightly browned.

Makes 24 cookies. *Doubles easily. Freezes well.*

 Save one portion per person for tomorrow's breakfast.

BREAKFAST
Heavy Artillery Cookie, Fruit of Choice , Hot Chocolate

LUNCH
Peanut Butter-Banana Sandwich,
Carrot Sticks, Milk

DINNER
Fusilli with Paprika Chicken, Steamed Green Beans,
Tossed Salad

SNACK
Frozen Yogurt <u>or</u> 1% Ice Cream

GAME PLAN

Prepare the sandwich below for lunch.

... continued page 170

PEANUT BUTTER-BANANA SANDWICH

This will bring you back to your school days!

---

2 slices whole grain bread

---

1 medium banana

---

1 tbsp (15 mL) reduced-fat peanut butter

---

1 tbsp (15 mL) fruit-only jam

No explanation is necessary... attack the banana any way you want: mash, slice dice, etc.

Makes 1 portion.

NUTRITION INFORMATION
See page 6 for standards used.

MENU ITEMS (single portion)	calories	carbs (grams)	protein (grams)	fat (grams)
Heavy Artillery Cookie — 1	168	32.1	5	3.2
Fruit of Choice	81	21	0.2	0.5
Hot Chocolate (made with water)	110	23	1	1
Peanut Butter-Banana Sandwich	360	68.6	9.4	7.7
Carrot Sticks — 1 medium carrot	31	7.3	0.7	0.1
Milk	86	11.9	8.3	0.4
Fusilli with Paprika Chicken	454	60.8	37.4	5.3
Steamed Green Beans — 1 cup (250 mL)	44	9.8	2.4	0.4
Tossed Salad	77	16.6	3.1	0.5
Frozen Yogurt — 1/2 cup (125 mL)	126	24	3	1.9
Total for day	1537	275.1	70.5	21
percentage fat ▶				12%

REMEMBER, these are the MINIMUM REQUIREMENTS of the Canada and U.S. Food Guides. Some people will need more calories.

...continued from page 169

Begin dinner preparations by making a tossed salad (use up any leftover red cabbage). Place in the fridge.

Follow the directions for **Fusilli with Paprika Chicken**. Steam the green beans while the pasta cooks. End of Story.

Total preparation and cooking time: **40 min.**

For tomorrow's lunch, scan your freezer for leftovers or plan to eat out!

Cut 45 minutes from tomorrow's cooking time by pre-cooking the rice for **Rice and Bean Casserole** tonight.

FUSILLI WITH PAPRIKA CHICKEN

The cuisines of many cultures blend well together — for instance, this recipe blends the cultures of Hungary and Italy.

1 cup	fat-free plain yogurt	250 mL
1 cup	fat-free sour cream	250 mL
¼ cup	all-purpose flour	50 mL
1 tsp	dry mustard	5 mL
1 tsp	canola or olive oil	5 mL
4	chicken breasts, boneless, skinless, all visible fat removed, cut in 1 " (2.5 cm) pieces	4
1	medium onion, diced	1
1	clove garlic, minced	1
1/2	red pepper, diced	1/2
1	green pepper, diced	1
1 tbsp	paprika	15 mL
¼ tsp	black pepper	1 mL
1	10 oz (284 mL) can chicken broth	1
⅓ cup	low-fat Parmesan cheese, grated	75 mL
1	12 oz (375 g) pkg fusilli or corkscrew pasta	1

1. Boil water in a Dutch oven.
2. Mix yogurt, sour cream, flour and mustard in a small bowl. Set aside.
3. Heat oil over medium-high heat in a Dutch oven coated with cooking spray.
4. Add chicken pieces and stir-fry until lightly browned.
5. Add onion and garlic. Cook until onion is translucent, stirring frequently.
6. Add peppers and cook for 2 to 3 minutes, stirring frequently.
7. Add paprika, black pepper and chicken broth. Bring to a boil. Cover. Reduce heat to low. Simmer for 20 minutes. Meanwhile cook pasta according to package instructions. Drain. Set aside.
8. Increase heat to medium, then slowly add yogurt mixture to chicken mixture, stirring constantly. Keep stirring until thickened. Add pasta. Mix well.

Makes 6 portions. *Doubles easily. Freezes well.*

SWEET AND SOUR PORK ON A
BED OF RICE NOODLES
page 25

BREAKFAST

Whole Grain Cereal of Choice, Fruit of Choice, Fruit Juice of Choice, Milk

LUNCH

T.G.I.F. (Use up leftovers or buy a lunch.)

DINNER

Rice and Bean Casserole, **Apple-Carrot Slaw**, Milk

SNACK

Treat Time!

SIXTH TIME WALKING:

You're ready for a longer walk today. Try 20 minutes, or better yet, challenge yourself to 30 minutes. Warm up, stretch, then find a route that includes a small hill. As you progress in your walking program, add more hills and make your route longer and longer. Cooling down and stretching become increasingly important as your exercise sessions become longer.

... continued on page 174

NUTRITION INFORMATION
See page 6 for standards used.

MENU ITEMS (single portion)	calories	carbs (grams)	protein (grams)	fat (grams)
Whole Grain Cereal of Choice	126	20.3	2.6	4.4
Fruit of Choice	81	21	0.2	0.5
Fruit Juice of Choice	80	20	1	0
Milk	86	11.9	8.3	0.4
Rice and Bean Casserole	280	47.4	15.6	3.4
Apple-Carrot Slaw	93.7	22.2	2.7	0.5
Milk	86	11.9	8.3	0.4
Total for day	832.7	154.7	38.7	9.6
		percentage fat ▶		10%

REMEMBER, these are the MINIMUM REQUIREMENTS of the Canada and U.S. Food Guides. Some people will need more calories.

Tonight, just follow the recipe for **Rice and Bean Casserole**. While it bakes, make the **Apple-Carrot Slaw**.

Total preparation and cooking time: **80 min.**
OR
35 min.
if you cooked the rice yesterday!

RICE AND BEAN CASSEROLE

This could become your favourite Mexican dinner.

1 cup	brown rice	250 mL
2 cups	water	500 mL
1	small onion, diced	1
1	14 oz (398 mL) can tomato sauce	1
1	14 oz (398 mL) can kidney beans, drained	1
1 cup	1% cottage cheese	250 mL
1 cup	low-fat cheddar cheese, grated	250 mL
1 tbsp	chili powder	15 mL
1 tsp	cumin	5 mL
¼ tsp	black pepper	1 mL

1. Bring rice and water to a boil over high heat in a large saucepan. Stir. Reduce heat to low. Cover and cook undisturbed for 45 minutes.

2. Meanwhile, purée cottage cheese in the blender (if you don't have to hide the cottage cheese from the picky eaters, skip this step).

3. Mix the cooked rice, cottage cheese, ¾ cup (175 mL) grated cheddar cheese and all remaining ingredients in the rice pan.

4. Pour into a 4 quart (4 L) casserole dish coated with cooking spray. Sprinkle with reserved ¼ cup (50 mL) grated cheddar cheese.

5. Bake uncovered at 375°F (190°C) for 30 to 40 minutes.

Makes 6 portions. *Doubles easily. Freezes well.*

APPLE-CARROT SLAW

Everyone loves coleslaw, and it's even better when freshly made. If you have leftover cabbage, make more of this delicious slaw... it's low-fat and low-calorie!

2 cups	green cabbage, shredded	500 mL
1	medium carrot, grated	1
1	green onion, chopped	1
1	medium apple, cored & diced	1
2 tbsp	fat-free sour cream	30 mL
1 tbsp	fat-free plain yogurt	15 mL
1 tsp	sugar	5 mL
¼ tsp	salt	1 mL
pinch	black pepper	pinch

1. Mix all ingredients together until well coated.

Makes 2 portions. *Doubles easily.*

CONGRATULATIONS!

You have now successfully followed the Canadian and U.S. Food Guides for a full month.

We hope that you enjoyed the recipes as much as our families enjoy them. You can now insert your own low-fat recipes into the meal plans, or just repeat the whole month as is!

To keep up with food trends and new products, we are designing a second book. Watch for it at your favourite book store, or write to us. If you are very kind, you will buy copies of this book for your family and friends. You will be telling them that you love them!

MEASUREMENT CHART

**Check your progress!
Take these measurements again:**

Neck _____ in/cm

Chest _____ in/cm

Bicep _____ in/cm

Waist _____ in/cm

Hips _____ in/cm

Thigh _____ in/cm

Calf _____ in/cm

You may have lost centimeters but not weight because muscle tissue weighs more than fat tissue. You have still made progress!

*... exercise program continued
for the rest of your life...*

Exercise program by

NOT A CONCLUSION – A PROGRESSION...

Did you ever have one of those days when you thought, "I put on pantyhose for this!" or for the gentlemen, "I shaved for this!"?

We all have, but how we dealt with the day or the circumstances probably varied. Some lose it and some use it. Know that everything happens for a reason and with everything that happens there is something to be learned; either about yourself, someone else or the circumstances. Use this information to your advantage. If you are sooo frustrated that your thoughts are impaired and unclear, take a walk, run, stretch, practice deep breathing, relax, or do whatever to clear your thoughts.

**Because all too often...
Thoughts become words,
Words become actions,
Actions become habits,
Habits become character,
Character becomes destiny.**

It takes six weeks to form a habit, healthy or otherwise, the choice is yours every moment of every day. You decide your own destiny. Unfortunately, turning the pages of this book or brushing the dust off of it do not a fit person make.

Following a regular exercise routine will a fit person make. You can start an exercise program at any age, so start now. Movement tones muscles, improves flexibility and strengthens your heart and lungs. If you believe that aging does not necessarily go with age, you will have no trouble continuing with an exercise program for "life". Stretching will keep you supple, toning will keep you tall and walking will keep you keeping on.

HOMEMADE PIZZA DOUGH

This is easier than thawing bread dough!

1¹/₂ cups	all-purpose flour	375 mL
1 cup	barley flour	250 mL
¹/₂ tsp	salt	2 mL
1 tbsp	dry instant yeast	15 mL
1 cup	hot water	250 mL
1 tbsp	oil	15 mL

1. Mix ¹/₂ cup (125 mL) all-purpose flour, barley flour, salt and yeast in a food processor. Add hot water and oil. Pulse for 5 seconds.

2. Add remaining flour and blend for 1 minute. Place on a floured surface. Knead for 1 minute. Let rest for 10 minutes. Spread on a 12″ (30 cm) pizza pan.

Makes 1 pizza crust, or 8 calzones.

Use your bread machine (if you have one) to make **Homemade Pizza Dough**.

HOMEMADE ITALIAN SAUCE

Okay, it's not 100% homemade but it tastes like homemade!

1	14 oz (398 mL) can tomato sauce	1
1	clove garlic, minced	1
¹/₄ cup	onion, diced	50 mL
¹/₂ tsp	basil	2 mL
1¹/₂ tsp	oregano	7 mL
pinch	black pepper	pinch

1. Cook onion and garlic for 2 to 3 minutes over medium heat in a nonstick skillet coated with cooking spray.

2. Add spices. Cook for 1 minute. Add tomato sauce. Cook only until sauce is heated through.

Makes 2 cups (500 mL). *Doubles easily. Freezes well.*

HOMEMADE CHICKEN BROTH

Canned chicken broth is no competition!

2 lbs	**chicken backs & necks**	900 g
	OR	
1	**stewing chicken, cut in large pieces**	1
1 tbsp	**oil**	15 mL
1	**medium onion, cut in chunks**	1
10 cups	**water**	2.5 L
1	**medium carrot, cut in chunks**	1
2	**stalks celery, coarsely chopped**	2
2	**cloves garlic, minced**	2
1	**bay leaf**	1
8	**whole peppercorns**	8
1 tsp	**salt**	5 mL

1. Add oil and bones (or stewing chicken) to a Dutch oven. Brown over medium heat for 10 minutes, stirring frequently. Add onion and cook for 5 minutes, or until lightly browned, stirring frequently.

2. Add water and remaining ingredients. Bring to a boil, uncovered, over medium heat. Once boiling, cover but leave lid slightly ajar and decrease heat to low. Simmer for at least 2 hours.

3. Remove from heat to cool. Strain in a colander, reserving liquid only. Discard all solids. Refrigerate for at least 4 hours. Skim off fat. It is now ready to use.

Makes 8 to 10 cups (2 to 2.5 L). *Freezes well.*

HOMEMADE SPICED APPLE SAUCE

You can make apple sauce in the Fall and preserve it. It's not only tastier than a commercial apple sauce, it's cheaper and ready to use at any time.

8 cups	apple, peeled, cored & coarsely chopped	2 L
¼ cup	white vinegar	50 mL
½ cup	water	125 mL
¾ cup	brown sugar	175 mL
1 tsp	cinnamon	5 mL
½ tsp	cloves	2 mL
½ tsp	nutmeg	2 mL

1. Place all ingredients in a Dutch oven. Cook, uncovered, over medium-low heat for 15 to 20 minutes or until apples are soft, stirring frequently.

2. Remove from heat. Mash with potato masher to remove large lumps.

3. Put hot apple sauce into hot sterilized canning jars, filling to ¾" (1.5 cm) from the top.

4. Place canning lids on jars. Process about 20 minutes in a hot water bath to seal. If unsure of processing time at your altitude, contact a local home economist.

Makes 4 pint (500 mL) jars.

If you don't have the equipment for home-preserving, **Homemade Spiced Apple Sauce** freezes well.

HOMEMADE VEGETABLE DIP

Like a good wine, this tastes better if aged — refrigerate for at least one hour before using.

½ cup	fat-free sour cream	125 mL
½ cup	fat-free plain yogurt	125 mL
¼ cup	dill pickle, finely chopped	50 mL
½ tsp	onion powder	2 mL
½ tsp	sugar	2 mL
¼ tsp each	garlic powder & salt	1 mL each
pinch	black pepper	pinch

1. Mix all ingredients together in a small bowl.

Makes 1¼ cups (300 mL).

HOMEMADE TACO SEASONING

Spice up your vitamin E — give wheat germ some zip!

½ cup	wheat germ	125 mL
1 tbsp	chili powder	15 mL
1 tsp	cumin	5 mL
1 tsp	sugar	5 mL
½ tsp	garlic powder	2 mL
½ tsp	onion powder	2 mL
¼ tsp	seasoning salt	1 mL

1. Mix all ingredients in a plastic bag.

Coats 4 meat portions.

HOMEMADE MESQUITE SEASONING

This is a cost-efficient alternative to the commercial variety. As an extra bonus, you get to control the amounts of seasonings.

¼ cup	all-purpose flour	50 mL
¼ cup	wheat germ	50 mL
2 tbsp	simulated bacon bits	30 mL
2 tsp	chili powder	10 mL
1 tsp	paprika	5 mL
2 tsp	sugar	10 mL
¼ tsp	garlic powder	1 mL
¼ tsp	black pepper	1 mL
pinch	cayenne pepper	pinch

1. Place all ingredients in a blender to crush bacon bits. Process for 10 seconds. OLÉ!

Coats 4 meat portions.

BREAKFAST YOU SAY?

This sounds so odd that you have to try it—keep your mind and mouth open!

1	**banana, sliced**	1
1	**avocado, sliced**	1
	lime juice, freshly squeezed	

1. Place banana and avocado slices in a small bowl. Sprinkle with lime juice.

2. Serve for breakfast or use any time as a side dish.

Makes 1 portion.

COUSCOUS SALAD

This recipe has a Moroccan flavour.

1½ **cups**	**chicken or vegetable broth**	375 mL
pinch	**nutmeg**	**pinch**
1 **cup**	**couscous**	250 mL
½ **cup**	**raisins**	125 mL
¼ **cup**	**dried apricots, chopped**	50 mL
1	**19 oz (540 mL) can chickpeas, drained**	1
3 **tbsp**	**olive oil**	45 mL
3 **tbsp**	**lemon juice, freshly squeezed**	45 mL
½ **tsp**	**lemon peel, grated**	2 mL
½ **tsp**	**salt**	2 mL
¼ **tsp**	**black pepper, freshly ground**	1 mL

1. Place broth and nutmeg in a medium saucepan. Bring to a boil over medium-high heat.

2. Remove from heat. Add couscous, raisins and apricots. Stir. Cover and let stand for 5 minutes. Fluff couscous with a fork. Cool slightly. Stir in chickpeas. Set aside.

3. Whisk oil, lemon juice, lemon peel, salt and pepper in a small bowl. Add to couscous mixture. Toss to combine.

4. Serve at room temperature.

Makes 4 portions.

RASPBERRY OR STRAWBERRY TEABREAD

No jam is required!

3	**eggs**	3
1 cup	**brown or white sugar**	250 mL
1 cup	**unsweetened applesauce OR any fruit puree**	250 mL
1 tbsp	**vanilla extract**	45 mL
2 cups	**all-purpose flour**	500 mL
1 tsp	**cinnamon**	5 mL
1 tsp	**salt**	5 mL
1 tsp	**baking soda**	5 mL
1 tsp	**baking powder**	5 mL
1½ cups	**quick oats**	375 mL
2 cups	**crushed raspberries or strawberries, fresh or frozen**	500 mL

1. Beat eggs and sugar in a large bowl. Add applesauce and vanilla. Stir well. Set aside.

2. Sift together flour, cinnamon, salt, baking soda and baking powder in a medium bowl. Mix in oats.

3. Add wet ingredients to flour mixture. Mix well. Add crushed berries. Stir only until combined.

4. Pour into 2— 4" x 8" (10 cm x 20 cm) loaf pans coated with cooking spray. Bake at 375°F (190°C) for 30 to 40 minutes or until toothpick inserted into centre comes out clean.

Makes 2 loaves.

RECIPE INDEX

CYNTHIA'S EXERCISE PROGRAM INDEX

YOU CAN OWN CYNTHIA KERELUK'S VIDEOS!

All of the exercises are knee, back, neck and spine safe.
When starting out, please do not get discouraged.
Exercise at your own pace.

BEST OF LIFE, LUNGS & LEG LIFTS

VIDEO I
Split screen, low impact and high impact aerobics, tummy, hips, thighs and upper body exercises plus a warm up and cool down.
45 minutes

VIDEO II
Split screen, low impact, some high impact and some beginner step aerobics. Since there is a split screen you do not have to step. Tummy, arms, chest, hips, thighs, neck, back and spine workouts plus a cool down.
60 minutes

VIDEO III
An all cardio-vascular workout. Split screen, low impact and no impact aerobics plus a stationary bike workout. Because there is a split screen you do not have to bike. A brief warm up and cool down. Great for burning fat!
45 minutes

VIDEO IV
An all toning and strengthening workout. Split screen, toning from chest to thighs plus a cool down.
45 minutes

REAR IN GEAR
Special emphasis on the rear! A special friend appears with Cynthia in this video that covers two levels of aerobics, two levels of toning exercises, a warm up, stretch and cool down.
60 minutes

VIDEO V
Starts with a warm up, then 20 minutes of split screen aerobics both high and low impact, tummy work and a cool down. Also upper body toning exercises with or without weights.
47 minutes

VIDEO VI
Begins with a warm-up, then 20 minutes of split screen high and low impact aerobics. Also lower body toning with or without ankle weights, some tummy torture and a stretch.
45 minutes

FOR EASY ORDERING, PLEASE SEE NEXT PAGE...

GET YOUR OWN COPY OF CYNTHIA'S WORKOUT VIDEO!

All of the exercises are knee, back, neck and spine safe. When starting out, please do not get discouraged. Exercise at your own pace.

BEST OF LIFE, LUNGS & LEG LIFTS!

ANY 3 VIDEOS $55.⁰⁰
(2 for $40.00)

Please send me:

Title/Product	Quantity	Price	Total
Video I		x $25.00 =	$
Video II		x $25.00 =	$
Video III		x $25.00 =	$
Video IV		x $25.00 =	$
Video V		x $25.00 =	$
Video VI		x $25.00 =	$
Rear in Gear Video		x $25.00 =	$
		Subtotal	$

QUALITY T-SHIRTS ETC.:

T-Shirt: white (one size fits all)		x $15.00 =	$
T-Shirt: white (imprinted with photo) ☐ M ☐ L ☐ XL		x $20.00 =	$
Sweatshirt: grey ☐ M ☐ L ☐ XL		x $25.00 =	$
Exercise Towel (with signature logo) ☐ white ☐ peach ☐ blue ☐ yellow		x $20.00 =	$
		Total enclosed	$

Price is subject to change. Prices include taxes, shipping and handling.

U.S. and international orders payable in U.S. funds.

Please make MONEY ORDER or CHEQUE payable to:

Cynthia Kereluk,
P.O. Box 75209, White Rock, B.C. Canada V4A 9N4

Please PRINT clearly

Name _____

_____

Street _____

_____

City _____

Prov./State _____

Country _____

Postal Code/Zip _____

PLEASE ALLOW 2 TO 6 WEEKS FOR DELIVERY.

Thank you from the physically challenged, S.P.C.A. and those that the Salvation Army Church help clothe and feed, as some of the proceeds of each sale will help these causes.

ORDER BOOKS FOR YOUR FRIENDS!
SHOW THEM YOU LVE THEM.

Over 200 pages of shopping lists, menus, recipes, exercises and tips to help you **Eat Well, Get Moving and Feel Better!**

WHY "WAIST" TIME IN THE KITCHEN?™

Title	Quantity	Price	Total
Fit to Cook– Why "Waist" Time in the Kitchen?		x $23.95 (Can)	$
		x $19.95 (U.S.)	$
	Shipping & Handling		$ 3.00
	Subtotal		$
7% G.S.T. (Canada only: subtotal x .07)			$
	Total Enclosed		$

G.S.T. Registration No. BN 88459 6164   Prices are subject to change.

U.S. and international orders payable in U.S. funds.

TO ORDER

CALL: 24-HOUR TOLL FREE NUMBER: 1-888-678-4044

(check one):   ☐ Visa   ☐ MasterCard

Account # _____ Expiry ____ / ____

Cardholder's Name _____

Signature _____

OR: Make MONEY ORDER or CHEQUE payable to:
FIT TO COOK INC.,
Send to: Box 51152 B.P.O. , Calgary, Alberta, Canada T3K 3V9

Your Phone Number: (   ) _____
(In case we have a question about your order)

YOU COULD RECEIVE A FREE BOOK!
See next page for details

DELIVER TO:

Please PRINT clearly

Name _____

_____

Street _____

_____

City _____

Prov./State _____

Country _____

Postal Code/Zip _____

PLEASE ALLOW 3 TO 6 WEEKS FOR DELIVERY.

Order 5 or more books* and receive a significant discount plus FREE shipping & handling!

For **fund raising** or volume purchases of 5 or more books, *sent to one address, Fit to Cook Inc. offers a **significant discount** plus **FREE shipping & handling**.
Please call, fax or e-mail us for details.

toll-free: 1-888-678-4044

fax: (403) 730-3492

e-mail: fittocook@shaw.wave.ca

SEND US YOUR RECIPES!

If we choose your recipe for our next book,
your name will be printed with the recipe and you will
RECEIVE A FREE COPY OF OUR NEW BOOK!

We know every family has favourite recipes, but sometimes those recipes are too high in fat for today's eating style. We would love to help you.

Mail your recipe to Fit to Cook Inc. with a brief history of its origin in 50 words or less. If we choose it, we'll make it low-fat and place it in one of our next books with your name beside it. If we choose your recipe, you will also receive a free copy of the book in which your recipe is printed. Be sure to print or type your name, address and phone number very clearly in case we need to contact you.

Meanwhile ...

EAT WELL, GET MOVING, FEEL BETTER!

SEND A COPY OF THIS BOOK TO YOUR FAMILY AND FRIENDS.
YOU'LL BE SHOWING THEM HOW MUCH YOU LOVE THEM!
Easy ordering information on reverse.